European and Transatlantic Studies



Springer
*Berlin*
*Heidelberg*
*New York*
*Barcelona*
*Budapest*
*Hong Kong*
*London*
*Milan*
*Paris*
*Santa Clara*
*Singapore*
*Tokyo*

**Titles in the Series**

---

B. Eichengreen, J. Frieden, J. v. Hagen (Eds.)
Monetary and Fiscal Policy in an Integrated Europe

B. Eichengreen, J. Frieden, J. v. Hagen (Eds.)
Politics and Institutions in an Integrated Europe

João Loureiro
Monetary Policy in the European Monetary System

Horst Entorf

# Mismatch Explanations of European Unemployment

## A Critical Evaluation

Acting Editor: Michele Fratianni

With 18 Figures
and 36 Tables

Springer

Professor Horst Entorf
University of Würzburg
Institut für Volkswirtschaftslehre
97070 Würzburg
Germany



ISBN 3-540-64056-8 Springer-Verlag Berlin Heidelberg New York

Cataloging-in-Publication Data applied for
Die Deutsche Bibliothek – CIP Einheitsaufnahme
Entorf, Horst: Mismatch Explanations of European Unemployment / Horst Entorf. – Berlin; Heidelberg; New York; Barcelona; Budapest; Hong Kong; London; Milan; Paris; Tokyo: Springer, 1998
(European and transatlantic studies)
ISBN 3-540-64056-8


Printed in Germany



SPIN 10548636 43/2202 - 5 4 3 2 1 0 – Printed on acid-free paper

# Preface by Series Editor

Mismatching between those who want a job and those who hire is the hypothesis of choice to explain higher unemployment rates in Europe. Horst Entorf shows, painstakingly, that the claims of this hypothesis fall wide short of the mark and challenges, by implication, the profession to develop a more complex model to understand why European unemployment rates are rising.

The basic line of inquiry of Horst Entorf can be summarised as follows. Traditional measures of mismatching are inversely related to unemployment rates, a contradiction of the claim made by the hypothesis. However, the obvious inference is not legitimate because the explanatory variables of matching functions have trends, and thus give rise to spurious statistical results. To get around the problem, Entorf uses disaggregated data --40 occupations for the period 1971 to 1992-- from the German labor markets that are devoid of trend, typical of macroeconomic time series. One inference from the tests applied to the new data is that matching functions respond more to short-term fluctuations than to long-term factors, making them less suitable for the rigid European labour markets than the flexible U.S. labour market. Other inferences are that more education, more training and increased availability of flexible-time or part-time jobs facilitate the matching process. Regulations, laws, practices, and the general reluctance of labor unions to accept more job flexibility hinder matching.

Even the disaggregated data show that mismatching is inversely correlated with unemployment rates. This result can be explained by the fact that the pool of qualified workers rises during rising unemployment, making vacancies easier to fill. So, we are back to the initial question: what can the matching hypothesis explain? This hypothesis has useful things to say about the way the pool of unemployed finds its way to employment, but is silent about the way mismatching influences unemployment rates. The challenge for labor market economists, Entorf concludes, is to build a model that develops the two mechanisms, and not just one.

Horst Entorf has produced a fine example of applied economic analysis. His work ought to be of interest, not only to labour economists, but also to macroeconomists and econometricians.

Michele Fratianni

# Acknowledgments

This volume on mismatch explanations of European unemployment is grown out of my "Habilitation" thesis presented at the University of Mannheim. I am indebted to Prof. Heinz König and Prof. Jürgen von Hagen for supporting this work in many ways. My research project benefited from financial grants given by the German Science Foundation (Deutsche Forschungsgemeinschaft) and by the Commission of the European Communities.

Part of the research presented in this book was performed during two stays at the Université Catholique de Louvain, Louvain-la-Neuve, and at CREST, Paris. I would like to thank both research groups for their hospitality and many stimulating discussions. I received helpful advice, comments and suggestions from Luc Bauwens, Irene Bertschek, Jacques Bughin, Jacques Drèze, David de la Croix, Stephane Gregoir, Francis Kramarz, Guy Laroque, Stephane Lollivier, Alain Monfort, Fatemeh Shadman-Mehta, Henri Sneessens, Alain Trognon and Hideki Yamawaki. Georges Bourdallé and Jean-Pierre Lemaître were indispensable for the access to local computer facilities.

I gratefully acknowledge the pleasant atmosphere at the University of Mannheim, where I benefited from discussions with my colleagues. For excellent research assistance I thank Michalis Kavalakis, Peter Schwarz and Christoph Sponda.

Special thanks go to the Editorial Board of *European and Transatlantic Studies*, especially Michele Fratianni and Jürgen von Hagen, for their comments and the encouragement to publish this volume.

Finally, I owe a great debt to my wife Irene for her patience, support and confidence while I was doing the research for, and writing, the book.

# Contents

# Mismatch Explanations of European Unemployment

## A Critical Evaluation

# 1. Introduction

## 1.1. European unemployment and the mismatch hypothesis

Relatively high growth rates of GDP make it difficult to explain the high European unemployment rates within the usual business cycle framework. Over the four year period 1987-90, for instance, real GDP increased by 13 % and the unemployment rate declined from 10.7% in 1986 to 8.3% in 1990 for EC12. High unemployment rates remained despite an average growth rate of output of 3.4%. The persistence of European unemployment stands in striking contrast to the cyclical pattern of unemployment in the United States. Many people attribute the rise in European unemployment to increased imbalances between the pattern of labour demand and supply - in other words, to greater mismatch.

In many countries, the increase in unemployment through the mid-1980s was very large indeed. The OECD-standardised unemployment rate for Germany, for example, rose from an average of 1.1% over the 1967-74 period to 8.6% in 1984. Comparable numbers show an increase from 3.4 to 13.2 in the U.K, from 5.6 to 10.2 in Italy, and from 2.7 to 20.1 in Spain. The studies prepared for the first Chelwood Gate conference, collected in *The Rise in Unemployment* (Bean et al., 1986), analyse the contribution of real wages and demand deficiencies to the increase of unemployment after the first oil price shock in 1973. In the late eighties, however, the persistence of high unemployment over time became the main issue. The second Chelwood Gate conference focused on this topic. Analysing the role of capital constraints and insider wage setting in generating persistence, the common findings across countries in the latter conference, as summarised by Drèze and Bean (1990), show that growing unemployment was accompanied by a growing imbalance between labour supply, capacity-determined employment and demand-determined employment.

Other studies confirm similar findings. Unemployment rates differ widely between occupations and between regions, as well as across age, race and sex. The striking result is the stability of these differences. In all countries youths have much higher unemployment rates than adults. In addition, with the exception of the United States, in most countries regional differences are highly persistent. For example, in the North of Germany and England, and in the South of Italy unemployment is always above the national average.

Recent policy initiatives (Drèze and Malinvaud, 1994) focus on imbalances between skilled and unskilled workers. High unemployment is heavily concentrated among unskilled workers. That feature could result from displacement of unskilled workers by more skilled ones, which, on the one hand, arises for purely cyclical reasons. On the other hand, there seems to be growing evidence of an additional structural trend in the skill composition of labour demand, meaning that the given demand for labour calls for a decling proportion of unskilled jobs. Since the relative cost of unskilled versus skilled labour has been rather stable in most European countries (in contrast with the downward trend observed in the U.S.), persistent disequilibrium on the labour market seems to be concentrated on the market for unskilled labour.

Deficient matching between labour supply and demand has become a natural suspect to explain these findings. The question is: have exogenous forces raised average unemployment by changing the structure of labour demand and supply? To answer this question we need to develop relevant measures of mismatch, consistent with the overall framework of explanation. Moreover, it is necessary to provide empirical evidence on the various dimensions of mismatch. The first steps in these directions are being taken, for example in the contributions to *Mismatch and Labour Mobility* (Padoa-Schioppa, 1991).

The major result of the volume edited by Padoa-Schioppa (1991) consists in highlighting the looseness of the "mismatch" concept which explains why different mismatch definitions lead to widely varying judgements on the same observable facts. One must state that the book reveals its major limitation in failing to find a unified interpretation of the "mismatch" phenomenon.

At least four approaches to mismatch emerge from the existing literature (Padoa-Schioppa, 1991, p.2). My first approach associates mismatch with short-run sectoral shocks, which usually balance out at the aggregate level but temporarily raise both unemployment and variances: Lilien's (1982) turbulence index reveals this kind of mismatch. The remaining three approaches view mismatch as a more permanent phenomenon: The differences between them correspond to divergences on the concept of equilibrium unemployment relative to which mismatch is evaluated.

The second approach stems from the idea that frictional unemployment is unavoidable. It defines mismatch as the distance of the unemployment rate from an optimal rate. "Optimal" means that, at given vacancy rates, unemployed persons are allocated among regions (occupations etc.) to maximise hirings. The optimal rate is obtained when the vacancy/unemployment ratio coincides in all micro markets. The corresponding mismatch indexes measure the intersectoral dispersion of the vacancy/unemployment ratios (Jackman and Roper, 1987).

The third approach defines mismatch as the distance of the unemployment rate from a minimum rate, compatible with price stability. This minimum is reached - under certain assumptions stemming from a theoretical NAIRU framework ("non-accelerating inflation rate of unemployment") - when all unemployment rates are identical in every micro market. The corresponding mismatch index measures the variance of the relative unemployment rates in the economy (Jackman, Layard and Savouri, 1991).

The fourth approach identifies mismatch within a rationing model, under the basic assumption that the short side of each micro market determines the actual employment level of the micro unit. At the aggregate level, given that the binding constraint is not the same in every micro market, unfilled vacancies in some sectors coexist with unemployment in others. Thus, actual aggregate employment is lower than the minimum of aggregate labour demand and supply. In this framework, the "equity unemployment rate" is the one which would arise if at the aggregate level the labour demand equalled supply: It is the structural unemployment rate and is attributed to mismatch (Sneessens and Drèze, 1986, Lambert, 1988).

A long list of possible explanations for the increase of these measures can be put forward (Abraham, 1991, p.454-457). Several of the following sources of increased unemployment seem likely to have been associated with increases in labour market mismatch: Insufficiently aggressive macroeconomic policy; sluggish adjustment of the real wage level following the OPEC oil shocks; increased turbulence in the economic environment, which might have taken the form of shocks to the allocation of jobs across sectors, shocks to the distribution of labour across sectors, or higher job or worker turnover rates; decreased responsiveness of workers to shifts in relative labour demand; decreased responsiveness of employers to shifts in relative labour supply; a deterioriation in the search intensity of unemployed persons; and greater caution in hiring on the part of employers. No clear consensus concerning the relative importance of the various potential underlying contributors to the increase in unemployment has yet been reached. Estimates of the absolute importance of mismatch unemployment, however, indicate significant though widely ranging values: Shares of mismatch unemployment in German unemployment have been estimated, for instance, to be 20% (the German council of economic experts, SVR, 1994, p. 254), one third (Jackman, Layard and Savouri, 1991, p. 71) and 45% (Entorf, Franz, König, Smolny) in the 1980s.

A particular reason to suspect that labour market mismatch might have become more important comes from available micro data, indicating that there have been significant declines in labour market turnover and geographical mobility. This has led to the speculation that European labour markets have become less responsive than they used to be, thereby contributing to increased mismatch. A problem here is the difficulty of identifying whether decreased mobility contributed to high unemployment, or whether high unemployment is the cause of decreased mobility.

Perhaps the best reason to believe that the mismatch explanation for growing unemployment deserved serious consideration is the outward shift in the relationship between the unemployment rate and the job vacancy rate, commonly referred to as the Beveridge curve (the *u/v* curve). Outward shifts of the Beveridge curve have appeared almost everywhere in Europe since the early 1970s. It seems as if labour markets with substantial increases in unemployment have experienced outward *u/v* shifts as well. Increases in unemployment may result either from factors that cause the economy to move to the right along a given Beveridge curve, such as an excessive real wage, or from factors that cause an outward shift of the Beveridge curve, such as developments that lead to worsening mismatch. The interpretations of u/v shifts are diverse. For instance, some researchers pay attention to declining search effort and to the unemployment persistence arising as an effect of long-term unemployment. However, while growing labour market mismatch is not the only possible explanation for outward shifts in the Beveridge curve, it is high on most analysts' list of likely reasons.

These observations and other anecdotal evidence stand in striking contrast to reported evidence of mismatch trends when these are based on the first three approaches. Hypotheses of increasing sectoral imbalances across industries, regions or occupations have been launched, but found only limited support (Jackman and Roper, 1987; Padoa-Schioppa, 1991; Layard, Nickell and Jackman, 1991; Bean, 1994). Most results suggest that mismatch is higher before 1975 than afterwards. The index based on rationing theory, on the other hand, suggests increasing mismatch after 1975 in most countries. Several researchers express their reluctance to accept the reported evidence. Abraham (1991, p. 478), after summarizing findings in Padoa-Schioppa (1991), concludes "*... that given all the problems that stand in the way of constructing a believable skill mismatch indicator I am unwilling, in spite of positive evidence, to conclude that skill mismatch has in fact not worsened*". Rosen (1991, p. 102) is wondering what other factors are left to explain the increasing aggregate unemployment rates. Concerning the evidence based on the measure by Jackman, Layard and Savouri (1991), he writes: *What has become of the dislocations caused by economic integration, privatisation and the rest? Have these gone so smoothly as not to show up in unemployment and vacancy statistics? Is the variance of relative unemployment rates sufficiently sensitive to measure these things?*

## 1.2. The conceptual framework followed in this book

The following chapters analyse the recent evidence in more detail, try to explain why contradictory conclusions exist, look for alternative evidence and explanations of mismatch, and open up the "black box" of aggregate matching to microeconomic foundations. A comprehensive coverage of matching problems needs, as a prerequisite, a clear description of what "matching" and "mismatch" means in detail. An operational definition is given by Turvey (1977), who defines that "*... there is a mismatch between vacant jobs and unemployed workers such that if the latter were available with different skills and/or in different places the level of unemployment would fall*". Based on this idea, most evidence drawn from economic time series compares unemployment and vacancies at a well defined disaggregate level (occupational groups, sectoral affiliation, regions). These comparisons have their background in approaches (1) to (4) described above.

The static nature of these "classical" approaches to mismatch makes them of limited use for the analysis of dynamic adjustment processes, e.g. when cyclical and frictional unemployment, temporal reallocation and permanent shifts in employment take place. Taking a dynamic view of structural unemployment, several influential papers by Blanchard and Diamond (1989, 1990, 1992) propagate the analysis of structural unemployment within a flow approach to the labour market, where filling vacant positions with unemployed workers reduce the stocks of both unemployment and vacancies. The quality of this matching process is decisive for the dynamic adjustment of both stocks, i.e. for the dynamic interaction between unemployment and vacancies, known as the Beveridge curve. Thus, the adequate formal description of the matching process serves as an important building block within a more general theory of the Beveridge curve. It provides an alternative way to model mismatch as a cause of structural unemployment.

Bypassing complex issues of aggregation, Blanchard and Diamond propose so-called "matching functions", which make matches (new hires) a function of the stocks of vacancies and unemployment. They derive a system of differential equations of unemployment and vacancies, in which the Beveridge curve can be analysed in response to several types of shocks. Blanchard and Diamond (1989) show that cyclical shocks (aggregate activity shocks) lead to counter-clockwise loops around the steady-state locus of the Beveridge curve, while shifts of the curve itself arise due to changes in the intensity of reallocation and changes in the efficiency of matching.

Suitable empirical analysis of matching functions is a basic requirement for a reasonable interpretation of the Beveridge curve. After analysing mismatch in the sense of Turvey (1977) in Chapter 2, I thus follow the idea of matching according to the concept of aggregate matching functions in Chapter 3. These functions serve to disentangle changing matching efficiencies and reallocation dynamics.

In order to investigate the role of occupational realloction in the matching process, particular attention is paid to changes in professional status and the reallocation problems caused by the need to match those who graduate from school with available apprenticeship positions. Search theory and a dynamic framework suggest that the concept of matching functions must be generalized to include more than one single aggregate group of workers when potential substitution processes and long-lasting adjustment dynamics need to be analysed.

The microeconomic underpinning of matches occurring at an aggregate level is unclear. It remains to be clarified under what circumstances individual characteristics of job seekers and job requirements lead to a match, and which allocational consequences such a match might have. The final approach to mismatch followed in this book (Chapter 4) opens the macroeconomic black box and analyses individual job mobility that arises as a result of matching workers' (unmeasured) abilities to cope with skill requirements of modern new-technology work places.

European evidence on the lack of skilled workers, on the one hand, and unemployed workers with low skills, on the other hand, suggests that mismatch related to the emergence of new technologies must be investigated in detail. The analysis is based on a model of time-variant abilities, where the same ability can be valued higher or lower by different firms depending on requirements dictated by installed technologies, and where learning causes the firms' evaluation of a potential match to vary over time. Workers with greater ability to adjust to new technologies will change to new-technology jobs, while workers with lower abilities are allocated to positions with conventional technologies. This framework can explain the higher wages paid for new-technology workers and positive wage changes of people who change from conventional jobs to new-technology positions. Conclusions with respect to wage dynamics and wage differentials between conventional and new-technology jobs complete the lessons drawn from previous macroeconomic approaches to matching.

## 1.3. Overview and results

The present book aims at analysing recent matching phenomena, tries to understand the evidence within an adequate theoretical framework, and attempts to derive general conclusions on the basis of suitable data and econometric methods. Chapter 2 starts with a critical evaluation of standard mismatch indexes, derived from time series of individual groups (for instance, a time series of regions). Most of the indexes do not indicate any worsening of skill mismatch and a falling rate of regional mismatch (Padoa-Schioppa, 1991). In contrast, estimates based on macroeconomic rationing models, for instance those presented in Drèze and Bean (1990), reveal steadily growing mismatch in Europe. Since measuring mismatch is an important issue in policy advice, it would be necessary to dispose of unambiguous evidence. Chapter 2 presents underlying theoretical frameworks and sheds some light on the performance of the most prominent measures of mismatch, i.e. the concepts introduced by Jackman and Roper (1987), Jackman, Layard and Savouri (1991), Lilien (1982) and Lambert (1988).

Using data on vacancies and unemployment in 40 occupational groups of the time 1951 to 1992, mismatch seems to be inversely correlated with general unemployment trends and with microeconomic measures of labour mobility. This would imply that other factors must have been more important to explain the increasing aggregate unemployment rates. However, several data problems prevent such clear and unambiguous conclusions. First, measurement problems and the problem of insufficient disaggregation in mismatch indexes are addressed. Vacancy data, for instance, need special attention since they are taken from official statistics that comprise only those job searchers who register as such at the labour office. Moreover, simple examples of aggregation show that aggregate indexes, as they are used in most applications because of unsufficient data, might give a completely different result than indexes based on disaggregate data.

The behaviour of different measures of mismatch over time depends critically on the nature of the underlying time series. It can be shown that "trending" time series of unemployment in regions, for instance, can easily lead to falling mismatch indexes. More precisely, the analysis of time series behaviour of mismatch indexes exploits recent results of the econometric theory of nonstationary time series. The reader interested in technical details is referred to the Appendix to Chapter 2, where several propositions reveal the behaviour of measures of mismatch in the presence of trending and nonstationary time series. This property of economic time series can explain why indexes such as the one by Jackman, Layard and Savouri (1991) mistakenly show falling mismatch, whereas the one by

Lambert (1988) erroneously reflects increasing mismatch, even though both indexes are based on the same set of trending time series without any true change of mismatch.

In order to evaluate the empirical relevance of these theoretical results, actual time series related to mismatch indexes are investigated. There is strong evidence that, for instance, the time series behaviour of unemployment rates fulfill required assumptions (i.e. they behave like nonstationary time series). Finally, since some of the analytical results are only valid in the asymptotic case, simulation studies help in understanding the performance of mismatch indexes in small samples.

Chapter 3 analyses mismatch within the flow approach to macroeconomics. After some introductory remarks, the chapter reviews the theoretical framework of matching functions, and explains their role within the theory of the Beveridge curve. One of the main purposes is to demonstrate the importance of analysing matching functions with disaggregate data. For this purpose, I compare estimates based on panel data with estimates based on aggregate data. Aggregate matching functions turn out to be unsatisfactory: Parameter estimates are insignificant and/or the specification of the matching function has low explanatory power. Like most economic time series, the components of matching functions are trending and might reveal problems of nonstationarity. In order to study the possibility of misleading interpretations of aggregate matching functions, they are analysed in the econometric framework of so-called spurious regressions (the technical details can be found in the Appendix to Chapter 3). In fact, aggregate matching functions seem to be spurious. Hence, new evidence needs to be found.

The quality of the econometric results changes when we follow Hall's (1989) proposal to take a more disaggregate view of the matching process. Using a panel of 40 occupational groups for the period from 1971 to 1992, econometric results are now satisfactory from a statistical point of view and lead to reasonable economic interpretations. Applied panel estimation techniques (see again the Appendix to Chapter 3 for the presentation of econometric methods) and the theoretical concept of matching functions allow for a reconsideration of the question raised in Chapter 2: Is mismatch increasing or decreasing? Estimations of a time-variant parameter on matching efficiency in matching functions reveal a nonlinear pattern. Mismatch is particularly low during times of high unemployment. The level of mismatch is higher in the 1980s than in the 1970s. This result confirms suggestions made in Chapter 2, saying that the evidence of falling mismatch derived from conventional mismatch indexes might be spurious.

I continue by explaining mismatch in terms of several economic indicators known as potential causes of structural unemployment. There is evidence that general labour force growth is positively associated with mismatch. A possible explanation might be insufficient mobility of new entrants. A higher share of people with no schooling degree leads to falling mismatch, reflecting the fact that aggregate matching functions are easily dominated by workers in high turnover jobs. Finally, times of extremely high unemployment are times of low mismatch, because during these periods the pool of job searchers is large enough, and it is easy to find adequate workers for vacant positions.

Finally, Chapter 3 highlights upward and downward shifts of the aggregate Beveridge curve that arise due to reallocation between occupational groups. I first present matching functions which analyse the matching of vacant positions and job seekers from competing occupational groups, i.e. unemployed from the occupational group of the vacant position *and* from other occupational groups who intend to change their profession. Secondly, the matching of vacant apprenticeship positions with school-leavers is analysed. According to official figures of the German labour office, school-leavers represent 13% of all job seekers per year. Thus, labour markets fluctuations are highly affected by the successful or unsuccessful matching of young school-leavers. The importance is reinforced by "time-to-build" problems (most apprenticeships last three years) when both groups, firms and applicants, exhibit backward-looking behaviour that makes their decision dependent on recent labour market experiences. According to the data of a panel of apprentices in 27 occupational groups for the period 1968 to 1991, there is in fact strong evidence that both groups base their matching decision on the recent labour market performance of occupational groups, i.e. on recent relative unemployment and vacancies figures.

Considering mobility and learning in an economy with imperfect information, the microeconomic matching framework of Chapter 4 predicts that i) the general wage level of new-technology workers is higher than for conventional jobs, ii) workers moving from a conventional job to a new-technology position experience a wage increase, iii) the wage differential between new-technology jobs and conventional jobs grows with experience, and iv) workers in high-wage groups should perceive a better match with a new-technology job than workers in low-wage groups.

The empirical analysis of Chapter 4 tests these theoretical predictions using individual labour-force data on the spread of new technologies and the organization of the work place. Available data allow for a comprehensive consideration of new technologies. Three main groups can be distinguished: "Computer-related new technologies with high autonomy of the user", "computer-related new technologies with average autonomy" and "production-related new technologies with low autonomy". With respect to hypothesis i) (see also Krueger's (1993) result that computer-related jobs are better paid than other jobs, all other things equal), the data allow an affirmative answer only for the subgroup of workers with relatively "low" skills (blue collar workers) and with "computer-related new technologies with high autonomy", whereas no significant wage differential remains for high-wage groups (managers etc.).

Panel data estimations that control for unobserved abilities (represented by so-called fixed effects in panel-data modelling) are used to identify a potential wage change of workers who improve their match via a switch between conventional and new-technology jobs. Whereas no immediate wage change of mobile workers can be detected (possibly due to insufficient panel data), econometric tests confirm that a longer experience with new-technology work increases the wage differential between new-technology workers and conventional positions. Finally, survey data on self-reported mismatch confirm hypothesis iv) that the matching of abilities to technologies leads to a lower "new-technology mismatch" (i.e. mismatch arising from the work with new-technologies) in high-wage groups.

A summary of the main results and concluding remarks can be found in Chapter 5.

# 2. Do aggregate measures of mismatch measure mismatch? A time series analysis of existing concepts

## 2.1. Introduction

Many researchers explained the persistent and high level of unemployment in Europe as a result of "mismatch", arguing that these economies are too inflexible to match their unemployed with available employment opportunities. Recent episodes of economic history, including the two OPEC oil shocks, are widely believed to have caused adjustment processes with significant shifts in employment across industrial sectors, skills and regions. Moreover, the introduction of new technologies during the late seventies and eighties suggests an increased pace of job reallocation, leading to increased mismatch among different skill groups, and - since new technologies are often concentrated in only a few regions - across different geographical areas.

Surprisingly, existing empirical measures of mismatch indicate little, if any increase in mismatch during the 1980s. Recent international evidence presented in Jackman, Layard and Savouri (1991), Layard, Nickell and Jackman (1991) and country papers edited by Padoa-Schioppa (1991) even suggests the opposite: In many cases, measured mismatch was higher before 1975 than afterwards (see Abraham, 1991, for a survey of the international evidence). In contrast, the country papers in Drèze and Bean (1990) show that measures of mismatch based on rationing models indicate a steady increase in mismatch after the first OPEC oil price shock.

This chapter tries to shed some light on the performance of the most prominent measures of mismatch, namely those presented by Jackman and Roper (1987), Jackman, Layard and Savouri (1991), Lilien (1982) and Lambert (1988). The purpose of the analysis is to see whether empirical results based on these measures are partly or completely determined by spurious factors arising from stochastic trends and/or global shifts in unemployment. Since mismatch seems to be negatively correlated with actual unemployment (see Section 2.2), the impact of global shifts in unemployment on indicators of mismatch is a natural starting point. Furthermore, given the incidence of nonstationarity (unit roots) in unemployment time series, properties of the measures are analysed in the presence of trending time series. The econometrically interested reader might refer to Section 2.6 and to Appendix A2 for formal proofs, where the asymptotic properties of the indices are analysed when the underlying stochastic processes are generated as random walks or as a random walks with drifts. Since some of the analytical results are only valid in the asymptotic case, the chapter also includes some small sample simulations.

The results reveal that conventional measures of mismatch depend on the nature of the underlying time series of employment, unemployment and vacancies. The puzzling existence of contradictory results can be explained by the trending nature of the underlying time series. Thus, conventional measures of mismatch cannot be interpreted in the way they are designed.

This chapter is organized as follows. Section 2.2 surveys some empirical evidence of measured mismatch and contrasts micro and macro results. The theoretical background of conventional mismatch indicators is discussed in Section 2.3. Sections 2.4 and 2.5 highlight problems of interpretation due to measurement error and insufficient disaggregation. The time series analysis of the indexes of mismatch follows in Section 2.6 (and in Appendix A2). Section 2.7 and 2.8 reveal the nature of time series underlying indexes of mismatch with respect to the degree of integration (stationarity versus nonstationarity) and inform about the nature of trends (drifts). Section 2.9 contains simulations which illustrate theoretical results and Section 2.10 offers a few concluding remarks.

## 2.2. Some puzzling evidence

Measuring mismatch is a popular topic in empirical economics and economic policy advice. However, as pointed out by Abraham (1991), existing studies do not reveal a clear pattern of mismatch after 1975. Abraham expresses a reluctance to accept the evidence concerning skill mismatch: She concludes "... *that given all of the problems that stand in the way of constructing a believable skill mismatch indicator I am unwilling, in spite of the lack of positive evidence, to conclude that skill mismatch has in fact not worsened*" (Abraham, 1991, p. 478). With respect to regional mismatch, she finds the empirical evidence less ambigous and concludes that increasing geographical mismatch does not seem to be a general problem.

With regard to Germany, one may also believe that regional mismatch has increased in the 1980s. Evidence from German time series does not show a clear trend, as can be seen from estimated measures of mismatch in Jackman, Layard and Savouri (1991), Franz and König (1986) and Franz (1991a). Franz (1991a, who presents an update of Franz and König, 1986), using 141 regional labour market districts and the concept by Jackman and Roper, 1987 (see below), detects an upward shift between 1976 and 1979 but no clear-cut positive or negative trend thereafter. The author concludes that " ... *regional mismatch does not seem to be able to contribute much to the outward shift of the Beveridge curve or the SURE* ["structural unemployment rate at equilibrium"] *in that decade* [in the 1980s]".

If mismatch has to do with insufficient mobility, as most people believe (see, for instance, Barro, 1988; Section 2.3 presents theoretical foundations of mismatch indexes), then Table 2.1.a provides some micro evidence consistent with the view of a *deteriorating* matching process which is hindered by decreasing mobility. Comparing the time periods 1955-1970 and 1971-1985, a study of the German employment institute (IAB, Institut für Arbeits- und Berufsforschung) reveals a clear decline in regional labour mobility: For the group of all male workers the share of people moving for professional reasons declined from 17.2% to 10.4% (for women the share was 7.7% for the second period). In particular, older people are getting more reluctant to change their place of work. Mobility increases with qualification; here it is interesting to distuinguish between employed and unemployed people: We observe that the largest drop (in terms of the share 1985/1970) occurred for the lowest skill category of employed workers.

Some authors argue that economic performance might worsen with increasing labour mobility, since turnover costs and other costs of mobility might offset potential gains from mobility (Schettkat, 1992). Regarding employed workers, such arguments are plausible but they do not hold empirically, at least for Germany and other European countries. An increasing percentage of firms report a lack of skilled labour (Kramarz and Lollivier, 1990, Von Rosenbladt, 1990, EEC, 1991, Van Dam et al., 1991, Nam et al, 1992), though such bottlenecks reveal strong cyclical patterns (see Dabouineau et al., 1993, for recent French developments and Wirtschaftswoche, 1993, for the latest German evidence. According to a survey performed by the "Industrie- und Handelskammer" 87% of firms suffered from a lack of skilled blue-collar workers ("Facharbeiter") in January 1990. This percentage had fallen to 53% in January 1993. Thus, if mobility had been higher at least for this group, perceived bottlenecks would have been reduced and the matching process would not have been rationed.

For unemployed people even the general economic reasoning is not very realistic, since under regular conditions moving should be preferable to being unemployed when one compares the individual welfare in both situations. However, as Table 2.1 reveals, mobility of unemployed people has decreased too.

A possible explanation of reduced worker mobility is increasing home ownership, including of low-skilled workers. Bover, Muellbauer and Murphy (1990) address the problem that high house prices might lead to a "mobility trap", i.e. a reduction of mobility due to local and financial commitments. Official statistics, summarized in Table 2.1.b, are consistent with this hypothesis: While the number of households in rented houses, flats etc. remained more or less stable, the number of owner occupied dwellings and owner-occupied houses increased steadily. The ratio between owning and lodging was 55.6% in 1972 and increased to 70.6% in 1985.

German time series evidence of occupational mismatch (Franz, 1991, p. 119, using 327 professions and the measure by Jackman and Roper, 1987) shows a more or less constant mismatch between 1976 and 1982 and a sharp drop afterwards. Again, micro evidence suggests the opposite. The share of people who never change occupation rose from 62.8% in 1979 to 72.8% in 1986. Recent anecdotal evidence of structural changes due to new technologies, oil price shocks and other disturbing influences leads many economists to thinking that the coincidence of such adjustment processes and the increasing reluctance to change occupations resulted in an *increase* of mismatch (Abraham, 1991, for instance).

A time series example and international cross section data published in Padoa-Schioppa (1991) highlight the puzzling relationships between the level of unemployment and the level of mismatch. For the measures of mismatch under consideration, the longest time series available is the one by Bentolila and Dolado (1991, p. 191, 1962-1989). Furthermore, Jackman, Layard and Savouri (1991) present a cross section consisting of measures of mismatch by occupation for 11 nations in 1987.

Figure 2.1 displays the striking negative correlation between the time path of Spanish unemployment and the index of regional mismatch (according to the definition of Jackman, Layard and Savouri, 1991). After Franco's death and the start of new political institutions in 1975, the negative correlation is almost perfect. In terms of Pearson's correlation coefficient, the correlation coefficient for the whole period 1962 - 1986 is -0.84 (t-value = 7.4).

Jackman, Layard and Savouri (1991, Table 2.3, see also Layard, Nickell, Jackman, 1991, p.288) calculate a mismatch indicator using the variance of relative unemployment rates and apply it to various countries using data for 1987. At a first glance, one again gets the impression that mismatch is more or less the inverse of unemployment. The calculation of Spearman's rank-correlation confirms that conjecture: The coefficient is -0.47; taking a more robust trimming approach that deletes outliers (here: maximum and minimum of both unemployment and mismatch) leads to a highly significant negative correlation of -0.73.

A further example is provided by Lilien's index of interindustrial dispersion calculated by Flanagan (1987, see also Franz, 1991). This index takes the following values: 2.64 in 1960-64, 3.21 in 1965-69, 3.21 in 1970-74, 2.29 in 1975-79 and 1.85 in 1980-83. During these periods, average unemployment rates were (in percent) 0.8, 1.1, 1.2, 4.4 and 6.7, respectively.

Table 2.1.: Some evidence on labour mobility

a) Regional mobility: Share of employed workers who changed their home for professional reasons during the years 1955-1970 and 1971-1985, in %

| Group | Men 1970 | Men 1985 | Men Ratio 85/70 | Women 1985 |
|---|---|---|---|---|
| All workers | 17.2 | 10.4 | 0.6 | 7.7 |
| Age: | | | | |
| ≤ 20 | 3 | 3 | 1 | 3 |
| (20,25] | 8 | 5 | 0.62 | 8 |
| (25,30] | 20 | 8 | 0.40 | 12 |
| (30,35] | 25 | 16 | 0.64 | 14 |
| (35,40] | 23 | 18 | 0.78 | 14 |
| (40,45] | 20 | 13 | 0.65 | 7 |
| (45,50] | 16 | 10 | 0.62 | 4 |
| (50,55] | 14 | 6 | 0.43 | 1 |
| ≥ 55 | 12 | 5 | 0.42 | 2 |
| Unskilled workers ("Hilfs-,angelernte Arbeiter) | | | | |
| - unemployed | 17 | 14 | 0.82 | 11 |
| - employed | 12 | 5 | 0.42 | 3 |
| Skilled workers ("Fach-,Vorarbeiter, etc.") | | | | |
| - unemployed | 13 | 11 | 0.85 | 8* |
| - employed | 11 | 5 | 0.45 | 3 |
| Low and medium ranked administrative and managerial employees ("einfache und mittlere Angestellte") | | | | |
| - unemployed | 29 | 13 | 0.45 | 10 |
| - employed | 19 | 10 | 0.53 | 8 |
| High ranked administrative and managerial employees ("gehobene und leitende Angestellte") | | | | |
| - unemployed | 43 | 35* | 0.81 | 18* |
| - employed | 33 | 20 | 0.61 | 15 |

Table 2.1a) is based on two surveys performed by the German "Institut für Arbeitsmarkt- und Berufsforschung" (IAB) in 1970 and 1985, containing 60973 men in 1970, and 8177 men and 5304 women in 1985

* Shares are calculated using less than 100 observations

*Source:* Institut für Arbeitsmarkt- und Berufsforschung der Bundesanstalt für Arbeit (1988), p.130-131

*Table 2.1.:* (continued)
b) Living in owner-occupied houses and owner-occupied dwellings

| Year | Owner-occupied residence | Others (rented house, flat, etc.) | Ratio "Owning/lodging" |
|---|---|---|---|
| 1972 | 7.5 | 13.5 | 55.6 |
| 1982 | 9.3 | 13.9 | 66.9 |
| 1985 | 9.6 | 13.6 | 70.6 |

*Source:* Statistical Yearbooks (Statistisches Jahrbuch), various issues

c) Skill mobility: Share of the German labour force that changed its occupation at least once[1)] - in %.

| | 1979 | 1985/86 |
|---|---|---|
| Never changed occupation | 62.8 | 72.8 |
| One change of occupation | 24.8 | 18.9 |
| More than one change | 12.4 | 8.3 |

1) The share is calculated using the response to the question: "After finishing your school respectively professional education did your professional activity change once or more than once to such a degree that one could refer to it as a change of occupation ("Berufswechsel")?

*Source:* Zentralarchiv für empirische Sozialforschung - ZA Studie 1243 (1979, p.325) and ZA Studie 1790 (1985/1986, p.77)

*Note:* The survey was initiated by the Bundesinstitut für Berufsbildung, Berlin, and the Institut für Arbeitsmarkt und Berufsforschung, Nürnberg. The data are collected by EMNID, GETAS and INFRATEST in 1979 (29769 observations) and during October 1985 and March 1986 (26361 observations). The *Zentaralarchiv für empirische Sozialforschung*, Köln, has prepared and summarized the data for scientific purposes.

Figure 2.1: Unemployment and mismatch in Spain

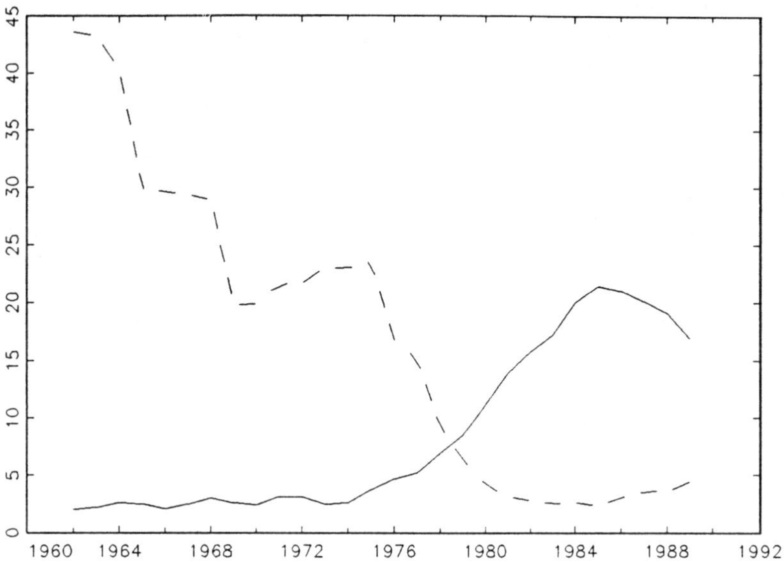


*Note*: Solid line: unemployment, dashed line: mismatch. Source: Bentolila and Dolado (1991)

In contrast, the country papers in Drèze and Bean (1990) provide estimates of mismatch based on a macroeconomic rationing model (Sneessens and Drèze, 1986, Lambert, 1988). For all European countries and the U.S., the mismatch index increases linearly over time and reaches its maximum at the end of the observation period (1986). Bentolila and Dolado (1991) also present some estimated indexes of mismatch based on this concept and confirm this relationship: Structural unemployment (SURE, see below) increased steadily and peaks about 10% in 1985.

It is not clear why that is so. The simultaneous existence of rising unemployment and both falling and increasing mismatch indexes is at least surprising. However, before (mis-) interpreting these results, the theoretical foundation of mismatch indexes has to be understood. Then, we can go on and analyse whether the statistical properties of actual time series might lead to false conclusions.

## 2.3. Measuring mismatch: Theoretical foundations

Several measures of mismatch exist in the literature. The most common ones are discussed in the contributions edited by Padoa-Schioppa (1991). They have their origin in the papers by Jackman and Roper (1987), Jackman, Layard and Savouri (1991), Lilien (1982) and Lambert (1988). With the exception of Lambert's (1988) concept of "smoothing by aggregation" which is based on a rationing framework, all measures are derived from equilibrium models.

Jackman and Roper (1987) start their framework by formalizing a general definition by Turvey (1977), who defines structural unemployment as existing where "*there is a mismatch betweeen vacant jobs and unemployed workers such that if the latter were available with different skills and/or in different places the level of unemployment would fall".* To make this measure operational, Jackman and Roper (1987) specify a job hiring function (a matching function using recent terminology) $H$ :

$$H_i = H(U_i, V_i), \qquad (2.1)$$

where $U_i$ and $V_i$ are the number of unemployed workers and vacancies in category *i* (sector, skill, region, ...) and $H_i$ is the number of job hires per unit time period. The concept of hiring functions goes back to Pissarides (1979). Following his proposals, $H$ is a convex, linear homogenenous function with

$$H_i = V_i h(U_i / V_i) \qquad (2.2)$$

$$\text{and} \qquad h' > 0, \quad h'' < 0.$$

Following Turvey (1977), Jackman and Roper (1987) define structural unemployment as that sectoral allocation of the existing stock of unemployment which, given the sectoral allocation of vacancies, maximizes aggregate hires, i.e.

$$H = \Sigma_i H_i = \Sigma_i V_i h(U_i / V_i) \rightarrow \max\ !, \qquad (2.3)$$

subject to $\Sigma_i U_i =$ constant and $V_i$ given.

Since the first order condition implies that $h(U_i / V_i)$ be constant for all i, the only possible solution to this allocation problem is that the ratio of unemployment to vacancies is identical across sectors. In turn, $U_1/V_1 = U_2/V_2 = \ldots = U_K/V_K$ gives $u_1 = v_1, u_2 = v_2, \ldots, u_K = v_K$ where $u_i = U_i/\Sigma_i U_i$ and $v_i = V_i/\Sigma_i V_i$. A natural way to define mismatch is thus

$$(2.4) \qquad M_1 = \frac{1}{2}\Sigma_i \,|\, u_i - v_i \,|,$$

which is zero in the case of no mismatch, i.e. $u_i = v_i$ for all $i$. The upper limit, $M_1 = 1$, occurs when all unemployment is concentrated in one single sector, while all vacancies can be found in another sector.

A particular form of the matching function (2.1) is given by

$$(2.5) \qquad H_i = \beta U_i^{1/2} V_i^{1/2},$$

and

$$H = \Sigma_i H_i = \beta U^{1/2} V^{1/2} \Sigma_i (u_i v_i)^{1/2}$$

in aggregate. (2.5) leads to a rectangular u/v curve (like isoquants for Cobb-Douglas production functions) and is therefore a very common approximation in empirical work. While initial proposals go back to Dow and Dicks-Mireaux (1958), very recent publications propagate the choice of $\alpha = 1/2$ in linear-homogenous Cobb-Douglas hiring functions (see Layard, Nickell and Jackman, 1991, p. 326, who justify their choice by refering to Pissarides, 1986, Blanchard and Diamond, 1990, and their own empirical evidence). Jackman and Roper use (2.5) to define an alternative index of mismatch,

$$(2.6) \qquad M_2 = 1 - \Sigma_i (u_i v_i)^{1/2}.$$

As before, optimal allocation of unemployment across sectors ( $u_i = v_i$ for all $i$ ) gives $M_2 = 0$. In case of no match at all, i.e. $u_i v_i = 0$ for all $i$, $M_2$ takes the maximum value of $1$.

Figure 2.2 displays some estimates for occupational mismatch in Germany, based on indexes $M_1$ and $M_2$. Both indexes are based on 40 professional classifications for the years 1951 through 1992. The long time series of $M_1$ and $M_2$ provide some interesting evidence beyond the time series published by Franz (1991), who calculated $M_1$ for 327 professions but only for the years 1976 to 1988. During these years, his $M_1$ decreased steadily, as it is also true for our 40 categories. Evidently, the much higher number of professions does not reveal diverging results.

$M_1$ and $M_2$ have some remarkable time patterns if one compares both time series with unemployment. Until the recession in 1975, mismatch seemed to be procyclical and parallel to unemployment. After 1975, however, mismatch and unemployment have been running in opposite directions.

Both $M_1$ and $M_2$ require job vacancy data, if possible at a disaggregate level. This is a prohibitive obstacle for many countries, where such data are not available. For instance, the U.S. even lacks *aggregate* vacancy data; therefore, American case studies use the "help wanted" index as an approximation for U.S. job vacancies (see Abraham, 1987). The advantage of the third index,

$$M_3 = \frac{1}{2} Var\left(\frac{U_i/N_i}{\Sigma U_i/\Sigma Ni}\right), \tag{2.7}$$

*Figure 2.2:* Occupational mismatch in Germany, 1951-1992

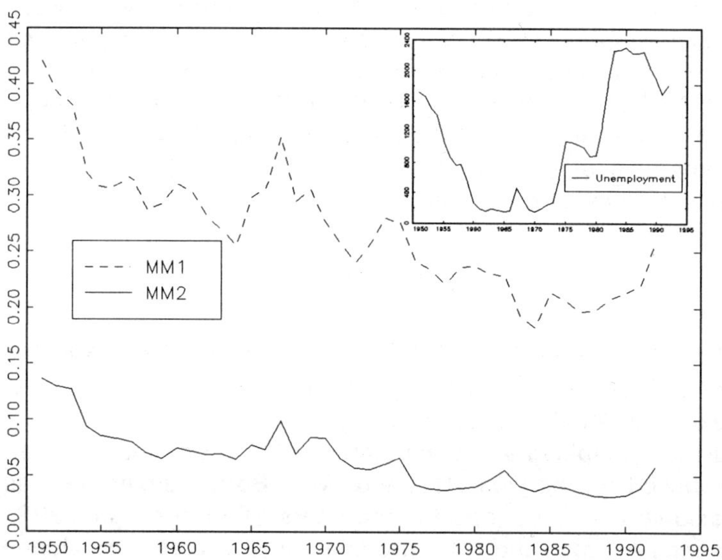


*Note:* For the period 1951 to 1961 only 37 categories are available. Here four professions (metal-oriented) are summarized as a single group.
*Sources:* Leupoldt and Ermann (1973), Ermann (1984), Ermann (1988); Bundesanstalt für Arbeit: Amtliche Nachrichten der Bundesanstalt für Arbeit, various issues

proposed by Jackman, Layard and Savouri (1991), is that it is exclusively based on unemployment rates ( $N_i$ = number of workers). These authors derive their index from a NAIRU-related theoretical framework.[1] Jackman, Layard and Savouri (1991) consider monopolistic competition and Cobb-Douglas technologies[2] with different types of labour (sectors, regions, ...) and constant returns to scale, leading to a cost function $Y \Pi_i e^{-\delta t} W_i^{\alpha_i}$, $\Sigma_i \alpha_i = 1$, where $W_i$ are wages of group i and $\delta t$ represents technical progress. The price level is determined by the elasticities of production and by demand elasticities, which, jointly with technical progess, are captured by $e^{-A}$ :

$$P = \Pi_i W_i^{\alpha_i} e^{-A}. \tag{2.8}$$

The next steps come from the principle underlying the NAIRU construction. Here, a crucial assumption is the particular form of the wage function, which is supposed to be double logarithmic (according to some quoted empirical evidence in Grubb, 1986): $\log W_i = \beta_i - \gamma \log ur_i$, where $ur_i = U_i / N_i$ . It is substituted into the price function (after taking logs) and the price level is set at unity. Some simple manipulations (adding $\gamma \log ur$ and $ur = \Sigma U_i / \Sigma N_i$ to both sides) give $\log ur = const - \Sigma \alpha_i \log(ur_i / ur)$. Finally, a Taylor expansion of $\log(ur_i / ur)$ around 1 yields

$$\log ur \cong const + \frac{1}{2} \Sigma \alpha_i \left( \frac{ur_i}{ur} - 1 \right)^2$$

$$= const + \frac{1}{2} var \left( \frac{ur_i}{ur} \right).$$

The minimum level of aggregate unemployment is thus given when the variance of $ur_i / ur$ is zero, i.e. when the unemployment rates are the same in all sectors. A natural index of mismatch is thus the difference between the actual and the minimum variance, as given by definition (2.7).

A standard index of industrial mismatch is Lilien's (1982) sigma, which is based on employment growth. This index measures the relative dispersion of growth rates among industries:

---

**1** See Layard and Bean, 1989, for a simple description of the NAIRU concept and Franz, 1987, for some critical remarks, in particular with respect to the history-dependent interpretation in the presence of hysteresis.

**2** In their Appendix, the authors show that very similar results hold for CES technologies with constant returns to scale (CES = "constant elasticity of substitution").

$$(2.9) \qquad M_4(t) = \left( \Sigma_i \frac{L_{it}}{L_t} (\Delta \log L_{it} - \Delta \log L_t)^2 \right)^{1/2},$$

where $L_t = \Sigma L_{it}$ is aggregate employment.

Lilien studies the importance of the dispersion in hiring conditions in determining the aggregate layoff rate. Here we sketch only those equations of Lilien's model which describe the role of Lilien's sigma in determining the level of unemployment. Lilien (1982) uses the flow approach to unemployment: $\Delta U_t = \theta_{1t} - \theta_{2t}$, where $\theta_{1t}$ is the flow into and $\theta_{2t}$ is the flow out of aggregate unemployment in period $t$.

The inflow is assumed to be $\theta_{1t} = F_t + a_0 + a_1 Q_t + \eta_{1t}$, where $F_t$ represents aggregate layoffs, $a_1 Q_t$ captures the proportion of voluntary labour turnover (voluntary quits without new job) as well as labor force entrants. $\eta_{1t}$ is a random disturbance. $Q_t$ is given by $Q_t = c_0 - c_1 U_t + \eta_{2t}$, i.e. quits vary inversely with tensions on the labour market.

The innovative element of the model is the formalization of layoffs. After defining layoffs at the firm level, $F_{it} = A_{it} - H_{it}$, where $A_{it}$ is the individual number of accessions, and after introducing some distributional assumptions for hirings, $H_{it} = H_t + \epsilon_{it}$, with $\epsilon_{it}$ distributed with mean zero and variance $\sigma_t^2$ and $H_t$ = aggregate hirings.[1] Aggregate layoffs in the model are linearized by

$$F_t = b_0 - b_1(\Delta L_t + Q_t) + b_2 \sigma_t + \eta_{3t}.$$

The model is closed by making the flow out of unemployment a function of the current and past unanticipated monetary policy, $\Delta M_{t-j}, j = 0, 1, \ldots k$, and last period's unemployment. Finally, solving the model (and using the identity $L_t + U_t = 1$ ) leads to the equation

$$(2.10) \qquad U_t = B_0 + B_1 \sigma_t - \Sigma_j \lambda_j \Delta M_{t-j} + B_2 U_{t-1} + \eta_t$$

Empirically, Lilien uses (2.9) as a proxy for $\sigma_t$, since he is particularly interested in measuring sectoral shifts. $\sigma_t$ turns out to be highly significant in equation (2.10), and he concludes that sectoral shifts represented by a highly procyclical $\sigma_t$ are an important source of cyclical unemployment.

---

1 Aggregate hirings = expected hirings, since Lilien considers the case of large numbers. Aggregate layoffs can be expressed as the expected value of individual layoffs, conditional on the parameters of the hiring process: $F_t = E(F_{it} \mid H_t, \sigma_t)$ (see Lilien, 1982, p. 782, for the eplicit formula).

Lilien's index is easy to compute because it does not require unemployment data by industry. The most severe criticism has been raised by Abraham and Katz (1986), who show that Lilien's sigma is not invariant with respect to aggregate demand fluctuations and, as a result, the pure "frictional" component of unemployment cannot be disentangled. Despite this problem, Lilien's sigma is one of the most popular indices of structural change in empirical work (see Brunello, 1991 and Franz, 1991, for some recent applications).

The last index under consideration is Lambert's (1988) *rho,* that is derived from micro-based macroeconomic rationing models.[1] Each micromarket consists of two components, labour demand, $D_{it}$, and labour supply, $S_{it}$. The observed, or transacted, value is the minimum of both latent components, $L_{it} = \min(D_{it}, S_{it})$. Assuming that $D_{it}$ and $S_{it}$ are log-normally distributed (see Smolny, 1993, for some empirical justification), i.e.

$$\ln S_{it} = s_t + u_{it},$$

$$\ln D_{it} = d_t + v_{it},$$

where $(u_{it}, v_{it}) \sim N(0, \Sigma_t)$ with $cov(u_t, v_t) = r_t \sigma_{dt} \sigma_{st}$ and variances $\sigma_{dt}^2$ and $\sigma_{st}^2$, Lambert shows that aggregate employment can be approximated by a CES function of aggregate components:[2]

$$L_t \cong \left(D_t^{-\rho_t} + S_t^{-\rho_t}\right)^{(-1/\rho_t)}, \tag{2.11}$$

where $D_t = \Sigma_i D_{it}$, $S_t = \Sigma_i S_{it}$, and $L_t = \Sigma_i L_{it}$. The parameter $\rho_t$ measures mismatch in the micromarkets, since it is inversely related to the dispersion of micro demands and supplies, more precisely to the difference of microeconomic disturbances (cf. Lambert, p. 124):

$$\rho_t = \frac{r_t}{\sigma_{*t}}, \tag{2.12}$$

$$\sigma_{*t}^2 = var(u_t - v_t) = \sigma_{dt}^2 + \sigma_{st}^2 - 2 r_t \sigma_{st} \sigma_{dt}.$$

1 See Sneessens und Drèze, 1986, for the theoretical analysis of a complete macroeconomic model and Drèze and Bean, 1990, for the estimation of country models of the main European countries and the U.S.

2 Lambert (1988) considers a large number *n* of micromarkets so that aggregate values can be replaced by expected values: The law of large numbers implies, for instance, $plim(\Sigma D_{it}) = nE(D_{it})$.

Empirical estimates of Lambert's *rho* are based on equation (2.11), which can be estimated by nonlinear least squares. To get time-variant indexes, $\rho_t$ is formulated in terms of linear time trends and dummies (see the country papers in Drèze and Bean, 1990) or in terms of explanatory variables (Entorf, König and Pohlmeier, 1992). The most appealing property of *rho* is its interpretation in terms of "structural unemployment at equilibrium", SURE, which measures the amount of unemployment which would arise due to mismatch despite a hypothetical situation of general equilibrium $D = S$. (2.11) reveals that such a situation leads to $L_t = 2^{-1/\rho_t} S_t$, and using the definition $UR = 1 - L/S$ gives

$$SURE_t = 1 - 2^{-1/\rho_t}. \tag{2.13}$$

Evidence based on German data (Entorf, Franz, König and Smolny, 1990) reveals that *SURE* is growing steadily throughout the estimation period, reaching about 4 percent in 1986.[1]

## 2.4. Measurement problems

Measures of mismatch require that unemployment and vacancies reflect supply and demand of the job market. Quality of data is always debatable, but the issue is particularly troublesome in the case of mismatch. The most evident drawbacks arise for indices based on unemployment and vacancy data.

*Unemployment:* The crucial question is whether unemployment in fact measures potential job offers or at least underutilization of labour. There are many flows such as quits, layoffs, hirings, entries into the workforce, exits into (early) retirement and employment-employment flows that moreover depend on economic situations and institutional setups. The dynamics and the flexibility of the matching process is much more complex than unemployment figures *alone* can reflect. For instance, during 1985 and 1990, employment in Western Europe grew by some 9.5 million people, whereas unemployment fell by roughly only three million (EEC, 1991). Other factors were not counted as a potential component of underutilization: The working-age population went up by four million (partly because of migration), 3.5 million women who were counted as

---

1 Using estimates of the goods market, some recent works also include results for "structural underutilization of capital at equilibrium", *SUCE,* which remains at a constant value of about 2 percent if all spillovers coming from the labour market are eliminated (see the discussion in König and Entorf, 1990, and Entorf, 1992).

inactive before changed their status (i.e. the female participation rate increased substantially), whereas one million men changed from active to inactive.

A second example comes from Eastern Germany, where employment fell by about 40% within two years after the German Monetary Union without an apparent effect on official statistics for many reasons (commuting, migration, early retirement, training etc.). For these reasons, indices based on employment instead of unemployment are more robust with respect to such hidden unemployment problems that are also affected by institutional and political arrangements.

*Vacancies:* Even more severe problems arise for indices based on vacancy data. Official data comprise only those job searchers who register as such at the labour office. Reyer et al. (1990) report the results of a survey conducted by IAB in 1990 (Institut für Arbeits-und Berufsforschung, German Employment Institute, Nuremberg), saying that only 40% of all vacant jobs are mediated by the labour office. This ratio is higher for unskilled blue-collar workers ("un-, angelernte Arbeiter", 47%) than for skilled blue-collar workers ("Facharbeiter", 38%). As for blue-collar workers, the reported ratio decreases with qualification for white-collar workers: 29% of the skilled white-collar workers ("Angestellte mit qualifizierter Tätigkeit") appear in official data, whereas 50% of simple white-collar jobs ("Angestellte mit einfacher Tätigkeit") are registrated at the labour office.

Firm size is represented asymmetrically in official data in the same way as the degree of qualification. While only 37% of all vacancies of small firms (less than 20 employees) are reported, 62% of all vacancies offered by large firms (more than 1000 employees) appear in the official statistics ( Reyer et al., 1990). Similar coverage problems arise for the respective sectoral affiliation. The public sector reports 50% of all vacant jobs, the manufacturing sector reports 45%, whereas the banking and assurance companies report only 15%.

Being aware of the pertinent problems of interpretation, Franz (1987, 1991b) assumes, that the average duration of job vacancies filled through the labour office is equal to the average duration of job vacancies filled without the assistance of the labour office, and he calculates corrected vacancy data based on the ratio of cumulated official vacancies and cumulated hirings within one year. Figure 2.3 displays official vacancy data, corrected vacancy data, the ratio official data / corrected data and the degree of capacity utilization. The figures show that the ratio mediated by the labour office seems to be affected by cyclical variations as represented by the degree of capacity utilization.

*Figure 2.3:* Vacancies and corrected vacancy data

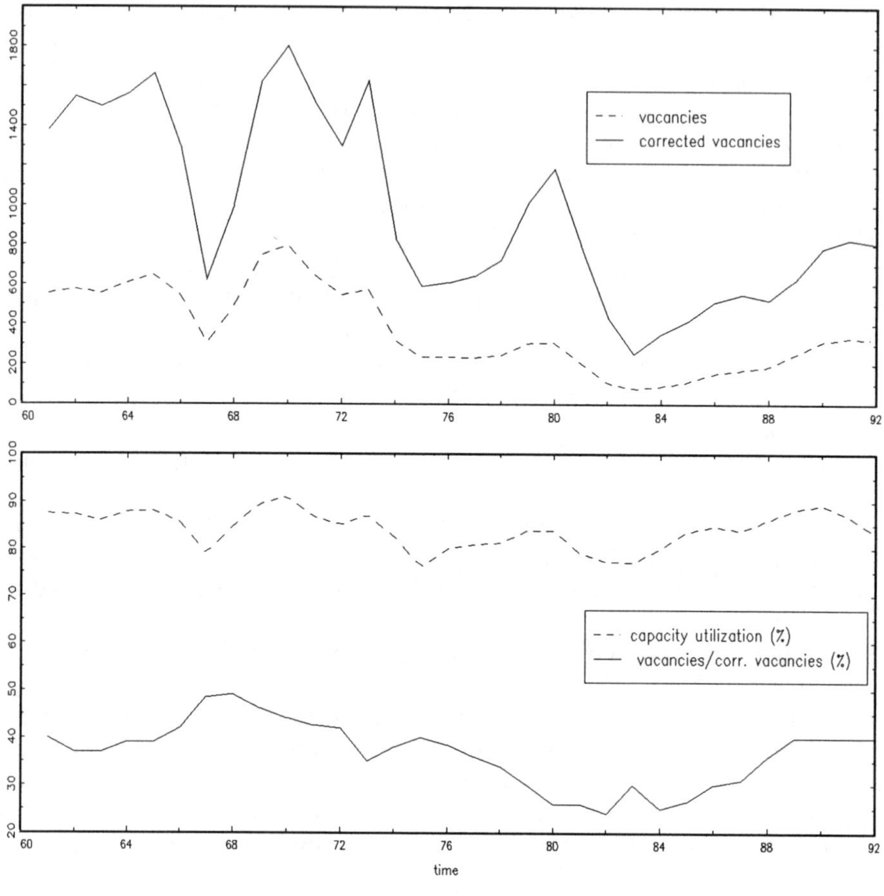


Franz (1991a) reports some interesting insights resulting from using both corrected vacancy data and official statistics. While the official data do not indicate any shift of the Beveridge curve since 1974, the data corrected for a fall from 45% to less than 25% of new hires mediated by the labour office show a substantial outward shift. Similar problems, though with opposite implied errors from the official data, are reported for Beveridge curves of the U.K (Jackman, Layard and Pissarides, 1989) and the U.S. (Abraham, 1987). Somewhat reassuring is the fact that both time series of adjusted and unadjusted vacancies reveal similar trends, though the adjusted time series are more sensitive with respect to cyclical effects at least until the beginning of the eighties (see Figure 2.1).

## 2.5. Disaggregation and unobserved heterogeneity

Conventional indexes measure mismatch as a one-dimensional phenomenon (cf. Padoa-Schioppa, 1991; Layard, Nickell and Jackman, 1991). The most common practice is to confront relative unemployment figures of a well defined category such as sector, skill or region with corresponding relative vacancies. The following example shows that a more disaggregate analysis of mismatch would be helpful.

We consider the simplest case of two regions, $A$ and $B$, and two skills, $a$ and $b$. Relative unemployment $u_i = U_i/U$ and relative vacancies $v_i = V_i/V$ are allocated as follows in two disaggregate matrices $U_{\text{dis}}$ and $V_{\text{dis}}$:

$$U_{\text{dis}} = \begin{pmatrix} u_{Aa} & u_{Ab} \\ u_{Ba} & u_{Bb} \end{pmatrix},$$

$$V_{\text{dis}} = \begin{pmatrix} v_{Aa} & v_{Ab} \\ v_{Ba} & v_{Bb} \end{pmatrix},$$

where $u_{Aa} = U_{Aa}/(U_{Aa} + U_{Ba})$ and $u_{Ba} = U_{Ba}/(U_{Aa} + U_{Ba})$ divide unemployed workers having skill $a$ into two regional components. Analogously, we define relative unemployment figures of category $b$ as $u_{Ab}$ and $u_{Bb}$ as well as corresponding relative vacancies.

Conventional indexes of mismatch are limited to either regions or skills, i.e. they focus on marginal entries:[1]

$$u_{\text{region}} = \begin{pmatrix} u_A \\ u_B \end{pmatrix} = \frac{1}{U_{Aa} + U_{Ab} + U_{Ba} + U_{Bb}} \begin{pmatrix} U_{Aa} & + & U_{Ab} \\ U_{Ba} & + & U_{Bb} \end{pmatrix},$$

$$v_{\text{region}} = \begin{pmatrix} v_A \\ v_B \end{pmatrix} = \frac{1}{V_{Aa} + V_{Ab} + V_{Ba} + V_{Bb}} \begin{pmatrix} V_{Aa} & + & V_{Ab} \\ V_{Ba} & + & V_{Bb} \end{pmatrix}$$

or

$$u_{\text{skill}} = \begin{pmatrix} u_a \\ u_b \end{pmatrix} = \frac{1}{U_{Aa} + U_{Ab} + U_{Ba} + U_{Bb}} \begin{pmatrix} U_{Aa} & + & U_{Ba} \\ U_{Ab} & + & U_{Bb} \end{pmatrix},$$

$$v_{\text{skill}} = \begin{pmatrix} v_a \\ v_b \end{pmatrix} = \frac{1}{V_{Aa} + V_{Ab} + V_{Ba} + V_{Bb}} \begin{pmatrix} V_{Aa} & + & V_{Ba} \\ V_{Ab} & + & V_{Bb} \end{pmatrix}$$

A numerical example reveals potential problems:

$$U_{\text{dis}} = \begin{pmatrix} 1 & 0 \\ 0 & 1 \end{pmatrix}, \quad V_{\text{dis}} = \begin{pmatrix} 0 & 1 \\ 1 & 0 \end{pmatrix}.$$

---

1 Assuming a one-to-one relationship between workers and jobs, i.e. excluding that the same worker is captured in more than one skill category, for instance.

This situation describes perfect mismatch: In region $A$, all unemployed people can be found in the category of skill $a$, while all jobs are available in $b$. In region $B$, all unemployment is concentrated in $b$ and all jobs are in $a$. Analogously, for skill $b$, all unemployment is in region $B$, while all vacancies are in $A$, and, for skill $a$, all unemployment can be found in $A$ and all vacancies are in $B$.

Looking at aggregate indexes after averaging out either regions or skills, both alternative indexes would indicate a perfect *match*! Both $M_1$ and $M_2$ are zero, since all aggregate $u_i$ are equal to aggregate $v_i: u_A = v_A = u_B = v_B = 1/2$ and $u_a = v_a = u_b = v_b = 1/2$.[1] This example demonstrates the extreme case, but it shows that the degree of disaggregation is very important and how multi-dimensional categories can easily produce contradictory results. Here, the correct way to deal with mismatch would be

$$(2.14) \qquad M_1' = \Sigma_{ij} \,|\, u_{ij} - v_{ij} \,|,$$

where $i = 1, \ldots, K$ indicate regions and $j = 1, \ldots, M$ represent skills. More disaggregate levels highlighting the performance of a particular skill in a well defined region *and* a well defined industrial sector, would be an additional improvement. The problem, however, is that data with such deep level of disaggregation are not available, at least for vacancies. A more detailed construction of analogous indexes solely based on employment or unemployment would be somewhat easier, although still very cumbersome. It does not exist in practical applications.

Even with very detailed levels of disaggregation, mismatch measurement remains subject to potential misinterpretations. Structural problems might occur due to missing mobility also *within* well defined sectors. Recent evidence reveals that workers tend to move within sectors, rather than across sectors (Berman, Bound and Griliches, 1993; Jovanovic and Moffit, 1990). Thus, the very important aspect of match and mismatch within sectors is not captured by the available data, and the idea that mismatch could be reduced by moving labour across sectoral borders may be misleading.

The emergence of new technologies provides a good example that even detailed data on vacancies and unemployment are not capable to reveal a potential mismatch within sectors. Suppose we observe a large number of unemployed secretaries despite a large number of vacant secretarial jobs in a narrowly defined region and for a well defined sector. Since available computer skills do not fit the requirements of searching firms,

---

1 Interpreting $u_i$ as unemployment rates $ur_i$, one can easily show that also $M_3$ is zero.

no hiring will occur. Thus, even when the number of unemployed secretaries coincided with the number of vacancies for secretaries, mismatch would persist. Unobserved heterogeneity of job characteristics remains in the data. Estimations of mismatch have to be interpreted with care.

## 2.6. Time series analysis

Five indexes of mismatch were presented in Chapter 2.3. The evidence in Figures 2.1 and 2.2 and other surprising results in Chapter 2.2. suggest that the interpretation of mismatch might be affected by trending employment and unemployment variables. The following analysis summarizes time series properties of $M_1, M_2, M_3, M_4$ and Lambert's *rho* in the presence of stochastic trends and, if possible, deterministic trends.

Starting with $M_1$, the following properties hold. More detailed results and proofs are presented in the appendix to Chapter 2 (Appendix A2).

*Proposition 2.1:*

*(a) Given identical vacancies $V_i = V$ for all i, but at least one i with $U_i \neq U_j$, $i \neq j$, a positive additive global shift in unemployment will decrease mismatch $M_1$.*

*b) If sectoral unemployment follows a random walk with drift $\delta$ and if individual vacancies are generated according to a random walk with drift $\theta$, then $M_1(t)$ tends in probability to zero as $t \to \infty$.*

*Proof:* Appendix A2 (Proposition A1.c and Corollary*)*

Whatever the sample size, Proposition A1.a of Appendix A2 implies that the concept $M_1$ very likely indicates mismatch if the economy is characterized by a coincidence of a high dispersion of unemployment and a relatively homogenous number of vacancies. Proposition 2.1.a above covers the limiting case of completely homogenous vacancies. Here simple upward shifts of unemployment increase mismatch.

Proposition 2.1.b reveals the spuriously decreasing behaviour of the mismatch indicator $M_1$ in the face of stochasticly growing time series. Some simulation studies below will highlight the performance in small samples.

In the case of Jackman and Roper's (1987) alternative proposal, the presence of random walks with drifts implies the same asymptotic property:

*Proposition 2.2:*

*If unemployment and vacancies behave like random walks with drifts $\delta$ and $\theta$, respectively, then $M_2$ converges to zero for large t.*

*Proof:* Appendix A2 (Proposition A2)

Jackman, Layard and Savouri's (1991) $M_3$ can be analysed in the presence of simple deterministic growth:

*Proposition 2.3:*
*If unemployment $U_i$ of individual groups i is globally shifting upward by an amount q (such that the new individual level is $U_i + q$ for all i), then the measure of mismatch $M_3$ decreases.*
*Proof:* Appendix A2 (Proposition A3)

Nonstationary data force Lilien's (1982) index to decrease:

*Proposition 2.4:*
*If sectoral employment $L_{it}$ follows a random walk (with or without drift), then Lilien's (1982) sigma $(M_4)$ converges to zero for large t.*[1]
*Proof:* Appendix A2 (Proposition A4)

The final concept of mismatch is different from previous measures of mismatch. Lambert's (1988) *rho* is based on disequilibrium theory, its empirical evidence indicates growing mismatch after OPEC I, and Proposition 2.5 shows that mismatch *increases* if underlying time series reveal stochastic trends:

*Proposition 2.5:*
*If at least one of the components $\ln D_{it}$ and $\ln S_{it}$ in the min-condition $\ln L_{it} = \min(\ln D_{it}, \ln S_{it})$ behaves like a random walk (with or without drift), then Lambert's (1988) rho approaches zero for $t \to \infty$, i.e. the measure of structural underutilization "SURE" converges to 100% if $t \to \infty$.*

---

1 The result in Proposition 2.4 seems to contradict Lilien's (1982) empirical result which presents a regression where sigma has a positive impact on unemployment, whereas Proposition 2.4 suggests that unemployment and *sigma* run in opposite directions. This result has however been found in a multiple regression. Moreover time series of U.S. unemployment (see Lilien, 1982) appear much more cyclical than European unemployment figures. The positive coefficient in the regression is due to the high coincidence of short-run cycles in unemployment and short-run cycles in Lilien's sigma (see Abraham and Katz, 1986, for an alternative interpretation which stresses the importance of aggregate demand shocks). Using Lilien's (1982) data on unemployment and sigma, I calculated corresponding *long-run* trends of both time series. Employing simple deterministic trends of order three gives a *negative* correlation of -0.43 between long-run unemployment trends and Liliens's sigma. This is in line with Proposition 2.4 and the result that (despite the relatively high variance of the time series) also U.S. unemployment behaves like a nonstationary variable (see Chapter 2.7).

*Proof:* Appendix A2 (Proposition A5)

So far, all proofs are based on additively growing time series, either in terms of deterministic growth or in terms of stochastic trends. It should be stressed that potential *multiplicative* increments do *not* affect presented measures of mismatch, as can be seen from the following remark.

***Remark:*** *If the individual components of the indices* $M_1 - M_5$, *i.e. sectoral unemployment, vacancies or employment series, grow with a multiplicative factor, then measures of mismatch do not change.*
*Proof:* Appendix A2 (Remark A1)

Summarizing Theorem 2.1 to Theorem 2.5, we may conclude that predicted time series behaviour of mismatch indicators coincides with their observed time series behaviour in the presence of trending time series: $M_1$ to $M_4$ increase while *SURE* decreases. Thus, mismatch trends based on mismatch indicators might be simple statistical artifacts. Such a conclusion would be reinforced if actual time series behaviour indeed reveal nonstationarity.

## 2.7. Testing for unit roots

Chapter 2.6. demonstrates that, in the presence of integrated time series, the evidence presented in Chapter 2.2 must be reinterpreted to avoid misleading conclusions. The correct procedure to test the relevance of Propositions 2.1.- 2.5. would be to analyse the disaggregate time series directly. Due to data limitations such a procedure is not feasible. We are however able to run tests for several aggregate time series. From the representation of integrated time series, we know that, if some aggregate time series are integrated of a particular order, then at least one of the components must be integrated of the same or a higher order.

Testing for unit roots implies distinguishing between a trend stationary time series $y_t$, which can be written as

$$y_t = a_0 + a_1 t + u_t, \tag{2.15}$$

where $t$ is a time trend and $u_t$ follows a stationary ARMA process, and a difference stationary process

$$y_t = d + y_{t-1} + u_t, \tag{2.16}$$

where again $u_t$ follows a stationary ARMA process. The choice between the two models is difficult and confusing, as can be seen from the following model which includes both (2.15) and (2.16) as special cases (see Bhargava, 1986):

$$(2.17)\qquad y_t = \gamma_0 + \gamma_1 t + v_t, \quad v_t = \alpha v_{t-1} + u_t$$

$$= \gamma_0 + \gamma_1 t + \alpha(y_{t-1} - \gamma_0 - \gamma_1(t-1)) + u_t.$$

Thus, when $|\alpha|<1$, (2.17) is identical to the trend stationary model (2.15) and it reduces to the difference stationary model (2.16) when $\alpha = 1$. In reparameterized form, (2.17) can be written as

$$y_t = \beta_0 + \beta_1 t + \alpha y_{t-1} + u_t,$$

where $\qquad \beta_0 \equiv \gamma_0(1-\alpha) + \gamma_1\alpha, \quad \beta_1 \equiv \gamma_1(1-\alpha).$

Unit root tests are performed after subtracting $y_{t-1}$ from both sides, leading to

$$(2.18)\qquad \Delta y_t = \beta_0 + \beta_1 t + (\alpha - 1)y_{t-1} + u_t.$$

Unit root tests are based on the hypothesis that $(\alpha - 1) = 0$ (where the inference is based on the nonstandard Dickey-Fuller distribution). A disturbing problem, however, is the fact that under $H_0$ $(\alpha = 1)$ the linear trend term should disappear $(\beta_1 = 0)$, i.e. *both* the presence and the absence of a deterministic trend would lead to a zero estimate of the time trend, whereas in the stationary $H_1$ case, the regression may include a non-zero linear trend. This treatment does not do justice to deterministic trends under the null.

Thus, since more than one parameter estimate is involved for the test of unit roots, the more adequate way to formulate the unit root test is to use Lagrange-Multiplier (LM) tests. Schmidt and Phillips (1992) propose a LM test which avoids the above described confusions arising in the presence of deterministic trends. They also mention further difficulties such as variation of the Dickey-Fuller distribution with respect to nuisance parameters even under the null hypothesis, inconsistency against trend stationary alternatives (if the test equations do not allow for trend under the alternative) and, if a linear trend is introduced as an additional regressor, introduction of a variable that is irrelevant under the null.

Testing for unit roots is subject to many limitations, in particular in small samples. Since there is no general agreement about the correct way to deal with unit root tests in practice, here both LM-tests and conventional ADF-tests are applied. All ADF-tests follow a well defined order to make replications of the presented tests possible.

The general idea of my ADF-testing procedure is to choose a parsimonious parameterization which avoids drawbacks due to irrelevant regressors. Moreover, since many of the relevant time series are rather short (about 30 observations), I do not apply the "general to specific" rule-of-thumb, because the estimation of many parameters would lead to few degrees-of-freedom such that the t-values of critical parameters might be affected by collinearity problems. Here, three consecutive steps are performed:

1) The first step is an ADF regression with trend and constant and no lagged difference (i.e. a Dickey-Fuller test). Then lagged differences are added until no misspecification due to serial correlation remains ($1.85 < DW < 2.15$). If the linear trend is significant (5% critical value), stop and calculate the ADF-statistic.
2) If the trend is insignificant, restart with a constant only, add lagged differences until no serial correlation remains. If the constant is significant, stop and calculate the ADF-statistic.
3) If the constant is insignificant, restart with neither constant nor trend, add lagged differences until no serial correlation remains and calculate the ADF-statistic.

The critical values of the ADF distribution are calculated according to MacKinnon (1991), who implements a much larger set of replications than those on which the original Dickey-Fuller tables are based. In addition, he estimates response surface regressions over these replications which permit the calculation of Dickey-Fuller critical values for any sample size and the three options "constant included", "constant and linear time trend included" and "neither constant nor trend included".

The procedure used by Schmidt and Phillips (1992) can be summarized in two sequential steps:

Calculate first

$$(2.19) \qquad S_t = y_t - y_1 + \quad mean(\Delta y)(1-t),$$

where $y_1$ is the first observation of the variable under consideration. Then run the regression

$$(2.20) \qquad \Delta y_t = \text{intercept} + \phi(S_t - 1) + \text{error}.$$

The test statistics are defined as $\tilde{\rho} = T\hat{\phi}$, where $\hat{\phi}$ is the least squares estimator of (2.20). $T$ is the number of observations, and $\tilde{\tau}$ is the usual t-statistic for $\phi = 0$ in (2.20). The distributions of $\tilde{\tau}$ and $\tilde{\rho}$ are tabulated in Schmidt and Phillips (1992).

Table 2.2. summarizes the results of both procedures for the unemployment rates of the main West-European countries France (F), United Kingdom (U.K.) and (West) Germany (D) as well as for Spain (E), Japan (Jap) and the United States (U.S.). The estimation period is 1960 until 1990. A second period is analysed in the case of the U.S., where Lilien's (1982) time series of 1948-1980 is of particular interest (see Proposition 2.4.).

Table 2.2. reveals that unemployment rates behave like nonstationary time series and have to be treated as I(1) or even I(2). There is some evidence in favour of I(2) for Spain (both tests), France (ADF-tests) and U.K. (Schmidt-Phillips test). Given the additional evidence for the presence of drifts and/or trends in German, Spanish and U.S. time series, we in fact have to doubt the appropriateness of mismatch indices based on unemployment figures.

A simple experiment based on unemployment rates reveals a direct implication of unit roots tests. We apply Jackman, Layard and Savouri's (1991) $M_3$, which is based on the variance of relative unemployment rates. The variance at each point in time is calculated using the unemployment rates and the weights of the main European countries U.K., France, Germany and of the U.S. Thus, $M_3$ can be interpreted as a measure of mismatch among some of the main industrialized countries and the index should show whether unemployment could be reduced by increasing international labour mobility. The result is no longer surprising and reflects the integrated nature of underlying time series: Figure 2.4. suggests a declining general trend of $M_3$, implying that only a minor part of unemployment could have been avoided in the eighties and a high percentage of unemployment could have been eliminated in the sixties and early seventies, a result which very likely is a mere mirror-image of general unemployment growth.

*Table 2.2.:* Unit root tests of national unemployment rates

| | F | U.K. | D | E | Jap | U.S. | U.S. (Lilien) |
|---|---|---|---|---|---|---|---|
| I. ADF-tests: | | | | | | | |
| a) $H_0$ = I (1) (against I(0) ) | | | | | | | |
| Order of lags | 3 | 2 | 1 | 1 | 1 | 1 | 1 |
| ADF-statistic | -1.97 | -0.007 | -2.54 | -2.46 | -1.21 | -2.19 | -3.27 |
| Linear trend significant? | no | no | yes | yes | no | no | yes |
| Constant significant? | yes | no | - | - | yes | yes | - |
| Mac-Kinnon critical value | -2.98 | -1.95 | -3.57 | -3.57 | -2.97 | -2.96 | -3.56 |
| b) $H_0$ = I(2) (against I(1) ) | | | | | | | |
| Order of lag | 1 | 1 | 0 | 1 | 0 | 0 | 0 |
| ADF-statistic | -1.52 | -3.81 | -3.56 | -1.72 | -3.81 | -4.93 | -5.73 |
| Linear trend significant ? | no | no | no | no | no | no | no |
| Constant significant? | no | no | no | no | no | no | no |
| Mac-Kinnon critical value | -1.95 | -1.95 | -1.95 | -1.95 | -1.95 | -1.95 | -1.95 |
| Result | I(2) | I(1) | I(1) | I(2) | I(1) | I(1) | I(1) |
| II. Schmidt-Phillips tests | | | | | | | |
| a) $H_0$= I(1) (against I(0) ) | | | | | | | |
| $\tilde{\rho}$ | -1.64 | -3.01 | -3.63 | -1.30 | -2.05 | -6.32 | -15.56 |
| $\tilde{\tau}$ | -0.87 | -1.19 | -1.31 | -0.77 | -0.97 | -1.78 | -3.04 |
| b) $H_0$= I(2) (against I(1) ) | | | | | | | |
| $\tilde{\rho}$ | -17.37 | -15.33 | -20.46 | -7.2 | -20.31 | -26.20 | -31.35 |
| $\tilde{\tau}$ | -3.32 | -3.05 | -3.74 | -1.92 | -3.72 | -4.52 | -5.64 |
| Result | I(1) | I(2) | I(1) | I(2) | I(1) | I(1) | I(1) |

*Notes:* Unemployment rates are taken from Layard, Nickell and Jackman (1991). The period is 1960 - 1990. "U.S. (Lilien)" is based on the unemployment rates of Lilien's (1982) work and covers the years 1948 until 1980. The critical value of $\tilde{\rho}$ is -16.0 and the critical value of $\tilde{\tau}$ is -3.17 (Schmidt and Phillips, 1992, Table 1A).

*Table 2.3.:* Unit root tests of "mismatch time series"

| | D | C | S | U | O | O (corr.) | L |
|---|---|---|---|---|---|---|---|
| I. ADF-tests: | | | | | | | |
| a) $H_0$ = I(1) (against I(0)) | | | | | | | |
| Order of lags | 1 | 1 | 2 | 2 | 2 | 1 | 2 |
| ADF-statistic | -3.90 | -4.00 | -1.81 | -2.44 | -0.48 | -3.64 | -0.90 |
| Linear trend significant? | yes | yes | no | yes | no | yes | yes |
| Constant significant? | - | - | yes | - | no | - | - |
| Mac-Kinnon critical value | -3.60 | -3.60 | -2.99 | -3.53 | -1.95 | -3.57 | -3.57 |
| b) $H_0$ = I(2) (against I(1)) | | | | | | | |
| Order of lag | - | - | 1 | 1 | 1 | - | 1 |
| ADF-statistic | - | - | -3.33 | -3.51 | -5.54 | - | -3.72 |
| Linear trend significant ? | - | - | no | no | no | - | no |
| Constant significant? | - | - | no | no | no | - | no |
| Mac-Kinnon critical value | - | - | -1.96 | -1.95 | -1.95 | - | -1.95 |
| Result | I(0) | I(0) | I(1) | I(1) | I(1) | I(0) | I(1) |
| II. Schmidt-Phillips tests | | | | | | | |
| a) $H_0$= I(1) (against I(0)) | | | | | | | |
| $\tilde{\rho}$ | -7.56 | -10.56 | -1.09 | -1.47 | -4.05 | -10.56 | -3.40 |
| $\tilde{\tau}$ | -1.96 | -2.41 | -1.31 | -0.84 | -1.41 | -2.39 | -1.28 |
| b) $H_0$= I(2) (against I(1)) | | | | | | | |
| $\tilde{\rho}$ | -18.98 | -19.89 | -14.72 | -20.5 | -28.2 | -24.92 | -14.57 |
| $\tilde{\tau}$ | -3.61 | -3.78 | -3.02 | -3.56 | -4.54 | -4.34 | -2.99 |
| Result | I(1) | I(1) | I(2) | I(1) | I(1) | I(1) | I(2) |

*Notes:* D = Demand determined employment, C = Capacity determined employment, S = labour supply; D, C and S, observed for 1960-1986, are taken from Entorf, Franz, König and Smolny (1990); U = unemployment in West-Germany, 1951-1992, O = vacancies in West-Germany, 1951-1992, O (corr.) = corrected vacancies in West-Germany, 1961-1992, the correction is based on Franz, 1991b; the figures in 1991 and 1992 are based on the assumption that 40% of all vacant jobs are mediated by the labour office (according to Reyer et al., 1990). L = Employment in West-Germany, 1960-1992 (Statistical Yearbooks).

Table 2.3. presents unit root tests for the remaining mismatch indices. The disaggregate time series underlying Lambert's *rho* only allow an ambigous conclusion, since the time series "demand-determined employment" $D$ and "capacity-determined employment" $C$ ("employment at full capacity", as defined in the work of the "European Unemployment Programme", see Entorf, Franz, König and Smolny, 1990, in Drèze and Bean, 1990) are I(0), while $S$ seems to be I(1) (note the poor power of unit root tests which are based on 26 observations). However, Theorem 2.5 implies that the presence of one single I(1) component suffices for a spurious increase of *rho*. Moreover, the Schmidt-Phillips test turns out to be more in favour of higher degrees of integration. $D$ and $C$ are I(1), while $S$ is I(2). Thus, there is some danger that the observed increase in *SURE* is the mere result of the nonstationarity of the data. Also employment $L$, measured for 1960-1992, is I(2) in terms of Schmidt and Phillips (1992) and I(1) in terms of traditional ADF-tests which raises doubts with respect to the validity of Lilien's index: The falling numbers presented in Franz (1991), for instance, might be spurious. Unemployment and vacancies, as they are used in Figure 2.2. turn out to be I(1). Corrected vacancies, however, are I(0), though they are only available for the shorter period 1961-1992. The Schmidt-Phillips test, however, again does not reject the I(1) hypothesis.

*Figure 2.4.*: International "mismatch"

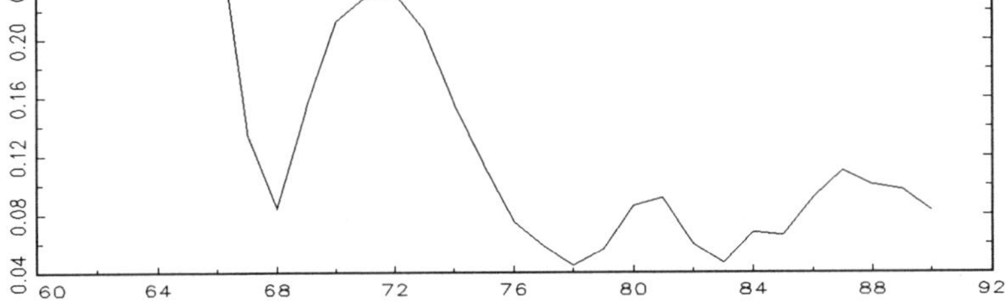


*Note:* $M_3$ based on weighted unemployment rates of U.K., France, Germany and U.S., 1960-1990; Data: Layard, Nickell and Jackman (1991)

## 2.8. On the magnitude of drifts in macroeconomic mismatch time series

Before a final conclusion based on Propositions 2.1.- 2.5. can be drawn, the nature of drifts in observed time series remains to be analysed. It becomes clear from simple regression analysis that the nature of drifts is well described by the ratio drift/noise, i.e. the ratio of $\gamma$ and $\sigma_\epsilon$ in $y_t - y_{t-1} = \gamma + \epsilon_t$ (see also Appendix A3.II). Hylleberg and Mizon (1989) investigate some macroeconomic time series and find ratios between -0.14 and 0.78 . Table 2.4. gives some impression of the magnitude of the drifts in the time series underlying the indexes of mismatch. The table contains consistent estimates of $\gamma$ and $\sigma_\epsilon$ which are obtained by regressing $\Delta y_t$ on a constant and by calculating the sample standard deviation of $\Delta y_t$. Moreover, Table 2.4. includes t-values of $\hat{\gamma}$.

The results show that one can hardly draw any unambiguos conclusions from all time series and for all time periods. Drift/noise ratios are rather heterogenous even for presented unemployment rates. While France and Spain have drift-noise ratios that exceed 0.35, Japan and in particular the U.S. are characterized by very low drift/noise ratios. This fact is also covered by low t-values.

Figure 2.5. gives some impression of the relationship between conventional t-values and drift/noise ratios. Based on $y_t = y_{t-1} + \gamma + \epsilon_t$, I have simulated stochastic processes with $\sigma_\epsilon = 1$ and (i) $\gamma = 0.2$ and (ii) $\gamma = 0.5$. Figure 2.5. presents the mean and percentiles of the estimate $\hat{\gamma}$ as well as corresponding t-values dependent on the length of time series, $T$. The results reveal that conventional t-values should be interpreted with care. For instance, if the ratio is $0.2$, which is a frequent value for economic time series, then *average* t-values for a sample size of about $T = 30$ are about $1.2$ and only for $T > 100$ t-values become larger than $2.0$. Moreover, -the distribution of t-values is widely spread and even for $T = 100$ the 5%-95% range is $0.4 - 4.7$. If $\gamma = 0.5$, t-values are higher, and average t-values range between $2$ (at $T = 15$) and $5$ (at $T = 100$) in Figure 2.5.

"Insignificant" conventional t-values do not imply that theoretical results based on the presence of drifts would not hold. All asymptotic results hold even for small drift/noise ratios and, thus, also for small t-values (i.e. below standard critical values of about 2.0). This fact will be demonstrated in some simulation study of the next Section. Moreover, as is the case for German unemployment, recent subperiods behave quite differently from the early data (see the period 1972-1992). The behaviour of the employment time series underlying Lambert's *rho* is different from the other time series since it reveals some negative drift ratios. In terms of Proposition 2.5., however, it should be reiterated that already the "simple"

I(1) property is sufficient for the convergence of *rho* towards zero (there is no drift needed for the weak convergence to zero). Employment over a longer period 1960-1992 has a more significant drift.

Based on the results of Table 2.4. we are now in the position to reinterpret Figure 2.2. Since the ratio of the variances of unemployment and vacancies (official data, as used in Figure 2.2.) is about 4/1 for the total period 1951 - 1992 and even 5.3/1 for the period 1972-1992, we may conclude that the variance of the unemployment time series dominates both $M_1$ and $M_2$ . The German unemployment series, however, reveals a highly significant (see Figure 2.5. for the evidence) drift for the period 1972 - 1992 while the other period has rather small drift terms. Thus, the falling mismatch indicators in the fifties (where we find *falling* unemployment rates) and the low level in the sixties might indeed come from a successful reorganization of the German labour market after World War II, whereas the falling mismatch indicator in the late seventies and eighties is very likely a spurious result of an unemployment time series that resembles an I(1) process with a strong positive drift.

*Table 2.4.:* The nature of drifts in observed time series

| Time series | Drift | Std.Dev. | Drift/ Std.Dev | t-value |
|---|---|---|---|---|
| Unemployment rates, 1960-90: | | | | |
| F | 0.24 | 0.48 | 0.5 | 2.7 |
| UK | 0.14 | 1.08 | 0.13 | 0.7 |
| D | 0.13 | 0.76 | 0.17 | 0.9 |
| E | 0.46 | 1.19 | 0.39 | 2.1 |
| Jap | 0.013 | 0.17 | 0.08 | 0.4 |
| US | 0.006 | 0.98 | 0.006 | 0.04 |
| US, 1948-80 (Lilien) | 0.10 | 1.21 | 0.08 | 0.5 |
| Unemployment *U*, 1951-92 | 2198 | 199715 | 0.011 | 0.07 |
| Unemployment *U*, 1972-92 | 77297 | 223577 | 0.35 | 1.6 |
| Vacancies *O*, 1951-92 | 4915 | 95538 | 0.05 | 0.3 |
| Employment (millions) *L*, 1960-92 | 0.095 | 0.33 | 0.29 | 1.6 |
| Demand determ. empl. *D*, 1960-86 | -0.07 | 0.60 | 0.12 | -0.6 |
| Capacity determ. employment *C*, 1960-86 | -0.08 | 0.30 | 0.27 | -1.4 |
| Labour supply *S*, 1960-86 | -0.02 | 0.20 | 0.10 | -0.4 |

*Notes:* See Table 2.2. and 2.3.; *D, C* and *S* are measured in millions.

*Figure 2.5.:* The distribution of $\hat{\gamma}$ and corresponding t-values

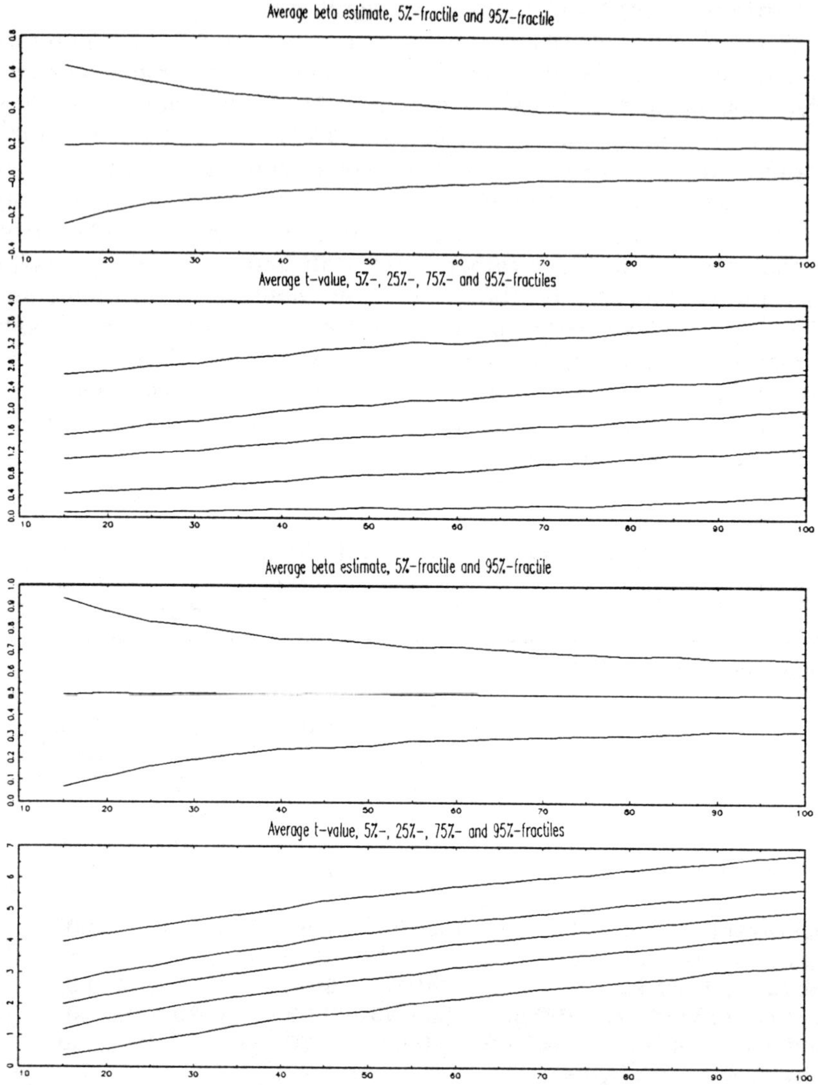


*Note:* The graphs show the distribution of $\hat{\gamma}$ of the regression $\Delta y_t = \gamma + u_t$, as well as conventional t-values of $\hat{\gamma}$. The percentiles are based on 5000 replications of the stochastic process $y_t = \gamma + y_{t-1} + \epsilon_t$, $\sigma_\epsilon = 1$. Starting values are zero which, however, is irrelevant since they cancel out in regressions including a constant, see the econometric results in Chapter 3.II. True values are $\gamma = 0.2$ and $\gamma = 0.5$, respectively.

## 2.9. Some simulation experiments

This section is devoted to the analysis of the behaviour of $M_1$ to $M_4$ in finite samples. We generate unemployment and vacancies according to

$$(2.21) \qquad U_{it} = \delta + U_{i,t-1} + \epsilon_{it}, \epsilon_{it} \sim N(0,1),$$

$$V_{it} = \theta + V_{i,t-1} + \nu_{it}, \nu_{it} \sim N(0,1), i = 1,\ldots,K, \quad t = 1,\ldots,T.$$

Starting values are uniformly distributed and randomly drawn from the interval [50,150]. Thus, with N(0,1) disturbances to unemployment and vacancies, most initial shocks are of a magnitude between zero and four percent with respect to the level of initial values. All time series are generated with identical realizations using the "seed" option of the GAUSS RNDNS random number generator.

Figure 2.6. displays some results with non-zero drifts. $T = 200$ observations are generated. The experiment is replicated 100 times. The first two windows display the average values of Jackman and Roper's (1987) $M_1$ and $M_2$. Following that is Jackman, Layard and Savouri's (1991) $M_3$ and finally Lilien's $M_4$. Note that the time series underlying $M_4$ are to be interpreted as disaggregate employment instead of unemployment as in the case of $M_1, M_2$ and $M_3$.

Panel a) starts with drifts $\delta = \theta = 0.10$. The number of groups (sectors, skills etc.) is $K = 5$. Despite the small drift/noise ratios, all indexes decrease when $T$ increases.

Panel b) demonstrates the effect when the drift/noise ratio of unemployment is $\delta = 0.5$ and the drift noise/ratio of vacancies is almost zero but still positive $(\theta = 0.02)$. When compared to Panel a), the graphs are smoother which is the result of a larger number of sectors $K$ and the effect of higher $\delta$ (see in particular $M_3$ and $M_4$ which are not affected by vacancies). An increase of $K$ leads to a general upward shift of mismatch, whereas higher drifts cause a faster convergence to zero.

Panel c) describes a situation with almost perfect match in the initial situation, that worsens afterwards, and that is eventually dominated by the trends in the data so that mismatch decreases again. An exception is Lilien's index which - apart from short-run fluctuations - decreases steadily in *all* experiments. This pattern was generated by assuming uniformly distributed starting values in the narrower range of [30,70] (instead of

[50,150]).[1] The other parameters are $\delta = \theta = 0.5$ and $K = 20$. This experiment shows that a decreasing path of mismatch is not simply the result of a very high variance of the initial situation.

In sum, these results suggest that the large-sample properties of mismatch indicators derived in propositions 2.1 to 2.5 also hold in small samples. This corroborates the view that empirical evidence suggesting decreasing importance of mismatch in the 1980s is severely biased by the nonstationarity of the data.

*Figure 2.6.:* Measures of mismatch on the basis of random walks with drift

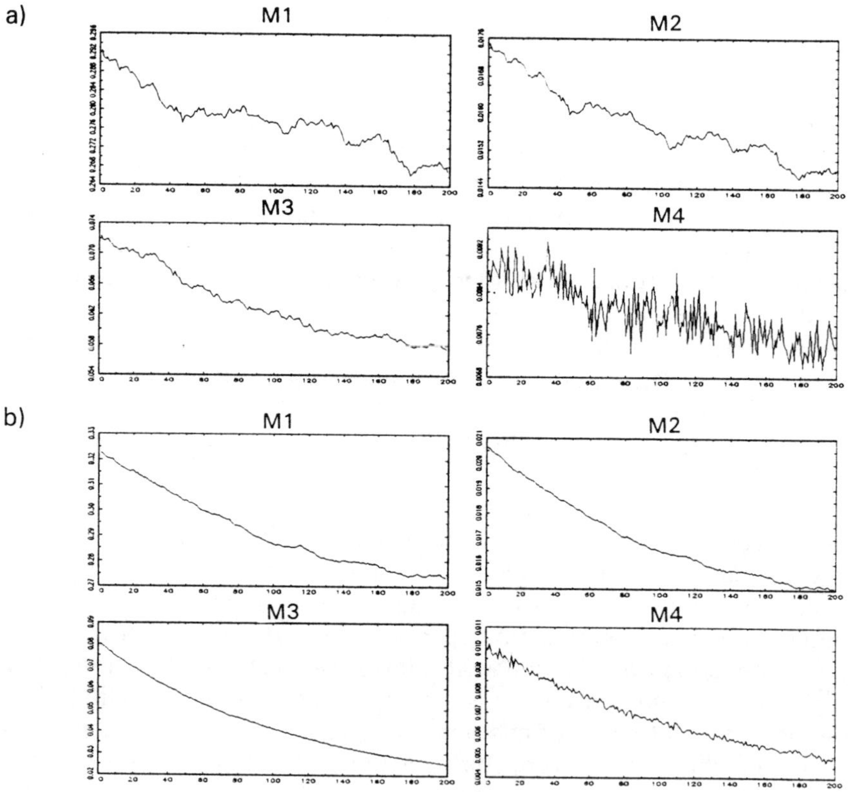


1 In the extreme case of identical starting values, mismatch would start with zero.

c)

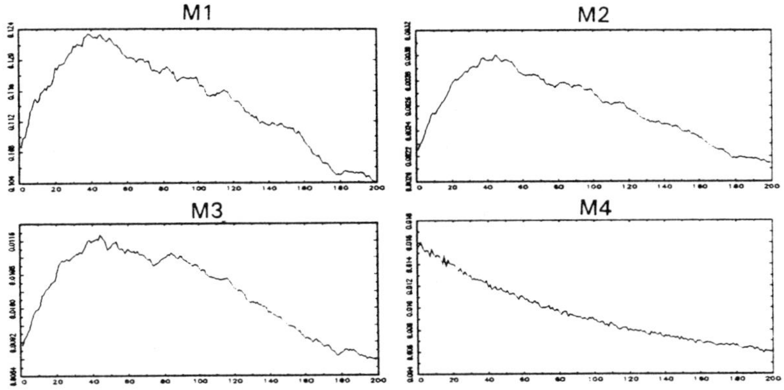


*Note:* All graphs represent the mean of 100 replications of model (2.21); Imposed parameters are as follows: Panel a): $\delta = \theta = 0.10$, $K = 5$; Panel b): $\delta = 0.5$, $\theta = 0.02$, $K = 20$; Panel c): $\delta = \theta = 0.5$, $K = 20$; Panel c) has different starting values: see the text for details.

## 2.10. Concluding remarks

Measuring mismatch is an important issue in policy advice. This chapter discusses the performance of five popular mismatch indices in the presence of globally growing unemployment. Measures of mismatch reported in literature do not indicate any worsening of skilled mismatch and a falling rate of regional mismatch (Padoa-Schioppa, 1991). On the other hand, estimates based on macroeconomic rationing models presented in Drèze and Bean (1990) reveal steadily growing mismatch in Europe. With respect to German data, Section 2.2. presents some micro evidence which suggests the same conclusion: Indicators of regional and occupational mobility reflect decreased mobility, most likely contributing to reported lack of skilled labour and high unemployment for wrongly skilled and unskilled workers.

The time series analysis of this chapter reveals that conventional measures of mismatch fail when unemployment figures reveal additive upward shifts. The results show that with both deterministic and stochastic shifts, measures of mismatch are likely to decline without any changes in the *relative* structure of sectors, skills or other grouping criteria. In contrast, Lambert's *rho* indicates *increasing* mismatch in such situations, i.e. it is biased in the opposite direction. Empirical tests show that these theoretical results have practical relevance, since unit roots and drifts are detectable in the data. The puzzle of contradictory results from different indicators can thus be solved by the observation that the underlying time series behave like nonstationary time series.

Existing measures of mismatch are designed for stationary (more precisely static) models (see the theoretical derivation of indexes of mismatch in Section 2.3.). Having said this, it is perhaps not surprising that results reported in the literature provide odd results. They should be supplemented by alternative measures, taking into account more realistic descriptions of the dynamics of mismatch phenomena.

Mismatch indices only reproduce the statistical properties of underlying time series. Of course, it is a disturbing idea that unemployment is I(1) since we know that there are natural limits which would constrain the growth of unemployment. However, in particular in the presence of short time series, computers are unable to distinguish recent, perhaps only temporary upward movements of unemployment from a perhaps stationary development in the long run. Indices of mismatch are dominated by recent upward trends, and the statistical procedure has to take consideration of this fact in order to avoid misinterpretation of statistical phenomena which are simply the result of computer aided number crunching and not of economic reasoning.

Would it be better to dismiss all results based on mismatch indices, given the problems addressed in this chapter? The message learned from the presence of trending time series and its implication for falling spurious mismatch is that potential *upward* movements could be interpreted in a non-spurious way: If we have nonstationary time series with drifts, and if we assume that these drifts are positive, upward movements of mismatch indicators are only possible if mismatch is indeed strong enough to offset the general inherent downward tendency which simply arises due to the trending nature of mismatch time series. The other downward direction would hold for Lambert`s *rho*, where we can argue that (despite stochastic trends in underlying time series) a *declining* mismatch index could only go along with a true reduction of microeconomic dispersion.

# Appendix A2

***Proposition A1:***

*(a) If*

$$\frac{1}{K^+}\sum_{i\in I^+} U_i > \frac{1}{K^-}\sum_{i\in I^-} U_i$$

*with*

$$I^+ = \{i \mid u_i > v_i\}, \qquad I^- = \{i \mid u_i \leq v_i\},$$

*$K^+$ = number of elements in $I^+$ and $K^- = K - K^+$, then $M_1$ decreases in the presence of additive shifts in unemployment measured as $U_i^* \equiv U_i + q$.*

*(b) If sectoral unemployment $U_{it}$ as well as sectoral vacancies $V_{it}$ are random walks, then $M_1(t)$ converges weakly to a Cauchy distributed random variable as $t \to \infty$.*

*(c) If sectoral unemployment follows a random walk with drift $\delta$, and if individual vacancies are generated according to a random walk with drift $\theta$, then $M_1(t)$ tends in probability to zero for large t.*

*Proof:*

(a) Let $U_i^* \equiv U_i + q$ for all i. Then $M_1$ becomes

$$M_1^*(q) = \Sigma \left| \frac{U_i^*}{\Sigma U_i^*} - \frac{V_i}{\Sigma V_i} \right| = \frac{\sum_{j\in I^+} U_j^*}{\sum_{i=1}^{K} U_i^*} - \frac{\sum_{j\in I^-} U_j^*}{\sum_{i=1}^{K} U_i^*} + \frac{\sum_{j\in I^-} V_j}{\sum_{i=1}^{K} V_i} - \frac{\sum_{j\in I^+} V_j}{\sum_{i=1}^{K} V_i}$$

We define $\Sigma^+ = \sum_{j\in I^+} U_j$, $\quad \Sigma^- = \sum_{j\in I^-} U_j$, $\quad S \equiv \Sigma_j U_j = \Sigma^+ + \Sigma^-$. The proposition follows if $\partial M_1^* / \partial q < 0$:

$$\frac{\partial M_1^*}{\partial q} = \frac{(K^+ - K^-)(S + Kq) - ((\Sigma^+ + K^+ q) - (\Sigma^- + K^- q))K}{(S + Kq)^2}$$

Using $S = \Sigma^+ + \Sigma^-$, $\quad K = K^+ + K^-$ and collecting terms leads to

$$\frac{\partial M_i^*}{\partial q} = \frac{2(K^+\Sigma^- - K^-\Sigma^+)}{(S + Kq)^2}.$$

Thus,

$$\frac{\partial M_1}{\partial q} < 0 \Leftrightarrow \frac{\Sigma^+}{K^+} > \frac{\Sigma^-}{K^-}.$$

(b) Let

$$(A1) \qquad U_{it} = U_{i,t-1} + \epsilon_{it} = \sum_{\tau=1}^{t} \epsilon_{i\tau} + U_{i0},$$

$$V_{it} = V_{i,t-1} + \nu_{it} = \sum_{\tau=1}^{t} \nu_{i\tau} + V_{i0},$$

where $\epsilon_{it}$ and $\nu_{it}$ are generated according to $\epsilon_{it} \sim \mathrm{IID}(0, \sigma^2_{\epsilon i})$, $\nu_{it} \sim \mathrm{IID}(0, \sigma^2_{\nu i})$ with $U_{i0}$ and $V_{i0}$ being non-zero starting values. Thus, taking expectated values, unemployment and vacancies could be interpreted as deviation from natural rates $U_{i0}$ and $V_{i0}$ . *IID* represents any well defined independently and identically distributed random variable.

Exploiting the same decomposition as in (a), we can write

$$(A2) \qquad M_1(t) = \frac{\sum_{j \in I^+} U_{jt} - \sum_{j \in I^-} U_{jt}}{\sum_{i=1}^{K} U_{it}} + \frac{\sum_{j \in I^-} V_{jt} - \sum_{j \in I^+} V_{jt}}{\sum_{i=1}^{K} V_{it}}.$$

As $t \to \infty$, asymptotic behaviour leads to the following expression for unemployment in category i $U_{it}$ (see Banerjee et al., 1993 for details about the transformation of integrated time series into Wiener processes):

$$(A3) \qquad t^{-1/2} \sum_{\tau=1}^{t} \epsilon_{i\tau} \Rightarrow A_{\epsilon i} \equiv \sigma_{\epsilon i} \int_0^1 dW(r),$$

where $\Rightarrow$ denotes weak convergence. In (A3), $A_{\epsilon i}$ is a random variable that boils down to a simple normal representation according to the central limit theorem: $A_{\epsilon i} \sim N(0, \sigma^2_{\epsilon i})$. Analogously, the asymptotic behaviour of individual vacancy terms is $B_{\nu i} \sim N(0, \sigma^2_{\nu i})$. Dividing numerator and denominator by $t^{1/2}$ leads to the following asymptotic ratio of normally distributed random variables (note that because of dividing by $t^{1/2}$ starting values play no role in the limit):

$$M_1(t) \Rightarrow \frac{\sum_{j \in I^+} A_{jt} - \sum_{j \in I^-} A_{jt}}{\sum_{i=1}^{K} A_{it}} + \frac{\sum_{j \in I^-} B_{jt} - \sum_{j \in I^+} B_{jt}}{\sum_{i=1}^{K} B_{it}}.$$

Thus, the limiting distribution is distributed as Cauchy and does not have a mean. (Here Slutsky's Theorem does not help in calculating asymptotic means, since both numerator and denominator have zero expectation).

(c) Let

$$U_{it} = \delta_i + U_{t.t-1} + \epsilon_{it} = t\delta_i + \sum_{\tau=1}^{t} \epsilon_{i\tau} + U_{i0}$$

$$V_{it} = \theta_i + V_{t.t-1} + \nu_{it} = t\theta_i + \sum_{\tau=1}^{t} \nu_{i\tau} + V_{i0}$$

with $\epsilon_{it}$, $\nu_{it}$, $U_{i0}$ and $V_{i0}$ defined as above. $\delta_i$ and $\theta_i$ are individual drift parameters.

We write $M_1$ as follows:

$$(A4) \qquad M_1(t) = \sum_{i=1}^{K} \left| \frac{U_{it} \sum_{j=1}^{K} V_{jt} - V_{it} \sum_{j=1}^{K} U_{jt}}{\left(\sum_{j=1}^{K} U_{jt}\right)\left(\sum_{j=1}^{K} V_{jt}\right)} \right| .$$

Looking at cross terms, for instance $U_{it}V_{jt}$, we see that the asymptotic behaviour is dominated by the product of the two deterministic trends $\delta_i \theta_j t^2$. All other terms grow with lower speed. See, for instance, the product $t\delta_i \Sigma \upsilon_{j\tau}$. According to (A3), this term grows with speed $t^{3/2}$.

Thus, dividing numerator and denominator by $t^2$ leads to the asymptotic result

$$M_1(t) \Rightarrow \sum_{i=1}^{K} \left| \frac{\delta_i \sum_{j=1}^{K} \theta_j - \theta_i \sum_{j=1}^{K} \delta_j}{\left(\sum_{j=1}^{K} \delta_j\right)\left(\sum_{j=1}^{K} \theta_j\right)} \right| .$$

Considering identical drifts $\delta_i = \delta$ and $\theta_i = \theta$ for all $i$ yields the result of Proposition A1 (c).

Proposition A1.(a) implies that the concept $M_1$ very likely indicates mismatch if the economy is characterized by a coincidence of a high dispersion of unemployment and a relatively homogeneous set of vacancies. For the limiting case of completely homogeneous vacancies, the following corollary applies.

***Corollary:***
*Given identical vacancies $V_i = V$ for all i, but at least one i with $U_i \neq U_j$, $i \neq j$, a positive additive global shift in unemployment will decrease mismatch $M_1$.*

*Proof:*
Identical vacancies imply $v_i = 1/K$. Since

$$I^+ = \left\{ i \mid U_i / \left( \sum_{i=1}^{K} U_i \right) < \frac{1}{K} \Leftrightarrow U_i > \frac{\Sigma U_i}{K} \right\}$$

$$I^- = \left\{ i \mid U_i / \left( \sum_{i=1}^{K} U_i \right) \geq \frac{1}{K} \Leftrightarrow U_i \leq \frac{\Sigma U_i}{K} \right\},$$

averaging $U_i$ of both sets $I^+$ and $I^-$ leads to

$$\frac{1}{K^+} \sum_{i \in I^+} U_i > \frac{\Sigma_i U_i}{K} \geq \frac{1}{K^-} \sum_{i \in I^-} U_i$$

***Proposition A2:***
*If unemployment and vacancies behave like random walks with drifts $\delta$ and $\theta$, respectively, then $M_2$ converges in probability to zero for large t.*

*Proof:*
We consider

$$\Sigma_i (u_{it} v_{it})^{1/2} = \frac{\Sigma_i (U_{it} V_{it})^{1/2}}{(\Sigma_i U_{it})^{1/2} (\Sigma_i V_{it})^{1/2}}.$$

As before, we assume $U_{it} = \delta_i t + \Sigma \epsilon_{i\tau} + U_{i0}$, $V_{it} = \theta_i t + \Sigma \nu_{i\tau} + V_{i0}$. Using (A3), we again make use of asymptotically dominating linear drift terms:

$$\Sigma_i (u_{it} v_{it})^{1/2} \Rightarrow \frac{\Sigma_i (\delta_i \theta_i)^{1/2}}{(\Sigma_i \delta_i)^{1/2} (\Sigma_i \theta_i)^{1/2}}.$$

This ratio converges to 1 in the case of common drift terms. Thus

$$M_2(t) = 1 - \Sigma (u_{it} v_{it})^{1/2} \Rightarrow 0$$

***Proposition A3:***
*If unemployment $U_i$ of individual groups i is globally shifting upwards by an amount q (such that the new individual level is $U_i + q$ for all i), then the measure of mismatch $M_3$ decreases.*

*Proof:*
We write $M_3$ as $M_3 = var(K_i U_i / (\Sigma U_i))$ with $K_i = \Sigma N_i / N_i$; in order to simplify notation, we assume constant weights for all sectors. It follows

$$(A5) \qquad var\left(\frac{U_i}{\Sigma U_i}K\right) = \frac{K}{(\Sigma U_i)^2}\Sigma U_i^2 - 1 \quad .$$

Inserting $U_i + q$ for all i and neglecting the constant term "-1" (which is negligible with respect to intended partial derivatives) leads to

$$M_3^* = \frac{\Sigma(U_i + q)^2}{(\Sigma U_i + Kq)^2}$$

Since

$$\frac{\partial M_3^*}{\partial q} = \frac{2(\Sigma U_i + Kq)[(\Sigma U_i + Kq)^2 - K\Sigma(U_i + q)^2]}{(\Sigma U_i + Kq)^4)}$$

we obtain

$$\frac{\partial M_3^*}{\partial q} < 0$$

$$\Leftrightarrow \qquad (\Sigma U_i + Kq)^2 < K\Sigma(U_i + q)^2$$

$$\Leftrightarrow \qquad (\Sigma U_i)^2 < K\Sigma(U_i)^2$$

which holds if at least for one pair i,j (i≠j) $U_i \neq U_j$.

***Proposition A4:***
*If sectoral employment $L_{it}$ follows a random walk (with or without drift), then Lilien's (1982) sigma ($M_4$) converges to zero for large t.*

*Proof:*
We can write

$$(A6) \qquad \Delta \ln L_{it} \approx \frac{L_{it} - L_{i.t-1}}{L_{it}}$$

and

$$\Delta \ln L_t \approx \frac{L_t - L_{t-1}}{L_t}.$$

When employment behaves like a random walk with drift, i.e. $L_{it} = \gamma_i t + \Sigma_\tau \nu_{i\tau}$, it follows from (A6) that

$$L_{it} - L_{i.t-1} = \gamma_i + \nu_{it}$$

and

$$L_t - L_{t-1} = \Sigma_i \gamma_i + \Sigma_i \nu_{it}.$$

According to the definition of Lilien's *sigma* (equation 2.9), and after taking squared values, we obtain

$$(M_4)^2 = \Sigma_i\left(\frac{\gamma_i + \nu_{it}}{L_{it}} - \frac{\Sigma_i(\gamma_i + \nu_{it})}{L_t}\right)^2 \frac{L_{it}}{L_t}$$

$$= \Sigma_i \frac{((\gamma_i + \nu_{it})L_t - L_{it}\Sigma_i(\gamma_i + \nu_{it}))^2}{L_{it}L_t^3}.$$

Following the same arguments concerning the speed of divergence of $\Sigma_\tau \nu_{i\tau}$ as above and inspecting highest linear trends in both numerator and denominator (which are found as *t* in $L_t$ and $L_{it}$ since $\Sigma_\tau \nu_{i\tau}$ diverges with speed $t^{1/2}$), the highest trend in the denominator is of order $t^4$ $(t*t^3)$, whereas the numerator is only of order $t^3$. The dominating term $(L_{it}\Sigma\nu_{it})^2$ implies an asymptotic linear time trend $(tt^{1/2})^2$. Thus, for large samples Lilien's sigma goes to zero.

If the drift term $\gamma_i$ is zero, then the dominating trend term is of order $t^{1/2}$. So the numerator grows with speed $t = (t^{1/2})(t^{1/2})$, whereas the denominator grows faster with speed $t^2 = (t^{1/2})(t^{3/2})$. Thus, irrespective of random walks contain drifts or not, Lilien's *sigma* converges to zero.

***Proposition A5:***
*If at least one of the components* $\ln D_{it}$ *and* $\ln S_{it}$ *in the min-condition* $\ln L_{it} = \min(\ln D_{it}, \ln S_{it})$ *behaves like a random walk (with or without drift), then Lambert's (1988) rho approaches zero for* $t \to \infty$ *, i.e. the measure of structural underutilization "SURE" converges to 100% if* $t \to \infty$.

*Proof:*
We first consider the case when both components are random walks with drifts:

$$\ln D_{it} = \gamma_d + \ln D_{i,t-1} + \epsilon_{it}^d = \gamma_d t + \sum_{\tau=1}^{t} \epsilon_{i\tau}^d$$

$$\ln S_{it} = \gamma_s + \ln S_{i,t-1} + \epsilon_{it}^s = \gamma_s t + \sum_{\tau=1}^{t} \epsilon_{i\tau}^s,$$

where both drifts can be zero. The stochastic components are sums of normally *N(0,1)*-distributed disturbances such that

$$E(\Sigma_\tau \epsilon_\tau^d) = E(\Sigma_\tau \epsilon_\tau^s) = 0,$$

$$E(\epsilon_\tau^d \epsilon_\tau^s) = r\sigma_d\sigma_s \quad \forall \tau = 1,2,\ldots,t, \quad E(\epsilon_\tau^d \epsilon_j^s) = 0 \quad \forall \tau \neq j,$$

$$E(\epsilon_\tau^d \epsilon_j^d) = 0 \quad \text{for } \tau \neq j, \quad E(\epsilon_\tau^d \epsilon_j^d) = \sigma_d^2 \quad \text{for } \tau = j,$$

$$E(\epsilon_\tau^s \epsilon_j^s) = 0 \quad \text{for } \tau \neq j, \quad E(\epsilon_\tau^s \epsilon_j^s) = \sigma_s^2 \quad \text{for } \tau = j.$$

In terms of the assumptions of Lambert's (1988) theorem, we write the two processes as follows (see Lambert, 1988, Appendix A):

$$\ln D_{it} = d_t + u_{it},$$

$$\ln S_{it} = s_t + v_{it},$$

where we define according to the assumptions concerning the components $\ln D_{it}$ and $\ln S_{it}$

$$d_{it} = \gamma_d t, \quad s_{it} = \gamma_s t,$$

$$u_{it} = \sum_{\tau=1}^{t} \epsilon_{i\tau}^{d}, \quad v_{it} = \sum_{\tau=1}^{t} \epsilon_{i\tau}^{s},$$

such that

$$\begin{pmatrix} u_{it} \\ v_{it} \end{pmatrix} \sim N\left( \begin{pmatrix} 0 \\ 0 \end{pmatrix}, \begin{pmatrix} \omega_{dt}^2 & \omega_{dst} \\ \omega_{sdt} & \omega_{st}^2 \end{pmatrix} \right).$$

where

$$\omega_{dt}^2 = var\left( \sum_{\tau=1}^{t} \epsilon_{\tau}^{d} \right) = t\sigma_d^2, \quad \omega_{st}^2 = var\left( \sum_{\tau=1}^{t} \epsilon_{\tau}^{s} \right) = t\sigma_s^2,$$

$$\omega_{dst} = \omega_{sdt} = E\left( \sum_{\tau=1}^{t} \epsilon_{\tau}^{d} \sum_{\tau=1}^{t} \epsilon_{\tau}^{s} \right) = tr\sigma_d\sigma_s = r\omega_{dt}\omega_{st}.$$

The assumptions concerning the structure of underlying variances and covariances allows for the application of Lambert's (1988) theorem and according to equation (2.12), we obtain Lambert's *rho*, which decreases with time $t$:

$$\rho_t = \frac{r}{var(u_t - v_t)} = \frac{r}{\omega_{dt}^2 + \omega_{st}^2 - 2r\omega_{st}\omega_{rt}}$$

$$= \frac{r}{t(\sigma_d^2 + \sigma_s^2 - 2r\sigma_d\sigma_s)}.$$

If only one of the components, e.g. $\ln D_{it}$, is I(1), the denominator of $\rho_t$ is dominated by the linear trend in $\omega_{dt}^2 = t\sigma_d^2$, because the covariance is of lower order $O(t^{1/2})$ (see (A3)).

***Remark A1:*** *If the individual components of the indices $M_1 - M_5$, i.e. sectoral unemployment, vacancies or employment series, grow with a multiplicative factor, then measures of mismatch do not change.*

*Proof:* $M_1$ and $M_2$ are based on ratios $u_i = U_i / \Sigma U_i$ and $v_i = V_i / \Sigma V_i$. Thus, the ratios do not change if we replace $U_i$ by $U_i(1+q)$ and $V_i$ by $V_i(1+m)$ since the factors cancel out in the ratio. This also applies to $M_3$, which is based on the ratio $(U_i/N_i)/(\Sigma U_i / \Sigma N_i)$. Lilien's index uses logged differences (so that the constant factor disappears) and the ratio $L_i/L$, with the same effect as above. Lambert's *rho* represents the dispersion of microeconomic supply and demand disturbances. Mean values of $\ln D_t$ and $\ln S_t$ do not enter the variance in (2.12) and, hence, multiplicative changes cannot affect Lambert's *rho.*

The following remark summarizes two properties with respect to starting values of underlying stochastic processes that have some economic interpretations in terms of "natural rates" of unemployment and vacancies:

*Remark A2: For finite samples the performance of* $M_1$ *to* $M_4$ *in the presence of random walks depends on starting values respectively "natural rates". If these values are sufficiently small when compared to the stochastic components of the variables (or equivalently, if the process lasts long enough), then the impact of "natural rates" is negligible also in small samples (the proof is identical to part (c) of the propositions).*
*On the other hand, if all individuals share the same starting value, then measures of mismatch will start from zero such that mismatch increases for small t (but it decreases again due to the behaviour in large samples). More precisely, if in case of* $M_1$ *and* $M_2$ $U_{i0} = U_0$, $V_{i0} = V_0$ *for all* $i$*, and if in case of* $M_3$ $U_{i0} = U_0$ *for all* $i$*, then measures of mismatch are zero at* $t = 0$*. (Proof: trivial).*

Propositions A1 - A4 depend on the presence of random walks with drift. Econometric tests to disentangle random walks with drift from I(2) variables and random walks with drift *and* linear trend have poor power. Anyhow, Remark A3 holds:

*Remark A3: All results concerning random walks with drift in Proposition A1 - A4 hold (a fortiori) in the presence of random walks with drift and linear trend as well as for I(2) variables with drifts (and higher order of integration).*

*Proof:* A random walk with drift and linear trend can be written as follows:

$$x_t = \gamma + x_{t-1} + at + \epsilon_t = \gamma t + x_0 + a \sum_{\tau=1}^{t} \tau + \sum_{\tau=1}^{t} \epsilon_\tau$$

$$= \gamma t + x_0 + a\frac{t(t+1)}{2} + \sum_{\tau=1}^{t} \epsilon_\tau = \left(\gamma + \frac{a}{2}\right)t + \frac{a}{2}t^2 + x_0 + \sum_{\tau=1}^{t} \epsilon_\tau .$$

The introduction of an additional linear trend gives a quadratic time trend. Thus, all reasoning presented in the proofs concerning $t$ can simply be replaced by terms $t^2$. Since the convergence properties depend on the simultaneous presence of trend terms in both numerator and denominator, the presence of the quadratic trend (instead of the linear trend) maintains the same ordering with respect to leading time trends and drift terms as in previous proofs. No asymmetric multiplication in numerator and denominator occurs so that a speed of convergence which diverges from previous results is excluded.

I(2) implies that we have to integrate a variable which is already I(1). After the integration of an I(1) variable $x_\tau = \gamma_x + x_{\tau-1} + \epsilon_\tau$, we obtain as I(2) representation

$$y_t = \gamma_y + y_{t-1} + x_t = t\gamma_y + \sum_{\tau=1}^{t} x_\tau$$

$$= t\gamma_y + \gamma_x t(t+1)/2 + \sum_{\tau=1}^{t} \sum_{j=1}^{\tau} \epsilon_j .$$

From Sims, Stock, and Watson (1990), we know that

$$\sum_{\tau=1}^{t} \sum_{j=1}^{\tau} \epsilon_j \Rightarrow t^{3/2} \sigma \int_0^1 W^2(t) dt .$$

Thus, as in the previous I(1) case with trend and drift, the deterministic part given by a drift term provides the leading (quadratic) time trend. In exactly the same way as before, the substitution of the linear trend by the quadratic time trend does not change any result.

# 3. Disaggregate matching functions, spurious mismatch and occupational reallocation in Germany

## 3.1. Introduction

The macroeconomic approach to labour markets has changed during the recent past. Several influential papers by Blanchard and Diamond (1989, 1990a, 1990b, 1992) propagate a flow approach to labour markets. The basic motivation of this new research agenda is the observation that, at any point in time, many firms are looking for workers, and many workers are looking for jobs. Some time series adjusted by Abowd and Zellner (1985) show that each month, roughly 7% of the U.S. labour force moves in or out of employment. In Germany, figures are smaller but still high: In 1987, a period of net job growth, each month 1.6% of the labour force left employment and 1.7% moved into employment (Burda and Wyplosz, 1990). Germany's employment office reported 3.7 million new cases of unemployment and 3.6 million exits from unemployment, or about 310,000 per month, while unemployment itself averaged only 2.2 million. Moreover, recent evidence by Davis and Haltiwanger (1990) shows that these gross flows do not simply consist of workers reallocating themselves across a given set of jobs. They find strong fluctuations in job creation and job destruction ("destruction" means that the job is not filled again). Using U.S. data of the period from 1979 to 1983, job turnover in manufacturing averaged some 10% per quarter.

How many hires result from a given number of vacancies and workers depends on several matching criteria, such as the geography of job destruction and job creation, on skill differences between workers and jobs, on occupational and geographical mobility, on how eagerly workers and firms are searching and so on. Bypassing complex issues of aggregation, Blanchard and Diamond estimate aggregate matching functions that express the flow of hires as a function of the stocks of vacancies and unemployment.[1] They find a stable, Cobb-Douglas matching function with a declining time trend, equal weight on vacancies and employment and constant or mildly increasing returns to scale. The estimated scale elasticity is interpreted as the presence or absence of "thick" markets (Diamond, 1982). When unemployment and vacancies are high (in Diamond's coconut parable, that is, many people are carrying coconuts looking for a trade), it is more likely that each person looking for a job and each firm searching unemployed will find a match. Increases in scale improve the efficiency of the search of workers or employers. Results on

1 Early applications of matching functions are in Pissarides (1979, 1986).

German data confirm the result of constant returns to scale (Buttler and Cramer, 1991, Burda, 1993, Burda and Wyplosz, 1994), however unemployment seems to dominate the matching process.[1]

The linear trend estimated in matching functions has its historical counterpart in Hick's measure of neutral technical progress. The decline suggests a shift of the Beveridge curve, i.e. the relation between unemployment and vacancies. Shifts of the Beveridge curve due to mismatch differ from expected movements of unemployment and vacancies in response to aggregate activity shocks, which generate counterclockwise loops around the steady-state locus (see, for instance, Blanchard and Diamond, 1989). Shifts in the Beveridge curve represent a simultaneous increase in *both* unemployment and vacancies, so that the matching of unemployment and vacancies is less effective. The estimate of the linear trend in matching functions therefore measures some general tendency of increasing or decreasing mismatch.[2] Results based on German placement data similar to the data used in this chapter (Buttler and Cramer, 1991, see Section 3.3 for the description of data) confirm the general impression of increasing mismatch in Germany presented in Chapter 2 (Table 2.1.), though the evidence is based on only a short period (1983-1990) and results are not satisfactory from a statistical viewpoint ($t$-value not significant, low Durbin-Watson statistic, potential problems with nonstationary data).

The Beveridge-curve framework has been critisized for several reasons.[3] The first bulk of arguments concerns the quality of data (see Section 2.3.). The second critical point is whether stable relationships between unemployment and vacancies can be identified. If not, Beveridge curves are simple descriptive tools without any structural economic interpretation. Hall (1989) makes the point that identifying a Beveridge curve might be difficult because of simultaneity problems in the matching function. Blanchard and Diamond (1989) use lagged right hand side variables and overall activity (industrial production) as instruments. Here, the crucial

---

**1** Using monthly data from the period 1983 - 1990, Buttler and Cramer estimate coefficients of 0.54 (unemployment) and 0.45 (vacancies). Burda's corresponding (preferred) estimates are based on a panel of Western German labour office districts (Arbeitsamtsbezirke) during the period of February 1990 - December 1992 are 0.88 and 0.11. Burda and Wyplosz (1994) use data for the period 1968:3-91:12 and find estimated parameters on unemployment ranging between 0.68 and 0.71, whereas corresponding parameters on vacancies range between 0.27 and 0.29.

**2** Blanchard and Diamond (1989) consider two different movements up and down a 45 degree line of the Beveridge curve. The first is due to the scale parameter $\alpha$ in $H = \alpha H(U,V)$, the second is due to changes in reallocation intensity (see below).

**3** Illuminating comments are given by R.E. Hall (1989) and Janet Yellen (1989).

identifying assumption is that economic activity does not simultaneously affect the matching process. Börsch-Supan (1991) finds evidence suggesting the stochastic endogeneity of the matching probablity. He shows that any shift in the Beveridge curve disappears after controlling for cyclical and demographic variables.

The third main point concerns the very high level of aggregation. Hall (1989) mentions the disproportionate role of certain types of workers in the turnover process. Teenagers and other high-turnover workers with very brief employment records dominate the matching process. Moreover, aggregate models cannot take into account changes in the occupational structure. Better matching in some groups may be offset by inefficient matching for other workers. Thus, aggregate matching may not indicate any change despite some strong disaggregate movements. Moreover, the asymmetry of unemployment and vacancies across different professions is well known. For example, during the eighties, computer based jobs behaved quite differently than jobs in the primary sector.

In view of these criticisms and following the discussion of Blanchard and Diamond's (1989) paper (Hall, 1989, and the comments by K.Abraham and C.Holt in the general discussion), the most promising direction for future work is a more disaggregate analysis of the matching process. This chapter presents estimations of matching functions based on a panel of 40 occupational groups of the period from 1971 to 1992.

Section 3.2 starts with a brief theoretical motivation of matching functions. Section 3.3. presents estimations of *aggregate* matching functions. An issue that arises frequently in macroeconomics is the possibility of spurious results arising from nonstationarity (unit roots) in underlying time series. In such cases, so-called spurious regressions might arise. Econometrically interested readers will find new theoretical results on spurious regressions for random walks with drifts in Appendix A3.II to Chapter 3 (the behaviour of the parameter estimates, the $t$-values, the DW-statistic, and the R-squared are analysed). The emergence of "spurious" matching functions is tested in Section 3.4. The hypothesis of spurious results cannot be rejected.

Section 3.5 provides panel estimations using a panel of occupational groups. Particular attention is paid to dynamic effects, measurement error, simultaneity and time-specific effects (see Appendix A3.III for the econometric specifications). In order to identify economic reasons of mismatch, the time-variant changes of the matching efficiency are related to several time series of economic variables which are widely acknowledged as potential sources of mismatch.

After discussing the results of Section 3.5., Section 3.6. turns to the analysis of occupational reallocation on the German labour market. Theoretical and empirical results show the crucial role of unemployment/vacancy relationships for the identification of structural adjustment processes. The adjustment process can be analysed using generalised matching functions, where the relevant pool of unemployed individuals consists not only of one occupational group, but also of competing occupational groups. Unemployment in an occupation with bad future prospects increases the relevant pool of unemployed workers in an competing occupation with good future perspectives. As a result, the direction of substitution in matching processes gives information about the changes in the occupational structure.

Subsection 3.7. is devoted to the access to apprenticeships at the occupational level. It is shown that the matching of demand and supply of apprenticeships is determined by the recent experience of occupational unemployment and vacancies. This result helps to explain inherent rigidities of labour force adjustments in the face of changing skill requirements. Section 3.8. concludes.

## 3.2. Aggregate matching functions: Theoretical framework

The matching function relates the aggregate flow of new hires during the measurement period that arises from stock of unemployment $U$ and vacancies $V$:

$$H = \alpha H(U, V), \tag{3.1}$$

where $\alpha$ is a scale parameter, and the behaviour of the function $H$ is analogous to the aggregate production function, i.e. $H_u > 0$, $H_v > 0$, $H_{uu} < 0$, and $H_{vv} < 0$.

(3.1) is often assumed to have constant returns to scale (but see empirical tests below). A particular matching function with constant returns to scale can be derived if one thinks of the matching process as one in which the unemployed draw "balls" (applications) from a box (the stock of vacancies) (see Blanchard and Diamond, 1990c, for this motivation based on Poisson processes, and Van Rijkeghem, 1993, for an attempt of a direct test of a Poisson matching process). If each unemployed worker applies to one randomly selected vacancy and if the number of vacancies and the number of applications are sufficiently large, the probability of a vacancy having no applicants will be $e^{-(U/V)}$.[1] The probablity that a vacancy has at least one applicant is thus ( $1 - e^{(-U/V)}$). As a result, aggregate hiring is equal to

1 For Poisson processes, the probability of no particles arriving during the interval (0,1) is $e^{-\lambda t}$. Here $\lambda$ (the mean number of particles arriving during (0,1) ) equals *U/V*, i.e. the mean number of applicants per vacancy during one time period.

$$H = V(1 - e^{(-U/V)}). \tag{3.2}$$

Hiring has constant returns to scale, i.e $H(cU, cV) = cH(U, V)$.

A similar motivation leading to the same matching function can be found in Jackman, Layard, Pissarides (1989). The main argument there is that only a proportion $p$ of the vacancies are filled per period, and that this proportion is the higher the higher the ratio of job-seekers to vacancies. This follows for example if each worker makes one application per period, the probablity that a given worker applies for a given vacancy is $1/V$, and the probability that there are no unemployed applicants for a single vacancy is $(1 - 1/V)^U$, which is approximately $\exp(-U/V)$ for large $U$, so that $p = 1 - \exp(-U/V)$ is the approximation for the proportion of vacancies get filled per period (see Hall, 1977, 1979). Again, the number of hires is $H = pV$ (see above). Since $p$ is a function of acceptable[1] unemployed workers, i.e. $p = p(U/V)$ with $p' > 0$, $p'' < 0$, the hiring (matching) function can be written as $H = H(U, V)$.

Matching functions assume the simultaneous coexistence of unemployment and vacancies. In an approach initially followed by Hansen (1970), an alternative formalization of aggregate relationships between unemployment and vacancies can be based on the aggregation of micromarkets. This is the framework extended by Lambert (1988) and applied by the researchers of the "European Unemployment Programme" (see Drèze and Bean, 1990, and contributions therein). Assume a large number of homogenous micro-units *i* (job-markets for a well defined position in a particular region), so that that the matching process of the micro-labour market can be described by

$$H_i = \min(V_i, U_i). \tag{3.3}$$

When vacancy and unemployment are lognormally distributed at the micro level,[2] the aggregate matching function can be approximated[3] as a CES-function

$$H = (V^{-\rho} + U^{-\rho})^{-1/\rho}. \tag{3.4}$$

---

**1** Blanchard and Diamond (1989) and Jackman, Layard, Pissarides (1989) argue correctly that only a proportion *cU* of unemployed workers are acceptable to employers. There are thus *cU* effective job-seekers. I keep the assumption $c = 1$ in accordance with most empirical approaches to matching functions.

**2** See Smolny (1993) for the approximation of labour supply and labour demand by a bivariate lognormal distribution.

**3** Entorf and Sneessens (1994) show that the approximation error is almost exact. Numerical experiments reveal a maximum error of 0.2%.

Thus, at the aggregate level, we are back to the simultaneous existence of unemployment and vacancies, unless $\rho < \infty$. The parameter $\rho$ measures mismatch prevailing on micromarkets, since it is inversely related to the dispersion of unemployment and vacancies at the micro level (confer Section 2.3.). If $\rho \to \infty$, the CES-function boils down to an aggregate minimum-condition.

Equation (3.4) demands an aggregate CES functional form. The standard matching function, however, is the more convenient Cobb-Douglas form. Most empirical tests seem to confirm constant returns to scale, at least for Great Britain and the U.S.[1]

In the particular case of constant returns to scale, the average duration of a vacancy and of unemployment can be calculated quite easily. The average duration of a vacancy is $(V/H)$. Thus, if the hiring function is of the Cobb-Douglas form $H = \alpha V^{\beta} U^{1-\beta}$, then the average duration is given by $\alpha^{-1}(V/U)^{1-\beta}$. Analogously, the average duration of unemployment is $\alpha^{-1}(U/V)^{\beta}$.

Changes in the scale parameter, $\alpha$, capture changes in geographic and skill distributions of jobs and workers, ceteris paribus leading to changing durations of vacancies and unemployment. In empirical approaches, the parameter of mismatch $\alpha$ is formalized as a linear trend. Blanchard and Diamond (1989, 1990b) find strong evidence of a declining trend for the U.S. (i.e. declining efficiency of the matching process, respectively increasing mis-match).

Proponents of aggregate matching functions such as Blanchard and Diamond (1990b) motivate their procedure by important advantages over conventional alternatives. It is more appealing than postulating a stock adjustment equation for employment. In the matching approach, where unemployment has an impact on hiring, filling vacancies depends on general labor market tensions which is more appealing than equating employment with labour demand. Here, unemployment would play no role in the matching process.

The matching function recognizes the fact of large labour market flows, and it serves as a building block for the Beveridge curve theory. In a "*minimalist model of vacancies and unemployment*" (Blanchard and Diamond, 1989), the equations of motion are given by a system of two differential equations:

$$(3.5) \qquad dU/dt = -\alpha H(U,V) + (q + \pi_0)(LS - U),$$

$$dV/dt = -\alpha H(U,V) + (q - \pi_1)(LS - U) + \pi_1 K - (\pi_0 + \pi_1)V.$$

---

1 See the evidence in Pissarides (1986), Layard, Nickell and Jackman (1991) and Blanchard and Diamond (1989, 1990b).

This bare-bones model takes labour force, $LS$, and the total number of jobs, $K$, as given. Outflows from unemployment and vacancies arise from matching unemployment and vacancies. However, the equations of motion also take account of important flows into and out of the labour force.

Inflows into unemployment are the result of (voluntarily) quitting employment $L = LS - U$ and of job destruction (job termination). $\pi_0$ is the probablity that a productive job becomes unproductive and q is the probability of quitting.

The vacancy dynamics in (3.5) might be understood more easily within the equation

$$dV/dt = -\alpha H(U,V) + q(LS-U) + \pi_1 I - \pi_0 V,$$

where the number of total jobs is $K$, the sum of filled jobs (employment) is $L$, vacancies are $V$ and the number of unfilled jobs with no vacancy posted (idle capacity) is $I$. Thus, $K = (LS-U) + V + I$. Inflows to vacancies arise from the need to replace workers who quit, i.e. $q(LS-U)$. $\pi_0 V$ represents an outflow from vacancies to unfilled jobs: vacancies become unproductive with the same probability $\pi_0$ as filled jobs (i.e $LS-U$). The second source of outflows is new hires. $\pi_1 I$ is the inflow of jobs which were previously unproductive and are productive now. Finally, in order to write the equations of motion as a function of $U$ and $V$, replacing $I$ according to the definition $I = K-(LS-U)-V$ gives equation (3.5).

Blanchard and Diamond (1989, 1990b) analyse the dynamics of *U* and *V* in terms of two types of shocks, which are assumed to change the parameters $\pi_0$ and $\pi_1$. For given $\pi_0$ and $\pi_1$, the proportion of potential jobs that are productive in steady state are given by $\pi_1/(\pi_0+\pi_1)$. This proportion measures the degree of aggregate activity. It is called $c$ (cycle).[1] The steady state proportion of productive jobs becoming unproductive is $\pi_0\pi_1/(\pi_0+\pi_1)$. This ratio is denoted $s$ and measures the intensity of reallocation in the economy. Solving for $\pi_0$ and $\pi_1$, we obtain $\pi_0 = s/c$ and $\pi_1 = s/(1-c)$, so that the dynamic system can be rewritten in terms of $s$ and $c$. The response of $U$ and $V$ to changes in $c$, aggregate activity shocks, is likely to produce counter-clockwise loops around the steady-state locus of the Beveridge curve.[2]

This is what economists have in mind when they refer to the dynamics of the Beveridge curve. If the economy is subject to $s-$ shocks, the curve will move up and down a 45 degree line (Blanchard and Diamond, 1989, p. 12). Thus, shifts in the theory of the Beveridge curve arise for at least *two* reasons, changes in the reallocation intensity and changes in mis-

---

**1** Empirically, *c* can be measured by the degree of capacity utilization, for instance.

**2** See Blanchard and Diamond (1989, p.12-13) for the proof.

match (captured in the parameter $\alpha$ ). Moreover, the presence of both shocks together leads to complicated, simultaneous movements along the Beveridge curve *and* shifts of the curve, so that identifying the true reason behind any movement of the Beveridge curve is impossible by analyzing the $UV$-curve *alone*.[1] Mortensen and Pissarides (1993) develop an extended model with endogeneous job creation and job construction, and show that, if there are simultaneous cyclical and reallocation shocks, the Beveridge curve ceases to be a useful tool of analysis, since there are two equilibrium curves in the vacancy/unemployment space depending on a similar set of parameters. However, these authors stress that the relationships between job matchings and job vacancies, on the one hand, and job matchings and unemployment on the other might shed more light on the sources of shocks than simple bivariate relations between the stock of unemployment and the stock of vacancies. Thus, linking the matching function to an extended[2] Beveridge curve framework should provide insights about the flow approach to labour markets, but not necessarily about the identification of the Beveridge curve itself.

## 3.3. Aggregate matching functions for West-Germany

U.S. and European experience (Blanchard and Diamond, 1989, Burda and Wyplosz, 1990) show that the size of the labour market flows is large relative to the stocks of both unemployment and vacancies. Figure 3.1 (see Buttler and Cramer, 1991, p.484, for the data) describes the matching process during the year 1990, as it appears in the data of the German labour office.

The data reveal a high number of outflows from vacancies (28.8% of initial stock + inflows) which most probably are flows into employment without mediation of the labour office. Partly, however, these are also jobs which change from being productive to unproductive. 4.7 million left the official pool of unemployment during the year 1990. According to a survey (IAB Mai/Juni Sonderuntersuchung) of the German Employment Institute (IAB, Institut für Arbeitsmarkt-und Berufsforschung) inquiring the background of leaving the unemployment register, 1.082 million people of the unemployed (stock+inflows=5.755 million) have found a job without the mediation of the labour office. 1.835 (31.9%) million have left the labour force. The latter flow out of the labour force is steadily

---

**1** See Börsch-Supan (1991) for a critique of the econometrics behind the identification of the Beveridge curve.

**2** Extensions of the theoretical model describe endogeneous movements of the labour force, give up the assumption of an homogenous pool of unemployed (see Blanchard and Diamond, 1989) and consider wage effects (Blanchard and Diamond, 1990b, 1992).

increasing. The share of workers registering as unemployed and who leave without being hired increased from 27.0% in 1986 to 46.2% in 1990 (Buttler and Cramer, 1991, p.485).

*Figure 3.1.*: Stocks and flows of the German matching process in 1990

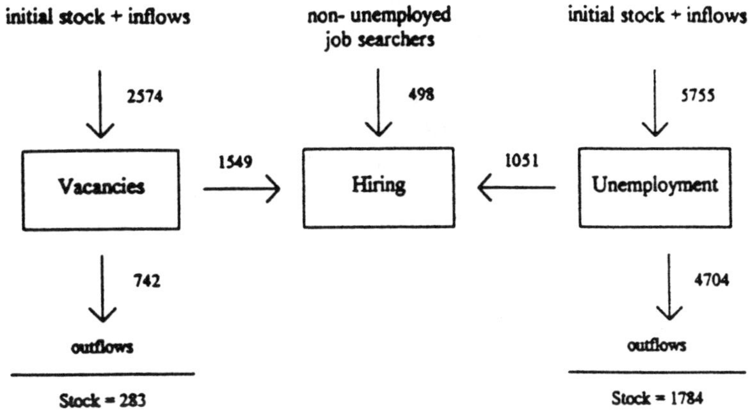


*Note:* in 1000, *Source:* Buttler and Cramer (1991), own calculations and representation

Additional problems concerning the availability of data on unemployment and vacancies are mentioned in Section 2.4. (see also Reyer et al., 1990). Given the unsatisfactory quality of data (which is even more disappointing in the U.S. and other European countries), is it reasonable to estimate matching functions? I think it is reasonable for at least five reasons. First, my approach will be a conservative test, including the possibility of a potential nonsense regression. Second, as Buttler and Cramer, 1991, I consider actual hiring data, though the matching process passes the filter of the German labour office. This is different from Burda and Wyplosz (1990, 1994) and Burda (1993), who use total exits from unemployment as the endogenous variable in estimated matching functions. Total exits from unemployment, however, are affected by cyclical factors, (early) retirement and changing female participation rates. Moreover, exits from unemployment fail to cover hirings from non-unemployed job-seekers, i.e. employment-to-employment changes and hirings from out of the labour force.

Third, the problem with placement data of the German labour force is the low mediation rate (see Section 2.4). Nevertheless, assuming a stable quality of the efficiency of the labour office, one can reasonably draw conclusions about the relative role of vacancies and unemployment and about general trends in the efficiency of the matching process that is the main interest in estimating matching functions here.

Fourth, admitting that the efficiency of the German labour office improves or deteriorates over time, the estimate of the time-variant scale parameter may give some information about the changing quality of the German labour office. Clearly, without further information, there is no way to distinguish between shifts of the "true" matching process and institutional shifts due to a changing matching quality of the German labour office, though, to the knowledge of the author, despite some recent deregulating of the tasks of the "Bundesanstalt für Arbeit" (the German labour office), there is no unambigous indication of declining efficiency (see Buttler and Cramer, 1991, for some discussion of recent efforts of the German labour office), while there is strong evidence of decreasing labour mobility (see Section 2.2.).

Fifth, and most importantly, panel estimations and matching functions at a disaggregate level are capable of shedding some light on heterogeneities of the matching process.

Given the high size of flows relative to the stocks, estimates of the matching function should use the highest frequency available. German data on unemployment and vacancies are available since 1951 (see Appendix A3.I). For this long period, data are available as annual averages of monthly stocks. The *UV*-curve in Figure 3.2. suggests a surprisingly stable Beveridge curve until 1983 (that represents the upward return in Figure 3.2), and the beginning of a single counterclockwise loop thereafter (Franz, 1991a, tries to correct vacancy data of the period 1960 until 1989 and finds a second shift in 1974, see also Section 2.4.).

In this chapter, aggregate matching functions are estimated for two reasons. First, the possiblity of spurious matching functions will be analysed, and second, aggregate matching functions will be compared with disaggregate matching functions based on panel estimation techniques. The panel is available for the years 1971 to 1992, hence aggregate functions (the total of all 40 occupational groups) will be estimated for the same period and can be compared with disaggregate results. Hires (placements) are available as the average of monthly flows.

Table 3.1. presents estimates of a basic Cobb-Douglas specification, with hires depending on current vacancies and current unemployment:

$$\ln(H_t) = \text{const.} + \alpha t + \beta \ln(V_t) + \gamma \ln(U_t) \tag{3.6}$$

Since reality is in continuous time, there is no clear-cut way of handling timing. While one would want to regress new hires during the month on the stocks at the same time of the month, the data are not available in that form. Blanchard and Diamond (1989) use lagged values (lagged one month) of $U$ and $V$ in order to take account of some delayed timing of new hires with respect to $U$ and $V$, which are measured at the end of the month. Such timing problems are averaged out and are of minor importance for averages of monthly flows, so that I prefer using current values of $U$ and $V$ in the matching equation.

*Figure 3.2.*: The unemployment-vacancies relationship, 1951-1992

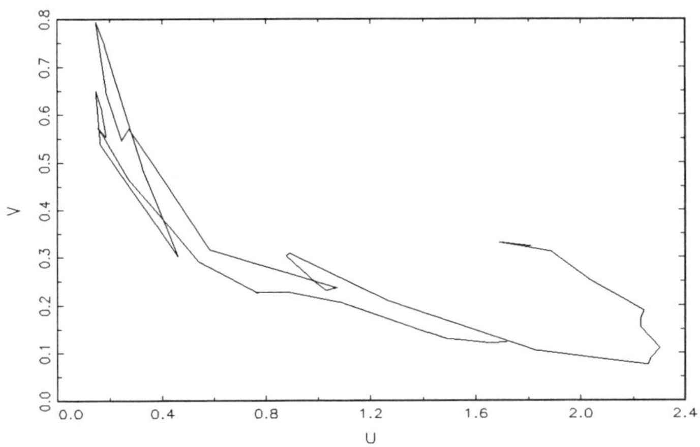


*Note:* In million, Source: see Appendix A3.I.

Results are presented in Table 3.1. The first two regressions estimate equation (3.6) with and without a trend.[1] The estimated degree of return to scales is far below unity (0.36 and 0.39, respectively), a result which is significantly confirmed using a Wald test of the restriction $\beta + \gamma = 1$ . Of course, these tests are included for merely descriptive reasons, since Chapter 2 informed about potential nonstationarities of unemployment and vacancies. Proceding in the same way as in Chapter 2, some additional tests analyse the time series used in Table 3.1. Without reporting the results in detail (which certainly suffer from the poor power of unit root tests in small samples), again tests do not reject the hypothesis of non-

1 Several attempts to estimate the aggregate CES function (3.4) failed due to convergence problems. The reason may be the short estimation period and the high divergence of unemployment, vacancies and hires.

stationarity.[1] Furthermore, a test checking for stationarity of the residuals in equations (1) to (4) in Table 3.1. does not support the hypothesis of a cointegrated matching function (according to Engle and Granger, 1987).

Somewhat surprisingly, the estimated coefficient on unemployment is small, indicating that only vacancies might play an important role in the matching process. The time trend does not reveal any significant change of the scale parameter.

Equations (3) and (4) use corrected vacancies $V_c$ instead of observed values $V$. When comparing (1) and (3), observed vacancies lead to a better fit (see R-squared) and to smaller parameter estimates. The estimates change if time is included. Neither vacancies nor unemployment remain significant, whereas there is some small significance of increasing matching efficiency, i.e. falling mismatch.

Given the poor power of unit root tests in small samples, I also treat the equation as a regression of stationary variables. Conventional diagnostic tests show that a simple AR(1) correction of the residuals does not suffice to remove serial correlation. A high portion of serial correlation comes from the presence of a strong residual moving average process of order one (MA(1)). The estimation of an ARMA(1,1) leads to the acceptance of several misspecification tests (see Table 3.1., notes 1. and 2.).[2] Except constant terms, no significant coefficient remains. Using $V_c$, the time trend is still 0.019 which would lead to a 50% decline in hires over the sample period, given unemployment and vacancies. However, the negative sign of unemployment and vacancies warns us that this result might be subject to co-linearity problems, which would possibly switch the signs of estimated parameters.

Given some positive correlation between the disturbance term to the hiring function and unemployment and vacancies (which can be the simple reflection of positive serial correlation in hires as well as in unemployment and vacancies), OLS estimation may lead to an upward bias in the estimated coefficients on unemployment and vacancies. Thus, equations (7) and (8) estimate the basic specification using the degree of capacity

---

**1** Additional tests use the procedure proposed by Hall (1989), who suggests that instrument variable estimation should be used in place of OLS in augmented Dickey-Fuller tests. The level instrumental variable used in place of $y_{t-1}$ is $y_{t-2}$. Hall's Monte Carlo results suggest that the method has higher power than usual ADF tests. Here the tests confirm the results of the ADF procedure.

**2** The ARMA estimation imposes a residual process $u_t = \rho u_{t-1} + \epsilon_t + \gamma \epsilon_{t-1}$. Results are achieved using Micro-TSP.

*Table 3.1.*: The aggregate matching function: Basic specifications

| | Independent variables: coefficients on | | | | | | |
|---|---|---|---|---|---|---|---|
| | const. | $\ln(V)$ | $\ln(V_c)$ | $\ln(U)$ | time | DW | $R^2$ |
| Dependent variable: $\ln(H)$ | | | | | | | |
| (1) OLS | 7.58 | 0.31 | - | 0.05 | - | 0.55 | 0.74 |
| | (6.1) | (5.4) | | (1.2) | | | |
| (2) OLS | 7.06 | 0.32 | - | 0.07 | -0.002 | 0.56 | 0.74 |
| | (2.5) | (3.6) | | (0.7) | (0.2) | | |
| (3) OLS | 9.04 | - | 0.24 | -0.01 | - | 0.39 | 0.50 |
| | (2.5) | | (2.3) | (0.2) | | | |
| (4) OLS | 13.9 | - | 0.08 | -0.22 | 0.018 | 0.37 | 0.56 |
| | (3.6) | | (0.6) | (1.6) | (1.7) | | |
| (5) ARMA[1)] | 9.34 | 0.20 | - | 0.02 | 0.002 | 1.75 | 0.91 |
| | (2.6) | (1.3) | | (0.1) | (0.2) | | |
| (6) ARMA[2)] | 16.0 | - | -0.05 | -0.25 | 0.019 | 1.72 | 0.88 |
| | (4.4) | | (0.4) | (1.6) | (1.7) | | |
| (7) IV | 7.99 | 0.14 | - | 0.16 | 0.004 | 1.84 | 0.85 |
| +ARMA[3)] | (1.8) | (0.8) | | (0.8) | (0.2) | | |
| (8) IV | 12.75 | - | -0.02 | -0.05 | 0.020 | 1.78 | 0.85 |
| +ARMA[4)] | (2.0) | | (0.1) | (0.2) | (1.5) | | |
| (9) OLS, | 6.22 | - | 0.27 | 0.14 | 0.017 | 1.44 | 0.97 |
| 1983-1992 | (2.7) | | (3.0) | (0.8) | (1.3) | | |
| (10) OLS, | 6.12 | 0.27 | - | 0.18 | 0.003 | 1.86 | 0.97 |
| 1983-1992 | (2.2) | (2.8) | | (1.0) | (0.2) | | |
| (11) OLS, | 2.55 | 0.13 | - | 0.50 | 0.040 | 1.60 | 0.97 |
| 1982-1992 | (0.8) | (1.3) | | (3.1) | (2.8) | | |
| (12) OLS, | -0.65 | 0.59 | - | 0.41 | -0.025 | 0.65 | 0.61 |
| restricted[5)] | (13.0) | (21.9) | | (15.2) | (4.8) | | |
| (13) OLS, | -1.33 | - | 0.65 | 0.35 | -0.020 | 0.60 | 0.13 |
| restricted[5)] | (15.2) | | (14.3) | (7.7) | (2.4) | | |

Period of estimation: 1971 to 1992;
Conventional t statistics in parenthesis;
1) AR(1) = 0.62 (2.4), MA(1) = 0.64 (3.2); Box-Pierce Q-Stat. with 2 (4) lags = 0.63 (1.70), Probablities = 0.73 (0.79); ARCH (2 lags): LM test (*T*R-squared*) = 0.41 (Prob=0.81); White test of heteroskedasticity: LM test = 7.10 (Prob=0.31); Ramsey reset(1) test: F-statistic = 1.03 (Prob=0.32)
2) AR(1) = 0.72 (5.0), MA(1) = 0.58 (2.6); Box-Pierce Q-Stat. with 2 (4) lags = 1.44 (1.97), Probablities = 0.49 (0.74); ARCH (2 lags): LM test (*T*R-squared*) = 2.98 (Prob=0.23); White test of heteroskedasticity: LM test = 7.29 (Prob=0.30); Ramsey reset(1) test: F-statistic = 1.59 (Prob=0.23)
3) AR(1) = 0.59 (3.9), MA(1) = 0.77 (4.0); instruments: $\ln(V)$, $\ln(U)$, one and two lags, $\ln(DUC)$, one and two lags
4) AR(1) = 0.71 (7.5), MA(1) = 0.71 (3.6); instruments: $\ln(V_c)$, $\ln(U)$, one and two lags, $\ln(DUC)$, one and two lags
5) $\beta + \gamma = 1$

utilization, $DUC$, with one and two lags as instrumental variables.[1] When compared with previous estimates, the estimated parameters of unemployment and vacancies further decrease.

The results do not confirm the existence of a stable, aggregate matching function for West Germany. Unemployment plays no role at all, and the impact of vacancies becomes insignificant after seriously controlling for serial correlation and a potential simultaneity bias.

Perhaps the result is more promising if we concentrate on times of high unemployment? Indeed, an estimation for the period 1982 to 1992 (equation (11)) reveals higher returns to scale (0.63). Note, however, that due to the short estimation period already slight changes of the estimation period lead to very different estimates (see equations (9) and (10) with returns 0.41 and 0.45, respectively), so that one cannot interpret these results at their face value.

Though not confirmed by a statistical test of constant returns to scale, equations (12) and (13) inform about the OLS estimation under the restriction $\beta + \gamma = 1$ . In accordance with previous estimates, the more important role of vacancies is confirmed (cf. (3) and (4)). For the first time, the trend is significantly negative (note that $t$-values are misleading due to misspecification and serial correlation). Equation (13) does not reject an F-test of zero parameters (results not reported, but confer the low R-squared).

Figure 3.3. displays the average duration of vacancies and unemployment calculated according to estimated parameters in equations (2)[2] and (12), and compares the estimates with registered vacancies appearing in the statistics of the German labour office. The estimated duration of vacancies follows quite closely the pattern of registered vacancies, though the estimate fails to represent the cycle 1979 to 1981. The problem of the aggregate matching function, however, is the poor representation of the registered duration of unemployment. The theoretical specification (3.6) implies a mirror of the duration of vacancies[3], i.e. it would require a cyclical pattern of unemployment. Unlike U.S unemployment, however,

---

1 See Blanchard and Diamond, 1989, 1990b, for a similar approach with industrial production as an instrument; this strategy, however, has been criticised by Hall, 1989, who argues that aggregate activity also activates the matching process, so that any cyclical variable is correlated with the disturbance term, making it less suitable as an instrument in the estimation of the matching function. This is also the crucial point in Börsch-Supan, 1991, who questions the stability of the Beveridge curve.

2 The average duration of a vacant position $V/H = (V^{1-\beta})/(\alpha U^{\gamma})$ , the average duration of unemployment is $U/H = (U^{1-\gamma})/(\alpha V^{\beta})$ .

3 This can be seen by inspecting the symmetric role of unemployment and vacancies in the numerator and denominator of $V/H$ and $U/H$ . Confer in particular the case of constant returns to scale: $(U/V)^{\beta}$ versus $(V/U)^{1-\beta}$ .

European (and German) unemployment is characterized by an increasing share of long-term unemployed[1], leading to a delayed and persistent increase in the average duration of unemployment (also referred to as the "hysteresis" problem of European unemployment).

*Figure 3.3.*: Observed and estimated durations of unemployment and vacancies

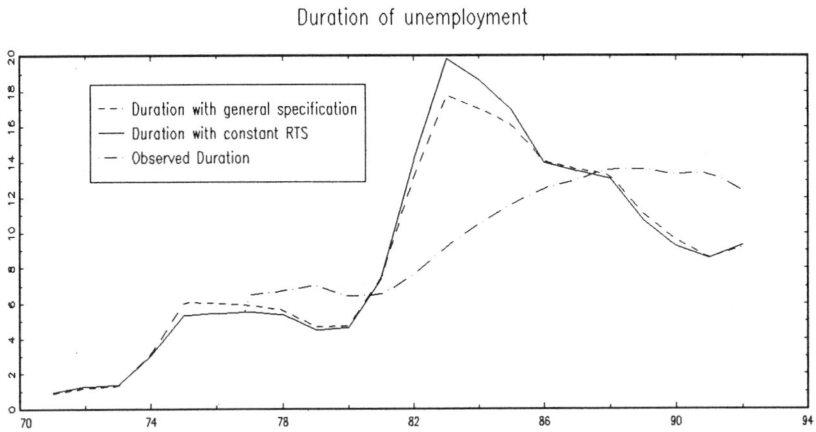


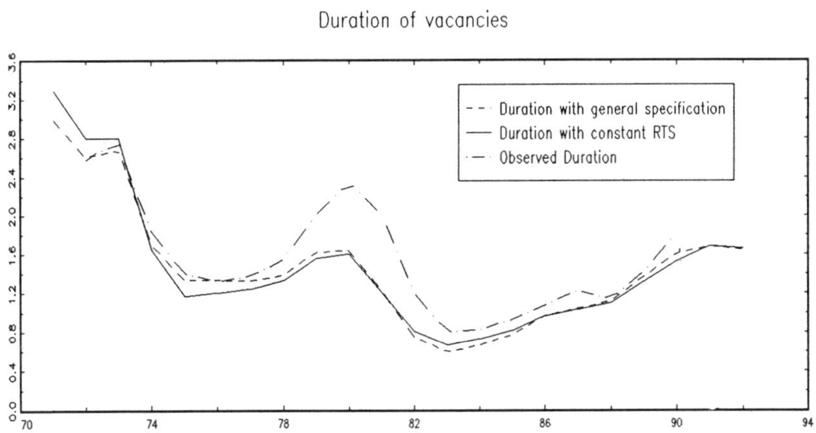


*Note:* Duration of a vacant position: Ermann (1988), p. 180-181, Buttler and Cramer, 1991, p. 84, for the period 1988-1990; duration of unemployment of the period 1977-1992: Amtliche Nachrichten der Bundesanstalt für Arbeit, 1985 and 1992

1 The share of long-term unemployed (more than one year) was 14.7% in 1978, increased steadily up to 32.6% 1988, and decreased slightly to 26.6% in 1992 (Source: Amtliche Nachrichten der Bundesanstalt für Arbeit, 1992).

To conclude, it is not surprising that matching functions yield reasonable results when applied to U.S. unemployment and vacancies, which are characterised by cyclical fluctuations of vacancies and countercyclical fluctuations of unemployment, with the latter resembling the mirror image of the first (confer Figure 5 in Blanchard and Diamond, 1989, p. 23). This German case study suggests that aggregate matching functions perform quite well in representing the time series of vacancies, but they fail in reproducing the pecularities of European unemployment, i.e. the persistent and non-cyclical behaviour of the duration of unemployment.

## 3.4. Spurious matching functions

### 3.4.1. The econometric theory of spurious matching functions

An issue that arises frequently in the analysis of economic time series is the possibility of spurious correlation resulting from unit roots in one or several of the series. Empirical macroeconomists have become aware of potential shortcomings in the interpretation of conventional test statistics. Such problems are aggravated by deterministic trends, that are easily encountered since many macroeconomic time series are considered to be random walks with drifts (Nelson and Plosser, 1982). Hence, estimating ordinary least squares with both regressor and regressand being random walks with drifts is a likely occurence in applied econometrics. In the case of random walks without drifts, such regressions have become known as "spurious regressions" (Granger and Newbold, 1974), and are studied analytically by Phillips (1986). *Theorem B1* of Appendix A3.II.1 extends Phillips (1986) to the non-zero drift case. Using the convergence properties of Wiener processes, the results reveal the asymptotic normality of the OLS estimator. OLS yields a consistent estimate of the ratio of drifts. Furthermore, it is proven that conventional $t$-values diverge with sample size, that the DW-statistic approaches zero and that the $R^2$ approaches unity as the sample size goes to infinity.

Previous unit root tests of the variables used in the matching functions do not preclude nonstationarity. Hence, since there is no indication of co-integration, are the regressions presented in Table 3.1. spurious? This would be the logical consequence of the non-cointegration of nonstationary variables that are integrated of order 1 (I(1) for short). Before accepting this conclusion, the next step should be a more direct test for spurious regressions.

Given I(1)-time series, the most conservative hypothesis is that a regression of placements $\ln(H)$ on vacancies and unemployment is completely spurious, so that any significance of conventional test statistics would lead to wrong conclusions. In fact, some regressions in Table 3.1. have the (rule-of-thumb) feature of a spurious regression, made popular by Granger and Newbold (1974), that the $R^2$ is larger than the DW, so that it is reasonable to test the hypothesis of a matching function consisting of independent random walks with drifts.

*Theorem B1* analyses the simple regression of two independent random walks with drifts, i.e $y_t = \gamma_y + y_{t-1} + \epsilon_y$ and $x_t = \gamma_x + x_{t-1} + \epsilon_x$. The *Remark* in Appendix A3.II.1 reveals that the *asymptotic* result does not apply in the presence of more than one regressor with drift, since any addititional regressor would lead to asymptotic linear dependency of the deterministic drift terms. In finite samples a regression with more than two random walks with drifts can be analysed in a Monte Carlo simulation. As can be seen in Appendix A3.II.3, the distribution of the slope parameter $\hat{\beta}$ in spurious regressions can be fully described by the ratios $\gamma_y/\gamma_x$ and the drift-noise ratios $\gamma_y/\sigma_y$ and $\gamma_x/\sigma_x$, where $\sigma_y$ and $\sigma_x$ denote the standard errors of $\epsilon_y$ and $\epsilon_x$. Accordingly, simulation studies have to obey these ratios when parameterizing the simulation scenario.

*Table 3.2.*: Drifts, standard deviations and drift-noise ratios

Period= 1971 - 1992:

| | $\ln(H)$ | $\ln(V)$ | $\ln(V_e)$ | $\ln(U)$ | $\ln(H/U)$ | $\ln(V/U)$ |
|---|---|---|---|---|---|---|
| Drift | -0.0067 | -0.033 | -0.030 | 0.109 | 0.115 | 0.142 |
| Std. Dev. | 0.087 | 0.280 | 0.307 | 0.240 | 0.301 | 0.500 |
| Drift/noise | -0.08 | -0.12 | -0.10 | 0.45 | 0.38 | 0.28 |

Period = 1982 - 1992 (see regression (11) in Table 3.1.):

| | $\ln(H)$ | $\ln(V)$ | $\ln(U)$ |
|---|---|---|---|
| Drift | 0.034 | 0.040 | 0.032 |
| Std. Dev. | 0.074 | 0.280 | 0.141 |
| Drift/noise | 0.46 | 0.14 | 0.23 |

*Note:* Drift $(y_t)$ = mean of $\Delta(y_t)$, Std. Dev. = standard deviation of $\Delta y_t$.

### 3.4.2. Simulated evidence

Table 3.2. contains parameters characterizing a time series under the assumption that these parameters, i.e. drift and noise, are estimated from the realizations of a random walk with drift. Hylleberg and Mizon (1989) draw attention to the particular role of drift-noise ratios when testing for unit roots. The Monte Carlo results in the Appendix of this chapter reveal that drift-noise ratios are important for the speed of convergence towards asymptotic results. High ratios lead to OLS estimates which are close to the asymptotic result even in small samples. Here the regression is a mixture of a fairly large drift-noise ratio (for unemployment) and small drift-noise ratios (for vacancies). Under the hypothesis that observed drift and noise are true parameters of the unobservable data generating process, subsequent Monte Carlo studies will show confidence regions of assumed spurious regressions.[1]

For illustrative reasons, the first experiment presents the simplest case of a spurious regression with one "explanatory" variable only. Omitting the time variable in equation (12) of Table 3.1 leads to the regression estimate (conventional *t*-values in parentheses)

$$(3.7) \qquad \ln(H/U) = \underset{(13.9)}{-0.80} + \underset{(24.0)}{0.68} \ln(V/U) + \hat{u}$$

$$R^2 = 0.966 \qquad DW = 0.40$$

In order to test consistency with a spurious regression outcome, six criteria are available: parameter estimates of constant and slope, corresponding *t*-values, *R-squared* and *DW*. The Monte Carlo study considers three independent random walks with drifts, $y_t = \gamma_y + y_{t-1} + \epsilon_y$, where drift and standard deviation coincide with the values of $\ln(H)$, $\ln(V)$ and $\ln(U)$ of Table 3.2. Starting values are the historical values of 1971, i.e. the first year of the regression period. Note that starting values are only important for the estimation of the constant term, whereas the slope parameter is independent of the initial level. Error terms are normally distributed.[2] Then, by subtracting the random walk simulations of $\ln(U)$ from the simulated series $\ln(H)$ and $\ln(V)$, the "spurious" variables replacing $\ln(H/U)$ and $\ln(V/U)$ in $(3.7)$ are created, so that the regression $(3.7)$ can be reestimated with simulated random walks with drifts. This experiment is replicated 5000 times. The length of the time series is extended as $T = 22 + i \cdot 50, i = 1, \ldots, 5$.

The Monte Carlo experiment is summarized in Figure 3.4. A comparison with the theoretical result of *Theorem B1* (Appendix A3.II), dealing with the regression of two independent random walks with drifts, seems to be straightforward. However, things are somewhat more complicated, because the imposed restriction implies the subtraction of $\ln(U)$ on both the left hand and right hand side, leading thus to an endogeneity bias

---

1 Note that simulated confidence regions represent marginal distributions of test-statistics, so that joint distributions of several parameters would yield smaller confidence bands. Thus, in tests with joint confidence regions, the rejection rate is likely to be higher.

2 Note, however, that Phillips' (1986) results as well as the results derived in the Appendix do just require the existence of any IID distribution.

(second order bias). In fact, some unreported simulations of small samples reveal that $\beta$ is smaller when only two unrestricted random walks with drifts were generated, where drifts and noise *directly* refer to $\ln(H/U)$ and $\ln(V/U)$ . Asymptotically, however, we obtain the convergence properties derived in *Theorem B1*: The mean value of $\beta$ converges to the ratio of drifts $\ln(H/U)/\ln(V/U)$ (which is *0.814),* corresponding *t*-values increase linearly, *DW* is of order $O(1/T)$ and *R-squared* approaches unity. The only difference is the constant term, where the speed of divergence, if any, seems to be much weaker as the simulation of unrestricted regressions would suggest (see Entorf, 1994, for evidence of the latter).

Figure 3.4. displays averages of simulated regressions, as well as percentiles of the spurious regression results (i.e the distribution of *R-squared*, *DW,* OLS estimates and corresponding t-values). Since the first scenario (the first $T$ in Figure 3.4.) assumes $T = 22$, the comparison with (3.7) reveals whether the actual regression violates any of the critical regions calculated in Figure 3.4. It should be noted that critical values of the constant term very much depend on starting values of the simulation process. I use observed values of the initial year in the sample that clearly is subject to additional stochastic fluctuations which renders the critical value of the constant to be less reliable. Here, however, all results including those of the constant term remain within the limits, though the *R-squared* is just below the critical value 0.97. Interestingly enough, the average estimate of $\beta$ is 0.70, which is close to the actual estimate 0.68. Thus, there is evidence that regression (3.7) is a spurious regression.[1]

The most important OLS results of Table 3.1. are analysed in the way described above. Table 3.3. shows spurious regressions with $T = 22$ and displays critical regions (5% and 95% percentiles), as well as averages (in parentheses) of simulated parameter estimates and test statistics (5000 replications). Simulated regressions (1) and (3) impose one "dependent" and two "explanatory" random walks with drifts according to drift and noise of the variables used in equations (1) and (3) of Table 3.1.; equations (2), (4) and (11) (the latter simulating $T = 11$ and using starting values of 1982) include an additional time variable. Equations (12) and (13) correspond to the example described above plus an additional time variable.

In the first regressions (1) and (2), using uncorrected vacancy data, most but not all test-statistics are in favour of a spurious regression. Besides some less reliable evidence due to the constant term, the more important evidence against a nonsense regression arises from the parameter estimate (and the corresponding *t*-value) of $\ln(V)$ , which is too high a value to be consistent with the hypothesis of a spurious regression.

---

1 Repeating the same experiment with drift and standard deviation of $ln(V_c)$ (results not reported) confirms the spurious regression result.

*Figure 3.4.*: The distribution of a spurious matching function

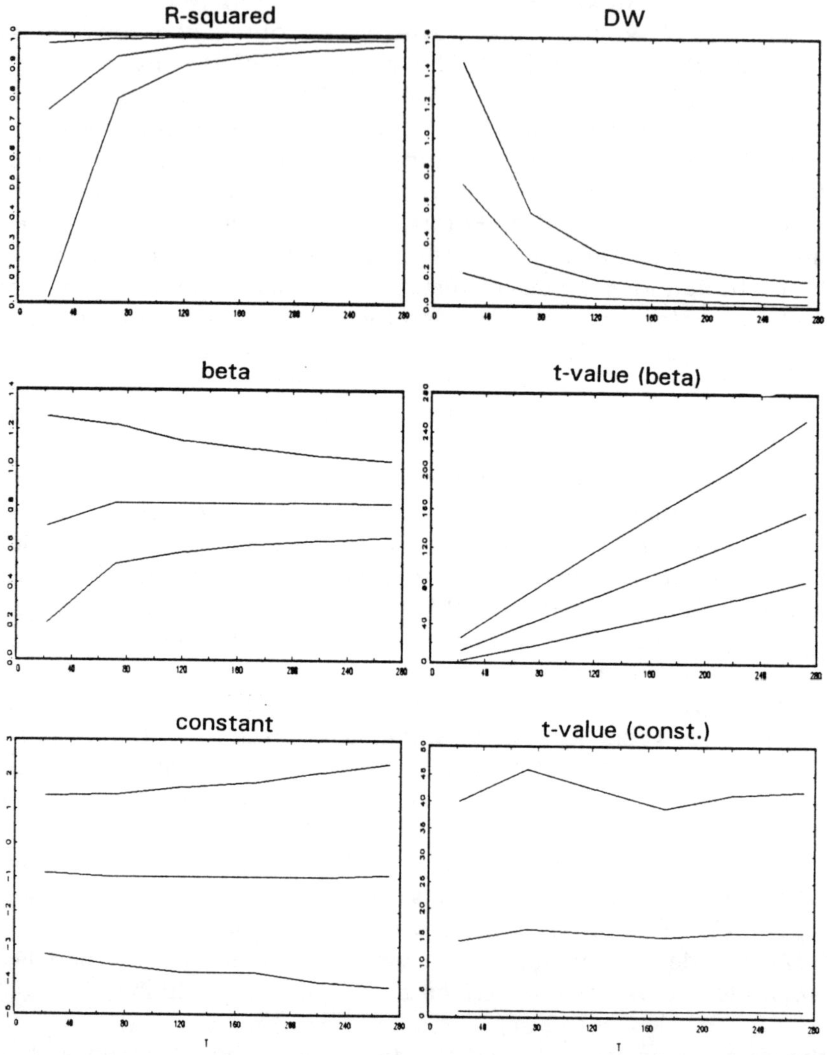


*Note:* Regression of three random walks with drifts; drifts and standard deviations: see Table 3.2.; the time series are restricted according to regression model (3.7): $T = 22 + i \cdot 50, i = 1, \ldots, 5$. For each $T$ the regression (3.7) is replicated 5000 times. Starting values = actual realizations of $\ln(V)$, $\ln(H)$ and $\ln(U)$ in 1971. The graphs represent averages as well as 5% and 95% fractiles of the simulated distributions.

*Table 3.3.:* Critical values of hypothetical spurious regressions

| | const. | | $\ln V$ ($\ln V_c$) | | $\ln U$ | | time | | DW | $R^2$ |
|---|---|---|---|---|---|---|---|---|---|---|
| | param. | *t*-value | param. | *t*-value | param. | *t*-value | param. | *t*-value | | |
| (1) | 7.6/17.8 | 4.0/27.9 | -.24/.26 | .1/5.0 | -.31/.23 | .2/8.4 | - | - | .38/1.73 | .06/.88 |
| | (12.6) | (12.8) | (.01) | (1.9) | (-.04) | (3.1) | | | (.97) | (.49) |
| (2) | 7.8/16.9 | 4.0/19.8 | -.22/.21 | .1/4.0 | -.25/.25 | .1/4.0 | -.05/.04 | .2/6.8 | .55/1.97 | .15/.93 |
| | (12.4) | (10.3) | (.00) | (1.5) | (.00) | (1.5) | (-.007) | (2.5) | (1.19) | (.61) |
| (3) | 7.7/17.6 | 4.1/29.5 | -.22/.24 | .1/4.9 | -.32/.23 | .2/8.4 | - | - | .39/1.76 | .06/.87 |
| | (12.7) | (13.6) | (.01) | (1.9) | (-.04) | (3.1) | | | (.98) | (.49) |
| (4) | 7.9/16.7 | 4.2/20.3 | -.19/.19 | .1/3.9 | -.25/.26 | .1/4.1 | -.05/.04 | .2/6.9 | .55/1.93 | .14/.93 |
| | (12.3) | (10.6) | (.00) | (1.5) | (.00) | (1.6) | (-.007) | (2.5) | (1.18) | (.60) |
| (11) | 4.7/18.8 | 1.1/10.6 | -.21/.20 | .1/3.2 | -.45/.45 | .1/3.2 | -.02/.09 | .2/9.9 | .94/2.85 | .29/.98 |
| | (11.6) | (4.9) | (.00) | (1.2) | (.00) | (1.2) | (.034) | (3.6) | (1.88) | (.78) |
| (12) | -2.2/1.6 | .4/16.1 | .04/.83 | .6/8.9 | (restricted) | | -.15/.05 | .3/12.4 | .41/1.77 | .53/.98 |
| | (-.3) | (5.6) | (.43) | (4.1) | | | (-.054) | (4.4) | (.99) | (.87) |
| (13) | -2.5/1.5 | .3/13.5 | .00/.76 | .5/8.5 | (restricted) | | -.16/.04 | .3/13.5 | .42/1.76 | .53/.98 |
| | (-.5) | (4.6) | (.37) | (3.7) | | | (-.063) | (4.9) | (.99) | (.87) |

*Note:* The entries have to be read as "5%-percentile/95%-percentile"; the numbers below (in parentheses) represent the average of 5000 replications of the simulation experiment. See Table 3.1. for the corresponding equation numbers and Table 3.2. for assumed drifts and standard deviations. Underlined values indicate that actual estimates violate the respective critical regions.

The same strong result does not hold for regression (3) which is based on *corrected* vacancies $\ln V_c$: Here only the *t*-value of the constant term is below the lower limit (2.5 instead of 4.1). Adding a time trend, however, makes the regression clearly non-spurious: Equation (4) of Table 3.2. has $DW=0.37$, whereas Table 3.3. reveals that the lower 5% critical value of a spurious regression is 0.55.

It is worth noting that a *DW* statistic in the area of two does not preclude the presence of a potential spurious regression: Equations (2) and (4) have 95% critical values larger than 1.90. Increasing the ratio "(number of regressors) / (number of observations)" worsens the credibility of the *DW* statistic in actual time series regressions: This becomes clear from equation (11) where the estimated *DW* statistic is 1.60. This value is far from being a proof against the presence of a spurious regression, since the small number of observations leads to a confidence interval [0.94,2.85], and the average *DW* is even 1.88. Nevertheless, there is evidence against a spurious relationship, since the estimated parameter of unemployment (0.50) exceeds the upper limit (0.45). Finally, the restricted regressions (12) and (13) of Table 3.1. have *t*-values of $\beta$ above critical values in Table 3.3.,[1] which again leads to the conclusion that aggregate matching functions are not spurious, unless we assume constant returns to scale without a time variable.

There is no evidence against spurious relationships coming from the deterministic trend. It is interesting to have a closer look at the unrestricted regressions where time is included. Since all results are in accordance with the spurious result, can we rely on the time variable in these aggregate results when interpreting time as a change of the scale parameter $\alpha$ ?

In order to understand the role of time in spurious regressions, *Theorem B3* (Appendix A3.II.4) reveals the asymptotic behaviour of the OLS estimate of the time parameter $\alpha$ (cf. eq. (3.6)) in spurious regressions, where both explanatory and dependent variables are random walks with drifts. It can be shown that it simply converges to the drift of the dependent variable. This also holds in small samples, as can be seen from the mean values of simulated trend estimates in Table 3.3. (confer the unrestricted regressions (2), (4) and (11)): Averaged simulated estimates coincide with the drifts of the "dependent" random walks, which are generated using the drifts of $\ln(H)$ reported in Table 3.2.

The theoretical result of *Theorem B3* raises doubts with respect to the use of *time* in actual regressions of Table 3.1. The only (unrestricted) significant time effect can be found in equation (11). Here the estimated parameter is 0.040, whereas the theoretically expected value which would be consistent with a spurious result is 0.034, i.e. the drift of $\ln(H)$ of the period 1982-1992. Thus, summing up, given the fact that no time parameter contradicted the spurious regression hypothesis, and that in case of the only "significant" relationship ("significant" in terms of conventional *t*-statistics) the actual estimate is close to the expected spurious result, we should be careful of giving the time variable too much economic interpretation in aggregate matching functions.[2]

---

1 Note that the *R-squared* in Table 3.1. does not correspond to the entry in Table 3.3., which required a regression with $\ln(V/U)$ on the left hand side.

2 The theoretically expected spurious regression result of the non-time parameters is as follows. From the Frisch-Waugh theorem we know that including a time variable is equivalent to running a regression using deviations from a (linear) trend. Durlauf and Phillips (1988, see also the extension formulated in Theorem B3 of Appendix A3.II.4) have shown that for a random walk with drift deviations from a linear trend lead to a random walk *without* drift (since the OLS estimate of a random walk with drift on time yields the drift). Thus, we are back to a spurious regression without drifts, as it is studied by Phillips (1986). Theorem B1 and the subsequent simulation study in Appendix A3.II.1 reveal that this yields average slope parameters around zero with a symmetric but nonstandard distribution. This explains the more or less symmetric range of the critical values in equations (2), (4) and (11).

# 3.5. Disaggregate matching functions using a panel of occupational groups

## 3.5.1. Occupational *UV*-curves

After excluding the possibility of a spurious regression, but also after some discouraging attempts to estimate aggregate matching functions, the next step is to extend the analysis to a disaggregate level. The data consists of a time series of 40 occupational groups of the period 1971 to 1992 (880 observations). Data on placements, vacancies and unemployment are available for all groups (see Appendix A3.I for data sources). Summing up all individual groups yields the aggregate data used in the previous section.

To give an impression of the heterogeneity behind disaggregate matching functions, Figure 3.5. provides a scatterplot of the "unemployment-v-acancies" relationship in all 40 occupational groups. Only a few examples fit the typical shape of a Beveridge curve, and potential counterclockwise loops, if any, only start in the eigthies (which becomes evident in the aggregate data: see Figure 3.2.).[1] Graph "1", for example, reveals that aggregate matching functions are dominated by particular groups of workers in the turnover process. It displays unemployment and vacancies of occupations related to agriculture and fishery. It is interesting to note that despite steadily *declining* employment in agriculture and fishery, both unemployment *and* vacancies steadily increase. Here seasonal workers with short-term contracts and other high-turnover workers with short tenure dominate the matching process (confirming Hall's, 1989, supposition). They replace the decreasing labour input of self-employed farmers.

A further observation sheds some light on the hypothesis that the occupational structure in Germany is changing towards a more service-oriented economy. Graphs "28" to "30" and the last two lines of Figure 3.5. show the situation for service-oriented and socio-cultural occupations, whereas lines two, three and four contain production workers. Whereas production workers provide several examples for typical *UV*-curves with less profound shifts, service-oriented and socio-cultural occupations are characterized by a profound counterclockwise loop in the eighties, indicating a reduction in unemployment which is accompanied by a strong increase in vacancies, an increase that is stronger than any one experienced before.

---

**1** Graph "17" is an exception in which "nutritionists" provide one single and completed loop.

*Figure 3.5.:* Unemployment and vacancies in 40 occupational groups

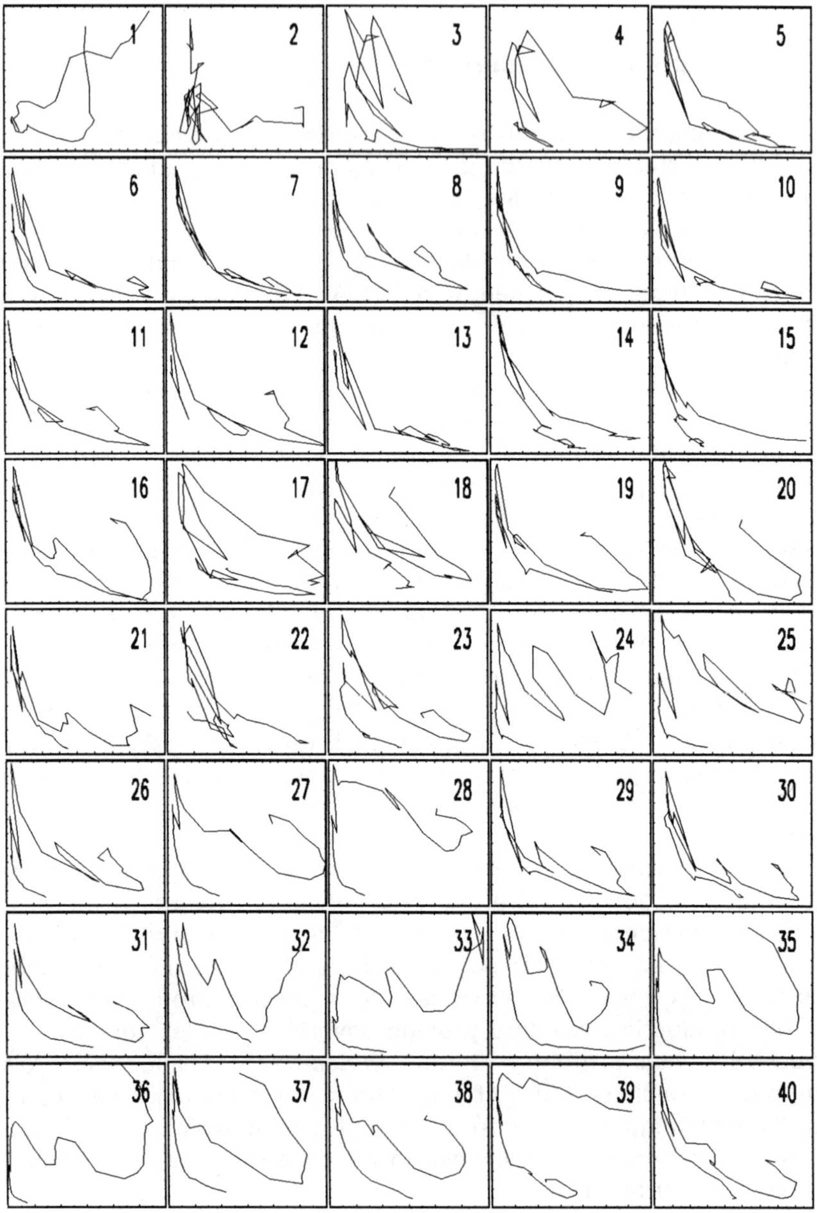


*Notes:* Horizontal axis: unemployment, vertical axis: vacancies; see Appendix 3.III for the list of occupational groups.

The most striking difference, however, is the reaction after the first oil price shock, where high unemployment figures go along with a persistently high number of vacancies. This is quite different from the situation for production workers, where vacancies decrease much faster (along a stable *UV* curve). Service-oriented and socio-cultural occupations, on the contrary, first start with a *clockwise UV* curve due to the persistently high number of vacancies after OPEC I which indicates the structural change in the service sector: The existence of new technologies leads to a growing demand for workers with computer skills, whereas wrongly skilled workers enter the pool of unemployment.

### 3.5.2. Nonsense regressions with panel data?

A suitable way to disentangle common features of different occupational groups is to run panel estimations. However, as with simple regression analysis, unit roots in individual time series may lead to misinterpretation problems of conventional t-values. Appendix A3.II.2 shows that spurious fixed-effects models (all individual time series are unrelated individual random walks but are estimated under the hypothesis that the true data generating process is a fixed-effects model) can lead to t-values above conventional critical values, in particular when individual drifts are high. Unfortunately, exact conclusions depend on the size of both *individual* drifts and standard errors.

In addition to the simulation experiments in A3.II.3, I ran a simulation experiment suitable to highlight the possibility of spurious t-values in the subsequent panel analysis. The Monte Carlo study is based on $K=40$ and $T=20$. Individual drifts are assumed to be zero (drift=0.0, standard error=1.0), which is a conservative choice since most drift-noise ratios are non-zero, especially in the cases of vacancies and placements. Moreover, the simulated fixed-effects regression is based on a model with only one regressor. Replicating the experiment 1000 times (i.e. generating 1000 times 40 individual random walks with drifts, and 1000 times estimating a fixed-effects model) leads to an average absolute t-value of the regressor of about 2.1 These results show that misleading conclusions can arise even for given sample sizes.

The importance of spurious interpretations in panel data models is confirmed by recent publications (Entorf, 1997a; Granger and Hyung, 1997). Of course, spurious regressions problems can only occur for nonstationary data, and known unit root tests have low statistical power in (short) time series. However, there has been progress in testing unit roots using panel data. Using the techniques by Levin and Lin (1992), Entorf (1997b) has shown that exploiting the higher power of panel unit root test vis-a-vis time series unit root tests allows us to conclude that unit roots in the panel data on placements, vacancies and unemployment used in this chapter are unlikely. These results reassure that potential t-values above two would be "real", and they cannot arise due to spurious fixed-effects models.[1]

### 3.5.3. Panel data estimations for disaggregate matching functions

After excluding potential interpretation problems due to unit roots in individual time series, panel data analysis should provide new insights when compared to aggregate time series analysis. It allows us to control for group specific and time specific effects that might be responsible for aggregation errors. Moreover, time specific effects in the matching function provide an interesting alternative to the simple time trend, since they can reveal potential nonlinearities in the matching efficiency. Below, the time pattern of these shifts in the matching efficiency will be related to some economic variables that are commonly believed as driving mismatch.

Several panel estimation techniques have been followed. The basic model for the panel of occupational groups is the so-called two-way-fixed effects model

$$\ln(H_{it}) = \beta \ln(V_{it}) + \gamma \ln(U_{it}) + \alpha_i + \omega_t + \epsilon_{it}, \tag{3.8}$$

where $t = 1,\ldots, T$ are the number of periods, and $i = 1,\ldots, K$ are the number of groups. Deviations from this model treat the term $u_{it} = \alpha_i + \omega_t + \epsilon_{it}$ in different ways: For instance, in the "one way fixed-effects" model, it is modelled as in the classical regression analysis: $\alpha_i$ is treated as a regressor (i.e. not necessarily independent of *ln(U)* and *ln(V)*) and it is estimated as an individual (occupational group specific) constant. The time effects are covered by a linear time trend. More details on the econometric panel specifications a) to k) used in Tables 3.4 and 3.5 are summarized in Appendix A3.IV.

Results (Table 3.4.) are quite different from aggregate estimations. All parameter estimates are highly significant, and most parameter estimates on *ln(V)* and *ln(U)* ($\beta$ and $\gamma$) range between 0.47 and 0.57 as well as between 0.30 and 0.45 respectively, giving more importance to vacancies in the matching process. The only exception is pooled OLS under the hypothesis of identical group-specific constants (equations (4) and (5)), where the coefficient on unemployment exceeds the coefficient on

---

1 The results reported in Section 3.5.2 are based on very recent developments concerning unit roots and spurious regressions in panel data. These papers were not available at the time of writing the book so that they cannot be incorporated into the text in more detail.

vacancies. Equation (5) seems to confirm previous estimates found in the literature, i.e. constant returns to scale, coefficients about 2/3 and 1/3 for unemployment and vacancies, and negative time trends. However, the assumption of identical constants is much to strong, and this hypothesis (model b), resp. $(B11)$ in A3.IV) is clearly rejected in favour of the presence of both group-specific and time-specific fixed effects (without reporting F-tests in detail).

The picture for the last ten years of the estimation period changes (no. (3) in Table 3.4.), where the coefficient on unemployment (0.45) is higher than the one on vacancies (0.36). In terms of fixed effect models, between 94% and 98% of the variance in hires is explained by the panel-data model of the matching function. The highest $R^2$ can be found for the subperiod 1983 to 1992, where thick markets (a large pool of unemployment workers) increase $R^2$ up to 0.988. There is mixed evidence with respect to constant returns to scale, though Wald tests reveal that estimating constant returns to scale is rather an exception (due to small standard errors the sum of coefficients has to be very close to unity).

As an alternative to fixed period effects, I estimate the model with a deterministic time trend (i.e., a constant scale parameter $\alpha$ ). Significant estimates range between -0.016 and -0.026 (leaving aside the estimate of pooled OLS, -0.045, which is less reliable due to significant fixed effects in models (1) and (2)). Accordingly, the decline in efficiency is between 16% and 26% which suggests a potential outward shift in the Beveridge curve (due to increasing mismatch). I return to this issue after presenting individual period effects.

The inclusion of (significant) period effects[1] leads to a higher coefficient on vacancies: Compare equations (1) and (2) as well as (10) and (11). Two-way-fixed-effects models and two-way-random-effects models lead to almost coincident results, as can be seen from (2) and (6). The Hausman test, however, is in favour of a random effects specification (model (6)).

All estimations reveal serial correlation in $\epsilon_{it}$, measured as $\hat{\rho}_{\epsilon} = \hat{Corr}(\epsilon_{it}, \epsilon_{i,t-1})$ in (1) to (6), though estimates are well below unity. Correcting for serial correlation yields results with constant returns to scale: see (7) and (8).

Equation (9) warns us that estimated coefficients might be too high due to measurement errors, but on the other hand, the very low *R-squared* (0.139) indicates that the assumption of multiplicative errors might impose a too simplistic model of measurement.

**1** F-tests are in favour of period effects models.

*Table 3.4.:* Panel-data models of matching functions

| No. | Method[1)] | *ln(V)* | *ln(U)* | *time* | $\overline{R}^2$ | Residuals | Tests |
|---|---|---|---|---|---|---|---|
| (1) | OLS, one way, a) | 0.48<br>(31.0) | 0.34<br>(16.1) | -0.016<br>(8.3) | 0.971 | $\hat{\rho}_\epsilon$ = 0.70 | Wald = 32.4* |
| (2) | OLS, two way, d) | 0.57<br>(32.4) | 0.34<br>(13.5) | - | 0.979 | $\hat{\rho}_\epsilon$ = 0.69 | - |
| (3) | OLS, two way, 1983-92, d) | 0.36<br>(11.5) | 0.45<br>(8.0) | - | 0.988 | $\hat{\rho}_\epsilon$ = 0.56 | - |
| (4) | Pooled OLS, b) | 0.45<br>(19.0) | 0.49<br>(19.3) | - | 0.595 | - | - |
| (5) | Pooled OLS, b) | 0.36<br>(14.2) | 0.63<br>(21.4) | -0.045<br>(8.7) | 0.628 | - | - |
| (6) | REM, two way, e) | 0.55<br>(34.0) | 0.32<br>(15.6) | - | 0.574 | $\hat{\rho}_\epsilon$ = 0.69<br>$\hat{\rho}_u$ = 0.93<br>$\hat{\rho}_\omega$ = 0.27 | Wald = 14.4*<br>Hausman = 5.7 |
| (7) | OLS, one way, *AR1*, f) | 0.55<br>(32.4) | 0.44<br>(18.2) | -0.026<br>(10.2) | 0.936 | $\hat{\rho}_\epsilon$ = -0.14 | Wald = 0.10 |
| (8) | REM, one way, *AR1*, h) | 0.54<br>(23.1) | 0.45<br>(13.5) | -0.026<br>(7.3) | 0.600 | $\hat{\rho}_\epsilon$ = -0.15<br>$\hat{\rho}_u$ = 0.64 | Wald = 0.07 |
| (9) | Measurement errors, i) | 0.26<br>(8.3) | 0.12<br>(2.9) | 0.001<br>(1.2) | 0.139 | - | - |
| (10) | IV, one way, j) | 0.47<br>(25.1) | 0.33<br>(12.6) | -0.016<br>(6.7) | 0.964 | $\ddot{\rho}_\epsilon$ = 0.59 | Wald = 13.0* |
| (11) | IV, two way, j) | 0.57<br>(24.0) | 0.30<br>(7.3) | - | 0.973 | $\hat{\rho}_\epsilon$ = 0.54 | - |
| (12) | IV, one way, *AR1*, j),f) | 0.47<br>(23.9) | 0.40<br>(13.7) | -0.019<br>(8.2) | 0.964 | $\hat{\rho}_\epsilon$ = 0.52 | Wald = 11.0* |

*Notes:* Estimation of a panel of 40 occupational groups for the period 1972 to 1992.
1) See A3.IV for a description of methods a) to j); * indicates significance at the 5% level, "Wald" is a Wald test testing constant returns o scale, i.e. $\beta + \gamma = 1$, "Hausman" is Hausman's chi-squared statistic for testing whether the GLS estimator is an appropriate alternative to the consistent fixed-effect (least squares) estimator; (absolute) t-values are in parantheses.

Equations (10) and (11) reveal only a minor reaction after using aggregate instrumental variables. The estimated returns to scales are somewhat smaller than before due to a simultaneity bias, and they decrease from 0.82 to 0.80 (equation (1) compared to equation(10)) and from 0.91 to 0.87 (equation (2) compared to equation (11)). A stronger impact of a potential simultaneity bias becomes evident after correcting for both endogeneity and serial correlation: While in equation (7) estimated return to scales is 0.99, it is reduced to 0.87 in the *AR1* estimation of model (12), so that the hypothesis of constant returns to scale has to be rejected.

A dynamic representation of the matching function is presented in Table 3.5. The first two columns show one way and two-way-fixed-effects models. The parameter on time has to be interpreted according to equation $(B15)$ (Appendix A3.IV). The indirect estimate of $\delta$ is -0.038. However, period effects turn out to be significant so that the two way model proves itself better suited. The parameter of serial correlation, $\rho$, is well below unity, so that unit root problems are not very likely. This holds in particular after instrumenting the lagged endogenous variable (according to Anderson and Hsiao, 1981).

*Table 3.5.:* Durbin's dynamic specification

| Explanatory variables (parameter) | OLS, one way, f) | OLS, two way, g) | Anderson/ Hsiao, k) | Anderson/ Hsiao, two way, k) |
|---|---|---|---|---|
| $\ln(V_{it})$ | 0.37 | 0.47 | 0.35 | 0.42 |
| $(\beta)$ | (18.4) | (21.5) | (18.6) | (18.8) |
| $\ln(V_{i,t-1})$ | -0.33 | -0.38 | -0.21 | -0.14 |
| $(-\rho\beta)$ | (17.4) | (16.2) | (11.5) | (6.6) |
| $\ln(U_{it})$ | 0.26 | 0.30 | 0.16 | 0.20 |
| $(\gamma)$ | (9.3) | (9.1) | (6.4) | (5.9) |
| $\ln(U_{i,t-1})$ | -0.16 | -0.19 | -0.07 | 0.02 |
| $(-\rho\gamma)$ | (6.3) | (6.0) | (2.9 | (0.5) |
| *time* | -0.0069 | - | -0.0042 | - |
| $(\delta(1-\rho))$ | (5.5) | | (5.2) | |
| $\ln(H_{i,t-1})$ | 0.82 | 0.80 | 0.34 | 0.61 |
| $(\rho)$ | (38.3) | (39.2) | (7.2) | (6.5) |
| *R-squared* | 0.990 | 0.993 | 0.518 | 0.589 |
| Wald Tests[1)] | - | 0.001 | 15.0* | 0.24 |

*Notes:* f), g) and k): see Appendix A3.IV; in the Anderson/Hsiao specification, variables are replaced by their differenced values (according to specification k)); see $(B15)$ for the identification of parameters;
1): Eq. (B15) implies that the hypothesis $\epsilon_{it} = \rho\epsilon_{i,t-1} + \nu_{it}$ yields the equation $\ln(H_{it}) = \alpha_i(1-\rho) + \beta\ln(V_{it}) - \rho\beta\ln(V_{i,t-1}) + \gamma\ln(U_{it}) - \rho\gamma\ln(U_{i,t-1}) + \rho\ln(H_{i,t-1}) + \nu_{it}$. Thus, this hypothesis and the additional hypothesis $\beta + \gamma = 1$ both hold if and only if $(\beta - \rho\beta + \gamma - \rho\gamma + \rho = 1)$.

Irrespective of modelling levels or first differences, the joint hypothesis $(\beta - \rho\beta + \gamma - \rho\gamma + \rho = 1)$, which consists of both a) $\epsilon_{it} = \rho\epsilon_{i,t-1} + \nu_{it}$ (i.e. the dynamic model $(B15)$ is the correct specification), and b) the matching function has constant returns to scale (see footnote 1 of Table 3.5), is confirmed for the (better fitting) two-way model (columns two and four).

### 3.5.4. Substituting the time trend by economic variables

Since models with period effects turn out to be superior to models with a linear trend, we may conclude that the linear time trend is too simple a model, though the negative sign of the linear trend is very stable throughout all specifications. The following one-way-fixed-effects regression shows that the linear trend ceases to be significant when economic variables which are potential candidates for explaining mismatch are added to the time variable in order to replace the scale parameter $\alpha$ (t-values in parentheses):[1]

$$(3.9)\ \ln(H_{it}) = \underset{(28.5)}{0.45}\ln(V_{it}) + \underset{(14.1)}{0.35}\ln(U_{it}) + \underset{(5.9)}{0.64}\ln(SEARCH_t)$$

$$- \underset{(4.9)}{0.18}RAT\_F_t + \underset{(4.6)}{0.02}DUC_t - \underset{(0.7)}{0.03}\ln(W/P_t) - \underset{(0.2)}{0.003}t$$

$$\hat{\rho}_\epsilon = 0.68, \quad \bar{R} = 0.974$$

A high number of non-unemployed job seekers, *SEARCH,* improve the matching efficiency, whereas a higher female participation rate, *RAT_F*, deteoriates the scale parameter. This may be explained by the fact that non-unemployed job seekers are better educated and lead to "thicker" job markets, whereas increases in the female participation rate imply job search by less experienced workers with low matching probability. "Good" economic situations lead to easier matching, as can be seen from the positive impact of the degree of capacity utilization, *DUC.* High real wages can be seen as a reason for firms to refrain from hiring, but the hypothesis is not confirmed since *W/P* turns out to be insignificant.

### 3.5.5. Period effects and the identification of mismatch

There are, of course, many other economic variables which are discussed as causes of mismatch. There are too many of them to include all in a single regression. Instead, the period effects in two-way-fixed-effects models provide a time-variant measure of the scale parameter in matching functions, hence, after switching signs, it measures shifts in mismatch.

---

**1** Eliminating the nonsignificant real wage *WP* leads to an even smaller t-value (0.004) on time.

Then, in a simple descriptive manner, it is straightforward to analyse correlative relationships between period effects and variables related to mismatch.

*Figure 3.6.:* Shifts of the scaling parameter in matching functions

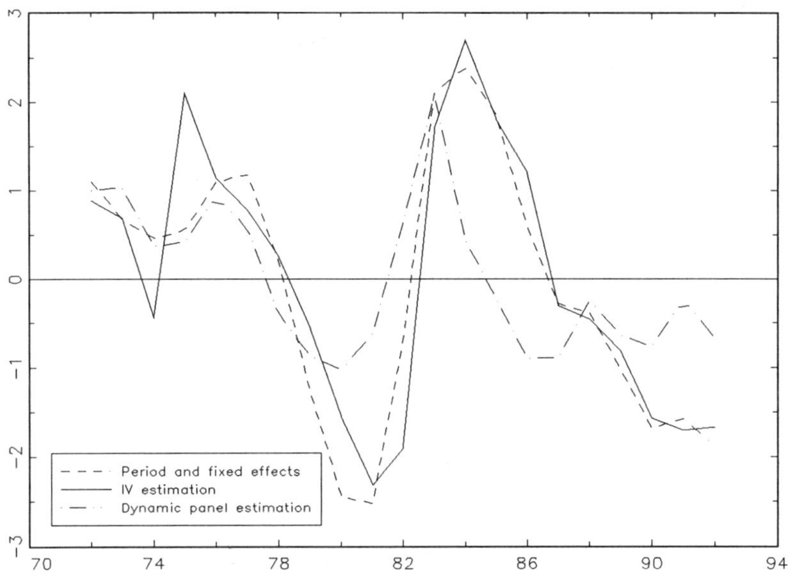


*Note:* Period effects of the following regressions: equation (2) ("OLS") and equation (11) ("IV"), both Table 3.4., as well as the dynamic regression "OLS, two way" from Table 3.5.

Figure 3.6. presents period effects from three different two-way regressions, i.e. OLS, IV and dynamic OLS. As is to be expected, period effects of the dynamic OLS regression behave like differenced period effects of the basic OLS regression, since the period effects of the dynamic regression must be interpreted as $\omega_t - \rho\omega_{t-1}$, where $\omega_t$ is the period effect of the basic OLS two-way-fixed-effects model. Figure 3.6. has to be interpreted under the restriction that period effects have mean zero. Recall, however, that unrestricted linear time trends in estimated matching functions are significantly negative. This is the result of a steadily decreasing matching efficiency after OPEC II (1982/83). Matching seems to be particularly easy in times of deep recessions, when the large number of people looking for a job improves the probability of a good match. In the case of OPEC I (1974/75), this is less obvious after using instrumental variables (compare the period effects of the simple two-way regression with the period effects of the IV estimation in Figure 3.6.): After a very small value in 1974, the period effect jumps to a local maximum in 1975.

Table 3.7. provides correlation coefficients between the period effects and potential explanatory variables of mismatch. Additional variables besides *SEARCH, DUC, W/P*, and *RAT_F* (see Chapter 3.5.4.) are presented below; Table 3.6. informs about general trends.

- *NO_SCHOOL* (share of unemployed without any schooling degree): This variable hints at educational mismatch. New technologies imply rising skill requirements so that insufficient schooling can be seen as a reason for not been hired (see, for instance, Freeman, 1991, and Soskice, 1991, and references therein).

- *POP* (German labour force): Inflows and outflows from the labour force determine the future (educational, occupational, regional) structure of the labour force, i.e. future matching probabilities. Discouraged workers and retired (including early retired) people leave the labour force, whereas foreigners and young workers search for employment. Related to *RAT_F* and *RAT_M, POP* changes in response to cyclical fluctuations (*RAT_M*) or as a general trend (*RAT_F*).

- *RAT_M* (male participation rate): During good (bad) economic situations, workers start entering (leaving) the labour force, particularly in high turnover jobs (construction, for example).

- $W_u/W_s$. (unskilled/skilled ratio of wages): In German business surveys (IFO Institute, Munich), firms report an increasingly important lack of *skilled* labour. In a neoclassical framework, this would imply an increasing wage of skilled labour relative to unskilled labour (in fact, Christl, 1992, uses $W_u/W_s$ as an indicator of relative demand shifts between skilled and unskilled labour). The historical development of $W_u/W_s$ informs us that no such effect occurs; the share is relatively stable, increasing slightly from 79.4% in 1973 to 81% in 1988 and again decreasing to 79.9% in 1992.[1] In the light of collective bargaining, this stable share confirms the hypothesis that the solidaristic wage policy of German trade unions prevented the relative wages of the least skilled workers from falling to the levels that would have been dictated by market forces. In terms of mismatch, the question is whether the failing neoclassical price mechanisms distort the optimal allocation of adequate skills. A further danger seen by many economists is that high wages of unskilled labour might lead to the export of unskilled jobs: Labour intensive production with low skill reqirements may take place in countries with lower wages ("outsourcing").

---

**1** Abraham and Houseman (1994) analyse the earnings inequality in Germany and find a relatively stable earnings distribution between skill groups, educational groups and age groups. These trends in Germany stand in striking contrast to recent trends in earnings inequality in the United States.

- *U_1YEAR* (share of unemployed being unemployed longer than one year): The rising share of long-term unemployed characterizes the hysteresis problem of European unemployment: Escaping from unemployment becomes more unlikely the longer the duration of unemployment because skills have depreciated since being unemployed.
- *AGE_50* (share of unemployed being older than 50): Structural changes in the German economy have led to a substantial share of frictional unemployment. However, when compared to better chances of young unemployed workers in Germany (where youth unemployment is relatively low), older workers have problems of reintegration, since firms are reluctant to hire them. The reasons are not perfectly clear, potential problems are relative high wage claims and suspected immobility. Buttler and Cramer (1991) analyse the duration of unemployment and find age as the dominant factor, in particular when age is accompanied by other "obstacles" of reintegration, for instance health problems. However, it is interesting to note from Table 3.6. that the share of older unemployed is not simply globally trending upwards. In times of deep recessions the share decreases because of a very high number of cyclical (short-term) unemployment (see the year 1984 in Table 3.6.).
- *MM_STOCK* (cross section volatility of stock market performance): Based on a paper by Brainard and Cutler (1993), the purpose of this new measure is to isolate reallocation shocks from aggregate shocks in a Beveridge curve relationship. Reallocation shocks, such as changes in tastes or technologies, cause changes within the sectoral pattern of stock returns, whereas aggregate shocks, in contrast, would affect *all* sectors at a time. Brainard and Cutler (1993) propose to distuinguish the two types of shocks by using the variance of sectoral stock market returns. According to this idea, I estimate a VAR using 12 sectoral indices of the period 1969 until 1992 (monthly data). Implementing the efficient market hypothesis, the VAR is based on one lagged value. The VAR is estimated as a "rolling regression", where the first result is available in January 1975, the second in February and so on. At each point in time I calculate the variance of the 12 sectoral residuals, which represent unexpected stock market returns. The time series of these sectoral innovations is *MM_STOCK* (after averaging monthly values). It should be low when aggregate shocks lead to a simultaneous movement of all sectoral stock markets, and it should be high when sector-specific shocks indicate reallocation.
- *STRUCT* (ratio "employment in manufacturing" / "employment in service sectors"): As can be observed in all industrialized countries, Germany faces a structural trend towards a more service oriented econ-

omy.[1] The adjustment process might lead to frictional unemployment/or reallocation problems, probably leading to shifts of the matching efficiency and/or the Beveridge curve.

- *FOREIGN* (ratio "foreigners / population"): The share of foreigners in West-Germany increased from 3% in 1967 to 10% in 1992. Some people argue that German "guest workers" ("Gastarbeiter", as they are called in Germany) fill vacancies of particular jobs where German workers are not available, whereas other arguments say that the high share of unemployed foreigners (14.4% in 1992) is a substantial source of the persistently high number of unemployed people in Germany.

*Table 3.6.:* The changing labour market

| | 1973 | 1980 | 1984 | 1988 | 1992 |
|---|---|---|---|---|---|
| *SEARCH*[1)] | 178.2 | 261.9 | 412.7 | 587.7 | 733.9 |
| *DUC*[2)] | 87.1 | 82.3 | 80.3 | 86.4 | 83.2 |
| *W/P*[3)] | 0.95 | 1.03 | 0.99 | 1.15 | 1.26 |
| *RAT_F*[2)] | 31.5 | 33.8 | 35.0 | 37.0 | 38.0 |
| *RAT_M*[2)] | 58.2 | 58.1 | 59.8 | 60.3 | 58.2 |
| *POP*[4)] | 27.4 | 27.9 | 28.7 | 29.6 | 30.9 |
| *NO_SCHOOL*[2)] | 18.7 | 22.8 | 30.3 | 28.7 | 28.1 |
| $W_u/W_s$[2)] | 79.4 | 79.7 | 80.6 | 81.0 | 79.9 |
| *U_1YEAR*[2)] | (n.a.) | 12.9 | 28.8 | 32.6 | 26.6 |
| *AGE_50*[2)] | 29.4 | 23.1 | 19.6 | 24.7 | 31.5 |
| *STRUCT*[5)] | 1.05 | 0.82 | 0.72 | 0.68 | 0.62 |
| *MM_STOCK*[6)] | (n.a.) | 12.0 | 107.8 | 292.6 | 1370.7 |
| *FOREIGN*[2)] | 6.4 | 7.2 | 7.1 | 7.3 | 10.0 |
| *UR*[2)] | 1.0 | 3.8 | 9.3 | 8.7 | 6.6 |

*Notes*: 1) in 1000, 2) in percent, 3) see Appendix A3.I, 4) in million, 5) ratio, 6) see text; Sources: see A3.I, own calculations, unemployment rate (*UR*): Bundesanstalt für Arbeit

Since most variables are trending, the correlation analysis is based on differenced values when high autocorrelation (unit root and near unit root) is evident. Therefore, the prefered fixed-effects model to be compared with is the dynamic estimation. Prefered (in a statistical sense) correlation coefficients where both variables most likely have the same order of integration I(0) are written in bold letters.

---

**1** The trend, however, is less profound than in other European countries and the U.S. (see EEC, 1991, for a comparison).

Positive signs indicate a positive correlation with the scale parameter representing matching efficiency, i.e. positive changes of variables with positive signs indicate decreasing mismatch, negative signs are related to growing mismatch. Significant relationships exist for *POP, RAT_F, W/P,* STRUCT and *AGE_50*. Evidently, new entrants of the labour force imply distortions of the matching technology, as can be seen from both *POP* and *RAT_F.* It is interesting to compare the latter with changes in *RAT_M*, which has a positive though insignificant correlation coefficient and which behaves similar to changes in *DUC*.

Real wage costs are positively correlated with mismatch. However, the negative sign in the correlation analysis is due to a general upward trend in *W/P* and the general downward movement in period effects. A stronger test would be to compare *changes* in real wage costs with the period effects of the dynamic OLS estimation. Here *W/P* remains negative but with insignificant t-values.

The negative correlation coefficient of *STRUCT* provides an unexpected result: It implies that further lowering the ratio "manufacturing/services" (i.e. increasing the relative importance of the service sectors) would imply easier matching. This contradicts the hypothesis that the trend towards service oriented industries represents temporary matching problems causing an outward shift of the Beveridge curve. However, one should be cautious before finally drawing such conclusions, since the service sector provides many high turnover jobs, so that "better matching" could be a misleading description: The high number of new placements following the structural change can possibly be due to a high number of non-permanent jobs, and hence, shifts in the matching function do not say too much about *long-run* matches of demand and supply.

The same reasoning applies to the role of *NO_SCHOOL*, where positive changes in the share of unemployed having no school degree lead to decreasing mismatch. Again, this must be interpreted in respect to the fact that a high number of less qualified workers seeking a job leads to a high number of placements into bad-quality jobs, which are characterized by low tenure and high fluctuation, again limiting the interpretation of the matching function to high turnover jobs.

The share of older unemployed workers, *U_1YEAR,* is negatively correlated with the scale parameter in the matching function, indicating that employers are indeed not willing to fill vacant jobs with older people, so that the Beveridge curve shifts outward in the presence of growing *U_1YEAR.*

At a glance, there is evidence that the rising share of foreigners increases mismatch. However, looking at the time series of the changes of *FOREIGN*, we can see that the share is always decreasing after cyclical downturns. This causes the problem that foreigners are missing in subsequent upswings. Foreigners cannot be treated as a factor of labour hoarding as

German workers, since many of them have to leave the country. In case of unemployment they are allowed to stay in Germany only after several years of employment. Thus, the time series pattern of foreigners in Germany is constrained by these institutional restrictions. However, we can learn what would happen in situations of upswings (downswings) if we would keep the level of foreigners as in recent "good times" ("bad times"). Therefore, I calculate the correlation between matching efficiency and the change in *FOREIGN* with a three years' lag. The high and positive coefficient says that matching would be easier since there would be a sufficiently large pool of workers. If these workers were released they would be missing in the subsequent upswing (according to the estimate, three years later).

*Table 3.7.:* Correlation analysis

| | Period effects of: | | |
|---|---|---|---|
| Variable | OLS | Dynamic OLS | IV |
| *ΔSEARCH* | 0.07 | **-0.14** | 0.05 |
| *DUC* | -0.27 | -0.39 | -0.27 |
| *ΔDUC* | 0.36 | **0.08** | 0.32 |
| *W/P* | -0.57* | -0.60* | -0.53* |
| *ΔW/P* | 0.17 | **-0.12** | 0.22 |
| *ΔRAT_F* | -0.28 | **-0.43*** | -0.23 |
| *RAT_M* | 0.10 | **-0.24** | 0.06 |
| *ΔRAT_M* | 0.20 | 0.04 | 0.16 |
| *ΔPOP* | -0.67* | **-0.67*** | -0.66* |
| *NO_SCHOOL* | 0.07 | -0.11 | 0.00 |
| *ΔNO_SCHOOL* | -0.05 | **0.47*** | -0.15 |
| $W_u/W_s$ | -0.14 | -0.38 | -0.18 |
| $\Delta W_u/W_s$ | 0.36 | **0.32** | 0.24 |
| *U_1YEAR* | 0.29 | -0.06 | 0.30 |
| *ΔU_1YEAR* | -0.02 | **-0.29** | 0.10 |
| *AGE_50* | -0.52* | -0.42* | -0.47* |
| *ΔAGE_50* | 0.02 | **-0.23** | 0.12 |
| *ΔSTRUCT* | -0.14 | **-0.41*** | -0.06 |
| *MM_STOCK* | -0.33 | -0.43 | -0.33 |
| *ΔMM_STOCK* | 0.02 | **-0.19** | 0.07 |
| *FOREIGN* | -0.54* | -0.39 | -0.54* |
| *ΔFOREIGN* | -0.64* | **-0.35** | -0.61* |
| *ΔFOREIGN*(-3) | 0.36 | **0.72*** | 0.21 |
| *ΔU* | 0.12 | **0.47*** | 0.04 |

*Note:* The table presents correlation coefficients between listed variables and time variant period effects; see text for details. * means a significant t-test at the 5% level. Bold letters indicate prefered estimates (see text).

The positive correlation between changes in *U* and period effects can only be understood after following the flow approach to the labour market. A high number of workers entering the pool of unemployed means "thick" labour markets so that matching becomes easier and the probability of a good match increases. Since we are not able to estimate time varying coefficients with panel data, the only way to capture these times of high matching efficiency is within the period effects of the matching function.

Of course, it would be preferable to explain mismatch in a multiple regression analysis where all potential causes of mismatch could interact. Unfortunately, such a regression is not suitable because of a small number of degrees of freedom. However, summarizing and completing previous correlation analysis, equation (3.10) presents a multiple regression result for demonstrative reasons. It contains the main labour supply variable, *POP*, and the main labour demand factor, *DUC*. To control for the size of the labour market, *U* is added as a regressor. The dependent variable, "mismatch", consists of period effects in the dynamic OLS fixed-effects model g), Table 3.5. These period effects are used with inverted signs so that positive changes in fact indicate growing mismatch. According to the construction of the dependent variable, all explanatory variables are implemented as *differenced* logged values. The error structure is well described as an MA(1) process (t-values in parentheses):

$$(3.10)\ \text{mismatch} = \underset{(1.7)}{38.6}\ \Delta\ln(POP) - \underset{(2.4)}{12.7}\ \Delta\ln(DUC) - \underset{(2.6)}{2.2}\ \Delta\ln(U), \quad u_t = \epsilon_t + \underset{(3.1)}{0.64}\epsilon_{t-1}$$

$Sample = 1972-1992, \quad \bar{R} = 0.550, \quad DW = 1.92, \quad F-stat = 7.10 \quad (p = 0.002)$

Equation (3.10) confirms that labour-force growth increases mismatch. However, after controlling for size effects measured in *U*, *POP* is only weakly significant (without reporting results, the same would apply to *RAT_F* as an alternative regressor). "Good" economic situtations, measured by the degree of capacity utilization, *DUC*, improve the matching efficiency. Here a multiple regression analysis helps understanding the bivariate correlation analysis in Table 3.7., where the role of *DUC* remained unclear. The result confirms the hypothesis that Beveridge curves tend to move backward in times of booming economies. Finally, the impact of *U* is positive and significant, confirming the reasoning of "thick" markets.

## 3.6. On occupational reallocation: Theoretical and empirical aspects

The equations of motion (3.5), describing a "minimalist model of vacancies and unemployment", reveal that shifts in the Beveridge curve arise for at least two reasons, changes in matching efficiency and changes in reallocation intensity. While in Chapter 3.5., I try to identify driving forces behind a changing scale parameter in matching functions, this chapter focuses on the impact of optimal reallocation for occupational unemployment and vacancies from the viewpoint of the search theory, and it presents empirical evidence on occupational change during the period 1951 to 1992.

### 3.6.1. Matching functions and the adjustment of unemployment/vacancy ratios

Reallocation between workers of different occupations may occur if it is profitable for an unemployed worker to change his/her occupation and search for a job in a new profession. Adapting a search model by Van Ours and Ridder (1995) which provides a framework for job competition between different educational levels, let us assume that an unemployed worker in occupational group *i* has to decide whether he searches a job within his group *i* or within a new group *j*. If he searches within *i* he is part of the pool of unemployed workers searching for a job *i*. The employment benefit of occupational group *i* is $W_i$ and the search duration is $T_i$. $W_i$ represents monetary and non-monetary job attractivity (wages, quality of working conditions etc.) *B* is fallback utility (unemployment benefit). $C_{ij}$ are adjustment and training costs (covered by the worker) of people changing from occupational group *i* to group *j*. Assuming that accepted jobs last forever, the discounted value of search for unemployed workers who search for a job in their own group *i* is

$$(3.11) \qquad S_{ii} = \int_0^{T_i} B e^{-rt} dt + \int_{T_i}^{\infty} (W_i) e^{-rt} dt$$

which can be written as

$$S_{ii} = B/r + ((W_i - B)/r) e^{-rT_i}.$$

If the duration of search $T_i$ is exponentially distributed with hazard rate $\theta_i$, $S_i$ becomes

$$(3.12) \qquad S_{ii} = B/r + \frac{(W_i - B)\theta_i}{r(r+\theta_i)}.$$

The value of search of unemployed workers who change their occupational group and who search in group *j* instead of their previous group *i* can be derived in the same way:

$$(3.13) \qquad S_{ij} = B/r + \frac{(W_j - C_{ij} - B)\theta_j}{r(r+\theta_j)}.$$

An unemployed worker in occupational group *i* is indifferent between searching in group *i* or changing to group *j* when $S_{ii} = S_{ij}$. Thus, according to (3.12) and (3.13) the worker is indifferent if

$$(3.14) \qquad \frac{\theta_i}{\theta_j} = \frac{(W_j - C_{ij} - B)}{(W_i - B) + (W_i - W_j - C_{ij})\theta_j / r}.$$

Note that in the equilibrium situation (3.14) $\theta_j > \theta_i$ if $W_j - C_{ij} < W_i$. This means that workers change occupation until *in equilibrium* the search duration of better paid workers is longer than for workers with lower wages.

Search durations depend on the matching technology and supply-demand conditions which are formalized in matching functions. Here, the matching function can be used to specify the relevant pool of unemployed workers looking for a job. According to (3.12) and (3.13), unemployed workers in occupational group *i* belong partly to the pool of unemployed workers with occupation *j*. In order to describe job competition, I assume that occupational group *i* is better educated, so that group *j* cannot compete with group *i* for jobs in *i*. Using a Cobb-Douglas technology with constant returns to scale, the matching function for both groups are:

$$(3.15) \qquad H_i = \alpha((1-\lambda_i)U_i)^{\beta} V_i^{1-\beta}$$

$$H_j = \alpha(U_j + \lambda_i U_i)^{\beta} V_j^{1-\beta}.$$

Since the hazard rate $\theta_i$ is equal to the ratio of the flow $H_i$ and the relevant pool of unemployed workers searching for a job in group *i*, the hazard rates can be written as

$$(3.16)\qquad \theta_i = \alpha(((1-\lambda_i)U_i)/V_i)^{\beta-1}$$

$$\theta_j = \alpha((U_j + \lambda_i U_i)/V_j)^{\beta-1}.$$

Equations (3.14) and (3.16) can be combined to

$$(3.17)\qquad \frac{(U_j + \lambda_i U_i)}{V_j} = \Phi \frac{(1-\lambda_i)U_i}{V_i},$$

where

$$\Phi = \left( \frac{(W_j - C_{ij} - B)}{(W_i - B) + (W_i - W_j - C_{ij})\theta j / r} \right)^{1/(1-\beta)}.$$

From (3.17) it follows

$$(3.18)\qquad \lambda_i = \frac{\Phi U_i V_j - U_j V_i}{\Phi U_i V_j + U_i V_i}.$$

Unemployed workers change from occupational group *i* to occupational group *j* if $\lambda_i > 0$, i.e. if the numerator in (3.18) is positive, so that

$$(3.19)\qquad \Phi \frac{U_i}{V_i} > \frac{U_j}{V_j}.$$

Hence, if $W_j - C_{ij} < W_i$ (so that $\Phi < 1$), a necessary but not sufficient condition for the existence of occupational change from group *i* to group *j* is that the *UV*-ratio of group *j* is lower than the *UV*-ratio of group *i*.

### 3.6.2. Empirical evidence

In order to highlight the direction of occupational changes more clearly, the 40 occupational groups of Chapter 3.5. are summarized into five main groups: Primary sector workers, *PRIM,* production workers, *PROD,* technical professions, *TECH,* service jobs , *SERV,* and socio-cultural professions, *SOCU* (see Appendix A3.III for exact definitions). Direct tests of the presence of job change would use a simultaneous estimation of the two matching functions in (3.15). Unfortunately, all attempts to achieve reasonable results failed. High collinearity and small degrees of freedom prevented a serious estimation of this highly nonlinear framework. I also refrain from looking for evidence on equation (3.19), which is a steady state relationship and therefore difficult to identify in the data.[1] I find it more appealing to look at the historical adjustment of *UV*-ratios, which indicate temporal disequilibria and reveal whether subsequent reallocation might have changed future *UV*-ratios.

Figure 3.7. presents *UV*-ratios for the period 1951 to 1992. The ordering of the ratio unemployment/vacancies with respect to occupational groups changes over time. While the post-war period faces an unfavourable *UV*-ratio for production jobs and socio-cultural professions, the situation changed during the sixties. This becomes obvious during the recession 1967-68. Now, the primary sector in particular suffers from a structural change, rendering many people unemployed whereas only a small number of vacancies is available. On the other hand, socio-cultural professions perform much better than in the fifties and are characterized by a relatively low *UV*-ratio in the eighties and nineties.

During the recession following OPEC I (1974-77), many workers with technical professions became unemployed and did not find vacant positions. However, the bad situation for technical professions only lasted until 1976. Evidently, supply and demand for technical professions adjusted after OPEC I, so that from 1978 on until 1990 the *UV*-ratio of technical professions even turns out to be the "best" in terms of unemployed workers per vacant position.

Analysing the performance of primary sector jobs over time, we see that the outflow from this occupational group seems to stabilize in the mid-seventies. Unemployed people of this group have found jobs elsewhere, so that the *UV*-ratio becomes relatively small.

The most recent development after OPEC II (1982) reveals some interesting occupational changes. First, we observe that the recession left many production workers unemployed. Also service jobs are hit by the deep recession, whereas socio-cultural jobs, the primary sector and in particular technical jobs are less affected by the cyclical shock. Then, during the eighties, service jobs faced the worst *UV*-ratio. This is somewhat surprising, since the German economy faces a general trend towards a service oriented economy, suggesting the presence of a sufficient number of vacant service jobs. A similar role of "services" can be found for the recession after OPEC I, when the recovery following the oil price shock witnessed a poor performance of service related professions. We may speculate that such a pattern was the result of a less cyclical service sector, whose recovery was slower than for production workers, that mainly belong to the most cyclical industrial sector. The poor performance of the service sector in the eighties and nineties (after finishing a downturn)

---

1 Note that average duration of unemployment reveals a general upward trend (due to increasing long-term unemployment), so that deciding about a steady state estimation period would imply a misleading assumption.

might also support the hypothesis that some of the shift from manufacturing to service employment is a statistical illusion. During the sixties and seventies, most manufacturing firms provided a wide range of services in-house. These days, however, they are more likely to buy in services from specialised service companies. Hence, data on output and sectoral affiliation of employment might indicate a strong change, while data on occupations do not reveal this change (a book-keeper remains a book-keeper, for instance).

*Figure 3.7.: UV*-ratios of occupational groups

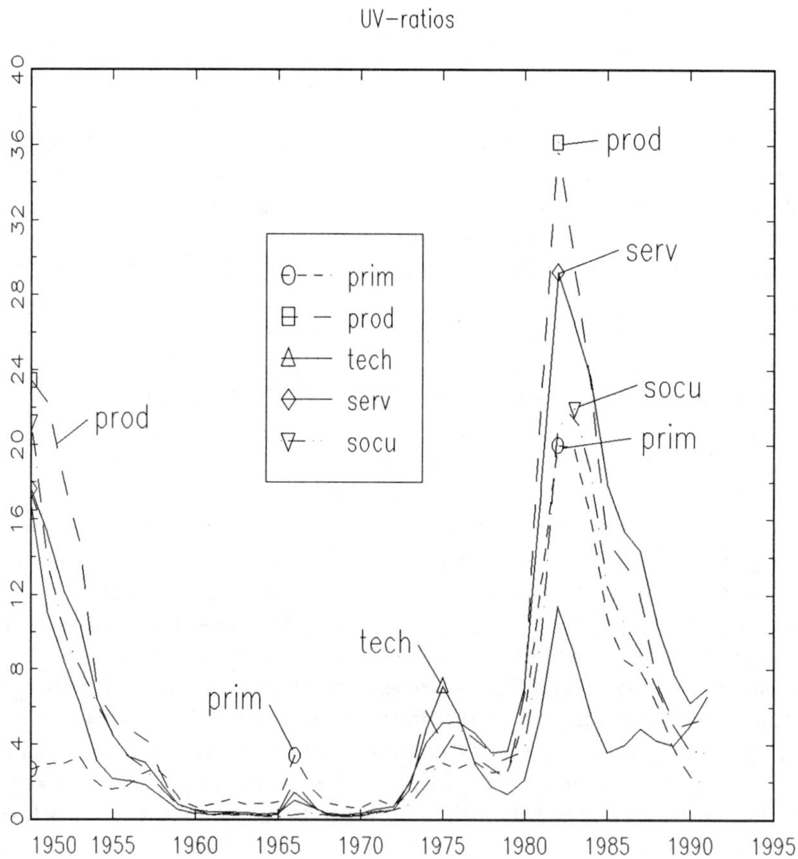


*Note:* See A3.III for the definition of variables.

Also surprising is that, at the end of the sample period in 1992, the primary sector had the lowest number of unemployed workers per vacant position. Inspecting these figures in more detail reveals that both unemployment *and* vacancies had the highest growth rates among all occupational groups in the nineties. As already discussed before, these figures reveal the changing nature of modern primary sector jobs that are characterized by increasing turnover and temporary contracts.

The performance of technical professions has deteriorated after 1990. In terms of occupational adjustment, such a situation is reasonable after the good performance of this occupational group in the eighties. Unemployed people from other occupational groups and young entrants into the job market (see Chapter 3.7.) have chosen this relative attractive occupational group during this period, finally rendering high supply compared to demand.

A direct test of occupational changes is presented in Table 3.8. It also suggests an answer to the question whether unemployed people of occupational groups belong to the relevant pool of unemployed workers of other occupational groups (see equation (3.15)). For this purpose, I estimate the (linear) matching function as follows:

$$(3.20)\quad \ln(H_{it}) = const. + \beta \ln(U_{it}) + \gamma \ln(V_{it}) + \delta \ln(U_{j,t-1}) + \epsilon_{it},$$

where *i* and *j* refer to main occupational groups, *i,j*=1,2,...,5. $U_j$ enters the matching function with lagged values in order to allow for some delay due to "time to adjust". (3.20) is estimated after first differencing the data so that t-values can be interpreted in a conventional way. Remaining serial correlation disappears after additional MA(1)-modelling of residuals.

Looking at Table 3.8. horizontally, we see that unemployed workers of other occupational groups do not change to primary sector jobs. This is not surprising since agriculture is a shrinking sector with poor future prospects. Production jobs are chosen by unemployed workers from three professional groups: From the primary sector (where people are forced to find alternative jobs due to structural changes), from technical professions and from service jobs. The change from technical jobs to production jobs might be interpreted as evidence in favour of job competition. During cyclical downturns better educated workers compete for scarce jobs with less educated people. Technical jobs are jobs with better educated workers than jobs with production workers. Higher educated workers of technical professions will take the jobs previously occupied by lower educated production workers (see Teulings and Koopmanschap, 1989, for econometric evidence of job competition between different educational levels). *SERV* and *PROD* seem to be substitutes, since unemployed workers change in either direction (see the line *SERV* where *PROD* is significant).

*Table 3.8.:* Checking the relevant pool of unemployed workers

| Dependent Variable: | Independent Variables: *PRIM* | *PROD* | *TECH* | *SERV* | *SOCU* |
|---|---|---|---|---|---|
| *PRIM* | - | 0 | 0 | 0 | 0 |
| *PROD* | 0.29 (2.6) | - | 0.22 (4.5) | 0.27 (3.7) | 0 |
| *TECH* | 0 | 0 | - | 0 | 0.28 (2.1) |
| *SERV* | 0.18 (2.5) | 0.11 (2.2) | 0.17 (4.0) | - | 0 |
| *SOCU* | 0 | 0 | 0 | 0 | - |

*Note:* The table presents the coefficient $\delta$ of the regression $\Delta\ln(H_{it}) = const. + \beta\Delta\ln(U_{it}) + \gamma\Delta\ln(V_{it}) + \delta\Delta\ln(U_{j,t-1}) + \epsilon_{it}$. t-values are in parentheses. "0" denotes a non-significant estimate of $\delta$.

The third line has technical professions as the dependent variable. There is only one group (socio-cultural professions) with a significant impact of unemployed job seekers. The worsening of the supply-demand ratio which is visible at the end of the observation period in Figure 3.7. is too short a period to have an impact on the estimation.

Service jobs in line four behave very much like the group of production workers, confirming the substitution effect of both occupational groups: Besides unemployed production workers, we again find evidence that technical workers and primary sector workers are matched with vacancies in service occupations (as for the matching of production workers in line two).

The socio-cultural group, finally, seems to be unattractive to unemployed workers of other groups. This might be due to poor working conditions and relatively low salaries, so that unemployed workers try other occupational groups or prefer to stay unemployed.

Alternatively, we can interpret Table 3.8. in terms of columns, which reveal *where* unemployed workers of a particular column are hired. For instance, column one shows that primary sector workers mainly find jobs as production workers or in the occupational group *SERV,* and the *TECH* column three shows that unemployed workers of this occupational group might be responsible for some "crowding out" of less educated workers in production and service jobs.

## 3.7. Understanding the matching of apprentices

### 3.7.1. The economic problem

The previous chapter has provided evidence for ongoing reallocation between occupational groups. The time of adjustment causes frictional unemployment. The probability of frictional unemployment increases if young entrants in the labour market are wrongly skilled, where "wrongly skilled" means that future supply of a skill exceeds its future demand. This chapter tries to shed some light on the question whether adjustment problems in the labour market are increased by matching demand and supply of apprenticeships. The analysis is related to the public discussion in Germany about cyclical unemployment/vacancies performances of certain professions, for instance teachers and engineers. Here, the role of delayed adjustment of skill formation is discussed.

Young school-leavers have to make decisions concerning their future profession. As they search for an apprenticeship in an "attractive" occupational group, apprentices may be heaped into particular groups, leading to potential future allocation problems when future labour demand undergoes some change. What does "attractive" mean to young school leavers? It certainly means discounting future income, so that individual factors such as preferences and education play an important role. However, from the viewpoint of a macroeconomist, time-specific aspects that would allow conclusions with respect to cyclical and structural unemployment are more appealing. The probability of job separation at time $t$ is a suitable indicator which helps approximating future income streams in response to the choice of a certain profession. Under uncertainty, current and recent unemployment figures of occupational groups proxy the probability of future job separations.

Adjustment problems increase if the reaction to recent unemployment figures is delayed due to a decision lag. Structural changes (due to technological shocks or changing tastes) can not be followed in a flexible way, so that fluctuations on the labour market may be more intense as if the reaction would be immediately.

A similar reasoning applies to the determination of the demand for apprentices in a certain profession, which itself is a function of the past labour market experience.[1] Instead of simply using lagged employment as a proxy of future labour demand, the stock of vacancies in occupational groups provides a better and direct indicator of the demand for workers

---

1 For instance, minimization of adjustment costs lead to autoregressive labour demand profiles.

with a particular skill. Once again, delayed reaction with respect to labour market signals might distort optimal reallocation and cause frictional unemployment.

The following framework analyses the matching process of the demand for and the supply of apprenticeships in occupational groups. This gives insights into a neglected field of the flow approach to labour economics, where the literature has focused on hires, quits and layoffs, while the analysis of young entrants (and of retirement) has been left to micro-economic and microeconometric research.

### 3.7.2. Towards a reduced-form matching function for apprentices

Relating the number of actual apprentices to applicants and available apprenticeship positions at a disaggregate level (occupational groups) is constrained by data limitations. The matching result, i.e. the number of new apprentices at time *t,* is not directly observable. Instead, data for a sufficiently long period are only available as the *total* number of apprentices, which combines new entrants with apprentices that began their careers during a certain number of previous years (in most professions, the duration of an apprenticeship is three years). Since matching functions describe the flow of new hires (i.e. the number of *new* apprentices) as a function of available jobs (the number of demanded apprentices) and of available job seekers (the number of applicants for an apprenticeship in the profession), the impact of recent unemployment and vacancy figures on apprenticeships (according to the presumed behaviour in 3.7.1.) is not obvious. Therefore, some clarifying remarks are in order.

Let $A_{it}$ be the total number of apprentices in occupational group *i* at time *t*, $E_{it}$ the number of apprenticeship-beginners in group *i* at *t*, $O_{it}$ the number of apprenticeship-leavers, $P_{it}$ the number of apprenticeship-dropouts (leavers without having finished apprenticeship) and *D* the duration of apprenticeship. Then $A_{it}$ can be written as follows:

$$A_{it} = \sum_{\tau=0}^{D} (E_{i.t-\tau} - O_{i.t-\tau}) + A_{i.t-D-1}, \qquad (3.21)$$

where $O_{it} = E_{i.t-D} + P_{it}$, since entrants in *(t-D)* finish their apprenticeship in *t.*

Furthermore, according to the economic reasoning in 3.7.1., apprencticeship-searchers make their choice given recent unemployment experience in occupational groups. The information set contains current and lagged unemployment figures:

$$E^s_{it} = f\Big(\underset{(-)}{U_{it}}, \underset{(-)}{U_{i.t-1}}\Big). \tag{3.22}$$

High unemployment figures in occupational groups are expected to reduce the number of applications in that group.

The demand for young workers with skills of occupational group *i* is determined by the recent stock of vacancies in that group:

$$E^d_{it} = g\Big(\underset{(+)}{V_{it}}, \underset{(+)}{V_{i.t-1}}\Big). \tag{3.23}$$

Matching demand and supply of apprenticeships yields

$$\begin{aligned} E_{it} &= h(E^s_{it}, E^d_{it}) \\ &= h_1\Big(\underset{(-)}{U_{it}}, \underset{(-)}{U_{i.t-1}}, \underset{(+)}{V_{it}}, \underset{(+)}{V_{i.t-1}}\Big), \end{aligned} \tag{3.24}$$

where $h_1$ is a reduced form, in which supply and demand for apprentices have been replaced by their explanatory variables unemployment and vacancies.

Inserting into (3.21), replacing $O_{it}$, and recursive solving of (3.21) leads to (the index *i* is neglected for simplicity):

$$\begin{aligned} A_t &= \sum_{\tau=0}^{D} (E_{t-\tau} - E_{t-D-\tau} - P_{t-\tau}) + A_{t-D-1} \\ &= \sum_{\tau=0}^{\infty} (E_{t-\tau} - E_{t-D-\tau} - P_{t-\tau}) \\ &= h_2(\underset{(-)}{U_t}, \underset{(-)}{U_{t-1}}, \ldots, \underset{(-)}{U_{t-D+1}}, \underset{(?)}{U_{t-D}}, \underset{(?)}{U_{t-D-1}}, \underset{(+)}{U_{t-D-2}}, \ldots; \\ &\qquad \underset{(+)}{V_t}, \underset{(+)}{V_{t-1}}, \ldots, \underset{(+)}{V_{t-D+1}}, \underset{(?)}{V_{t-D}}, \underset{(?)}{V_{t-D-1}}, \underset{(-)}{V_{t-D-2}}, \ldots). \end{aligned} \tag{3.25}$$

Dropouts $P_{it}$ are assumed to have no effect on the extended reduced-form matching function $h_2$. Expected signs of unemployment and lagged unemployment are negative up to a lag *(t-D+1)*. Thereafter the impact is not clear for *(t-D)* and *(t-D-1)*, because a negative impact from $E_{t-D-1}$ and $E_{t-D}$ may be offset by a positive impact of apprenticeship-leavers $O_t$ and $O_{t-1}$ (note that $O_t = E_{t-D} + P_t$). Parameters on unemployment with lags before *(t-D-2)* are expected to be positive (due to absolvents in *(t-1), (t-2),...,* i.e. beginners in *(t-D-1), (t-D-2),...* . With opposite signs, the same arguments hold for the impact of vacancies.

In Germany, most apprenticeships have a duration of *D=3*. Hence, (3.22)-(3.24) produce the following expected signs on unemployment and vacancy parameters:

$$(3.26)\qquad A_t = h_2(\underset{(-)}{U_t}, \underset{(-)}{U_{t-1}}, \underset{(-)}{U_{t-2}}, \underset{(?)}{U_{t-3}}, \underset{(?)}{U_{t-4}}, \underset{(+)}{U_{t-5}}, \ldots;$$

$$\underset{(+)}{V_t}, \underset{(+)}{V_{t-1}}, \underset{(+)}{V_{t-2}}, \underset{(?)}{V_{t-3}}, \underset{(?)}{V_{t-4}}, \underset{(-)}{V_{t-5}}, \ldots).$$

If we analyse first differences instead of levels, the lag structure becomes simpler:

$$(3.27)\qquad \Delta A_t = E_t - O_t = E_t - E_{t-D} - P_t,$$

and the matching function is

$$(3.28)\qquad \Delta A_t = h_3(\underset{(-)}{U_t}, \underset{(-)}{U_{t-1}}, \underset{(+)}{U_{t-D}}, \underset{(+)}{U_{t-D-1}}, \underset{(+)}{V_t}, \underset{(+)}{V_{t-1}}, \underset{(-)}{V_{t-D}}, \underset{(-)}{V_{t-D-1}})$$

which produces

$$\Delta A_t = h_3(\underset{(-)}{U_t}, \underset{(-)}{U_{t-1}}, \underset{(+)}{U_{t-3}}, \underset{(+)}{U_{t-4}}, \underset{(+)}{V_t}, \underset{(+)}{V_{t-1}}, \underset{(-)}{V_{t-3}}, \underset{(-)}{V_{t-4}})$$

in the case of *D=3.*

### 3.7.3. Panel estimations

Before testing the above equations empirically, they have to be corrected for temporary aggregate disturbances. For instance, the size of cohorts leaving school and starting an apprenticeship would dominate the variance of $A_{it}$, and cyclical effects would distort the analysis of unemployment and vacancy effects. Therefore, instead of considering absolute numbers, the analysis is based on the relative size of groups, i.e. we define $u_{it} \equiv U_{it}/\Sigma_i U_{it}$, $v_{it} \equiv V_{it}/\Sigma_i V_{it}$, $a_{it} \equiv A_{it}/\Sigma_i A_{it}$.

The empirical evidence is based on a subset of the occupational groups used in previous chapters. Data on apprentices are available for a long period, but 13 of our occupational groups do not have data on apprentices (not all professional careers start with an apprenticeship), so that the estimation is based on 27 occupational groups of the relatively long period 1968 to 1991 (648 observations).

Figure 3.8. provides a descriptive analysis of the lag structure between apprentices and unemployment as well as between apprentices and vacancies. The figure presents correlation coefficients which are averaged over occupational groups. Signs are as expected. Apprentices are negatively correlated with unemployment for all of the first five lags. Vacancies are positively correlated with the exception of lag one for levels and lag five for first differences. The first impression is that the time delay of the apprenticeship decision is longer than expected: Inspecting first differences, we see that the maximal correlation occurs for a lag of one year, but thereafter the impact dies out very slowly, whereas the contemporaneous correlation is rather weak. This conclusion is confirmed using data in levels, where a maximum impact seems to occur after two and three years (note that these results do not contradict each other because of the complex lag structure in (3.26)).

*Figure 3.8.:* The lag of apprenticeship decisions

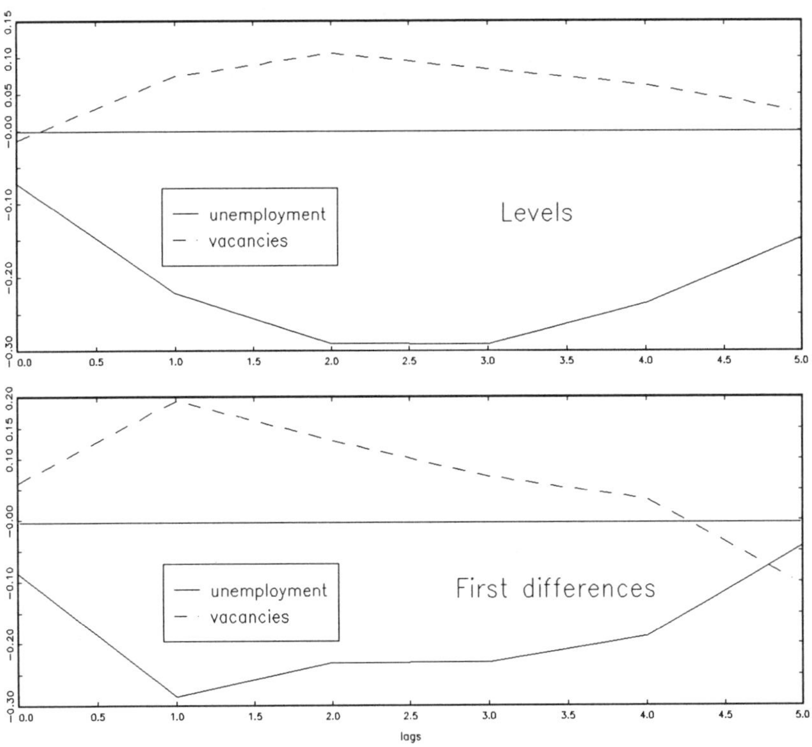


*Note:* Averages (over *i*) of $Corr(a_{it}, u_{i,t-\tau})$, $Corr(a_{it}, v_{i,t-\tau})$ and $Corr(\Delta a_{it}, \Delta u_{i,t-\tau})$, $Corr(\Delta a_{it}, \Delta v_{i,t-\tau})$.

Table 3.9. presents a distributed-lag structure estimated as a two-way-fixed-effects model (as it is introduced in equation $(B13)$). The signs of the estimated parameters in column (1) confirm the lag structure of the simple correlation analysis, but only one parameter ($u_{i.t-3}$) is significant. This is the result of some multicollinearity as becomes clear when comparing column (1) with columns (2) - (5). Eliminating lags of third order (column (2)) reveals that in particular lags 2 and 3 of unemployment are highly collinear, since lag 2 becomes significant after dropping lag 3.

Columns (3) and (4) are estimated after eliminating insignificant variables. Undominated specifications (based on likelihood-ratio tests) contain lagged vacancies and either unemployment with a second lag or with a third lag. (Including both lags would lead to an insignificant lag of second order).

Signs are as expected, but the response of matched apprentices with respect to the recent labour market experience takes longer than expected: Neither contemporaneous vacancies nor contemporaneous unemployment are part of the relevant information set of apprenticeship beginners and apprenticeship providing firms. In particular young school leavers looking for a job seem to have a delayed memory, giving much weight to the unemployment performance of occupational groups two and three years ago. Firms react quicker, but here again a one year lag remains, while there is no support for a simultaneous impact from demand pressures measured in terms of vacancies.

All estimations reveal high serial correlations in residuals. Column (5) of Table 3.9. presents Durbin's specification of a one-way fixed effects model, using the lag structure of column (4), i.e.

$$(3.29) \qquad a_{it} = \alpha_i(1-\rho) + \beta v_{i.t-1} - \rho\beta v_{i.t-2} + \gamma u_{i.t-2} - \rho\gamma u_{i.t-3} + \rho a_{it-1} + \nu_{it},$$

where $\epsilon_{it} = \rho\epsilon_{it-1} + \nu_{it}$ is the residual process of the original model (see equation $(B15)$; $\nu_{it}$ is a "white noise" process). In fact, the estimate of $\rho$ turns out to be 0.90. Again the signs confirm previous estimates, though the collinearity between lags 2 and 3 of unemployment prevents a clearer confirmation of the result in column (4).

Besides the theoretical arguments derived above, the high serial correlation is also a good reason for re-estimating the model using first differences. Furthermore, starting from the simple one-way fixed effects model, dealing with fixed effects is no longer necessary since they are differenced out. Because differencing allows for a more direct identification of the lag structure (see equations (3.27) and (3.28)), the results shown in Table 3.10. reveal immediate insights into the underlying lag structure. Nevertheless, Table 3.10. confirms previous suggestions. It becomes clear that apprenticeship applicants base their decision on relative unemployment figures of the last three years without any simultaneous reaction, and that a significant response with respect to vacant positions in occupational groups occurs after one to two years. Again there is no sign for a contemporaneous effect.

*Table 3.9.:* Dynamic apprenticeship decisions

| Explanatory variables | Dependent variable: Number of apprentices $a_{it}$ | | | | |
|---|---|---|---|---|---|
| | (1) | (2) | (3) | (4) | (5) |
| $v_{it}$ | -0.07 | -0.06 | - | - | - |
| | (1.2) | (1.0) | | | |
| $v_{i,t-1}$ | 0.10 | 0.18 | 0.16 | 0.10 | 0.14 |
| | (1.1) | (2.0) | (5.1) | (3.4) | (7.6) |
| $v_{i,t-2}$ | 0.08 | -0.02 | - | - | -0.06 |
| | (0.9) | (0.4) | | | (3.4) |
| $v_{i,t-3}$ | 0.04 | - | - | - | - |
| | (0.7) | | | | |
| $u_{it}$ | -0.06 | -0.03 | - | - | - |
| | (0.1) | (0.3) | | | |
| $u_{i,t-1}$ | -0.10 | 0.14 | - | - | - |
| | (0.7) | (1.0) | | | |
| $u_{i,t-2}$ | 0.08 | -0.37 | - | -0.31 | -0.08 |
| | (0.6) | (4.5) | | (9.1) | (3.4) |
| $u_{i,t-3}$ | -0.33 | - | -0.33 | - | 0.00 |
| | (4.1) | | (10.6) | | (0.2) |
| $a_{i,t-1}$, | - | - | - | - | 0.90 |
| resp. $\rho$ | | | | | (54.5) |
| $\hat{\rho}_{\epsilon}$ | 0.74 | 0.74 | 0.76 | 0.76 | 0.43 |
| *R-squared* | 0.990 | 0.988 | 0.990 | 0.989 | 0.998 |

*Notes:* Two-way-fixed effects estimations based on 27 occupational groups; the time period is 1968 - 1991 (648 observations); see A3.I and A3.III for data; specification (4) follows Durbin's procedure (confer equation $(B15)$ of the Appendix).

*Table 3.10.:* Dynamic apprenticeship decisions, first differences

| Explanatory variables | Dependent variable: Number of apprentices $\Delta a_{it}$ | | | |
|---|---|---|---|---|
| | (1) | (2) | (3) | (4) |
| $\Delta v_{it}$ | 0.01 | - | - | - |
| | (0.4) | | | |
| $\Delta v_{i,t-1}$ | 0.07 | 0.07 | 0.07 | 0.07 |
| | (3.4) | (3.4) | (3.2) | (3.6) |
| $\Delta v_{i,t-2}$ | 0.05 | 0.05 | -0.00 | 0.05 |
| | (2.0) | (2.1) | (0.1) | (3.0) |
| $\Delta v_{i,t-3}$ | 0.02 | - | - | - |
| | (1.0) | | | |
| $\Delta u_{it}$ | -0.03 | - | - | - |
| | (0.9) | | | |
| $\Delta u_{i,t-1}$ | -0.07 | -0.08 | -0.03 | -0.08 |
| | (2.0) | (2.5) | (1.0) | (2.9) |
| $\Delta u_{i,t-2}$ | -0.02 | -0.00 | -0.08 | - |
| | (0.4) | (0.0) | (2.9) | |
| $\Delta u_{i,t-3}$ | -0.11 | -0.14 | - | -0.14 |
| | (3.9) | (6.0) | | (6.7) |
| *R-squared* | 0.124 | 0.124 | 0.066 | 0.125 |

*Notes:* Estimation of (3.29) based on 27 occupational groups; the time period is 1968 - 1991 (648 observations); see Appendix A3.I and A3.III for data.

### 3.7.4. Backward-looking behaviour and future rigidities

If the apprenticeship decision is based on a backward looking behaviour, structural adjustment problems are likely to occur. This can be seen from a simplified flow equation of employment in group *i*, $L_{it}$:

$$L_{it} = L_{i,t-1} + E_{it} + R_{it}, \tag{3.30}$$

where *E* represents apprenticeship-beginners who base their decision on past labour market experience. According to estimations results, there is evidence in favour of

$$E_{it} = f(U_{i,t-1}, U_{i,t-2}, U_{i,t-3}, V_{i,t-1}, V_{i,t-2}). \tag{3.31}$$

$R_{it}$ covers remaining components of the flow equations (hirings, layoffs, quits). Using the definition $U_{it} = LS_{it} - L_{it}$, treating the functional form $f$ in a linearized form, and replacing $E_{it}$ by (3.31), equation (3.30) turns out to be a stochastic difference equation of at least second order. Thus, cyclical adjustment processes after sectoral unemployment shocks can be reinforced by a myopic[1] and backward looking behaviour of apprentices. Similar arguments apply to the behaviour of firms: They forecast future demand for skilled workers in terms of past vacancies, so that their demand for apprentices is likewise based on past labour market experiences which again accelerate employment fluctuations.

Conclusions for economic policy are straightforward. School absolvents have to be informed about the consequences of their delayed decision. A good performance of a profession in the recent past is no guarantee that future professional unemployment/vacancy ratios are still superior to other ratios when many apprentinces start in the same profession. Labour offices who advise school leavers should provide them with "rational expectations", i.e. inform them that other apprenticeship beginners may have the same information set, and that they should form their expectation *given* that other apprentices too may choose occupational groups with a good past labour market performance. Labour offices should avoid to advise school leavers by simply informing them about the *past* opportunities.

## 3.8. Concluding remarks

Matching functions are important building blocks of the more general framework of Beveridge curves (in the way described by Blanchard and Diamond, 1990 a, b, and c, 1992, and Mortensen and Pissarides, 1993). Bypassing complex issues of aggregation, matching functions map the hiring of new workers dependent on the number of vacant positions and unemployed workers. Empirical estimates enable the researcher to measure the degree of matching efficiency (mismatch) over time through a time-variant scale parameter.

Chapter 3 starts by considering matching functions based on highly aggregate time series. As in most economic time series, components of matching functions also reveal problems of nonstationarity which lead to interpretation problems similar to those encountered in spurious (nonsense) regressions. Here some new results are derived which analyse spurious regressions in the case of random walks with drifts (extending Phillips, 1986). Though the application of this theoretical econometric

---

1 The lag 1 can be partly explained by the mandatory period of practical work in the year before leaving school, so that the relevant decision might be taken in *t-1*. This, however, does not explain the presence of lags of higher order.

finding to aggregate matching functions reveals non-spurious results (Section 3.4), estimates nevertheless turn out to be unsatisfactory: these parameters are insignificant and/or have low explanatory power.

The picture changes after taking up Hall's (1989) proposal of a more disaggregate view of the matching process. Panel estimation techniques provide a satisfactory solution to the challenge. Hence, this chapter uses data on 40 occupational groups for the period 1971 to 1992. The most important advantages of these techniques are

1) a larger number of observations (880 instead of 22), which allow for the inclusion of additional explanatory variables,
2) the possibility to cover coexistent divergencies in subgroups (in aggregate data such movements would be cancelled out), and
3) a greater flexibility in specifying and estimating the time-variant matching efficiency in terms of time-specific fixed effects and/or explanatory variables.

Contrary to evidence based on time series, econometric results based on panel data lead to reasonable results which are also satisfactory from a statistical point of view. The possibility of nonsense regressions is addressed by using a new theoretical result for spurious fixed-effect models, but the probability for the occurence of the latter is found to be low for the data used in this chapter. The econometric specifications presented in Section 3.5 include one- and two-way-fixed effect models as well as random effect models. These models stress the role of dynamics in panel data estimations (consistent estimation of serial correlation in the residual process), and implement instrument-variable techniques (because of potential endogeneity problems and errors of measurement).

Most parameters on vacancies range between 0.5 and 0.6, whereas most weights of unemployment in the matching process are about 0.4. The estimation of constant returns to scale in the matching function is more or less an exception. Thus, when compared to results found in the literature, the disaggregate estimating strategy produces results that are different in that they do not confirm the hypothesis of constant returns to scale, and in that they give a larger weight to vacancies than to unemployment in the matching process. However, the analysis of the matching process in the more recent period from 1982 until 1992 suggests that the process varies with the prevailing economic situation. In this period, high and persistent unemployment lead to parameters of the matching function that indicate a change towards a more unemployment-oriented matching process.

Matching efficiency is declining over time. This is a robust result of our performed one-way-fixed effect models, in which the scaling parameter of the matching function is replaced by a linear time trend. In addition, the linear trend is replaced by economic variables that are widely accepted as determinants of match and mismatch. This attempt to endogenize mismatch leads to the preliminary conclusion that good economic performance as well as a large number of non-unemployed job-seekers improve matching efficiency, while increasing female participation rates have a positive impact on mismatch.

A more detailed analysis of the reasons behind mismatch is based on the period effects in two-way-fixed-effect models. The time series pattern of the period effects reveals a highly nonlinear shape, where periods of easy match can be found during the times of excessive unemployment in 1975/76 and 1983/84, and the general level of mismatch is higher in the eighties than in the seventies. This observation holds a fortiori during the relative stable times of 1972-1974 and 1987-1992. This result contradicts findings based on traditional indices of occupational mismatch in Germany (see Franz, 1991a, and Figure 2.2), and again hint at the possibility that earlier estimates of matching functions were based on spurious results (see Chapter 2).

In an explorative way, a mismatch time series based on the estimated time-variant parameter of matching efficiency in matching functions is analysed with respect to potential relationships with several economic variables that could drive mismatch. Only a few of them can be identified as determinants of mismatch. It becomes obvious that high unemployment is accompanied by lower mismatch. This may be explained by the large pool of job seekers that makes it easy to find adequate workers for vacant positions. In the terminology of Diamond (1982), there are "thick" markets. It is interesting to note that a similar result holds for (completely different) rationing models based on the "smoothing-by-aggregation" principle (Sneessens and Drèze, 1986, Lambert, 1988), where no mismatch occurs when all micromarkets face excess capacity, and, simultaneously, there is no micromarket with excess demand (see König and Entorf, 1990, Entorf, 1992). Such a situation corresponds to a recession and a period of high unemployment at an aggregate macroeconomic level.

There is evidence that a growing labour force as well as a growing female labour force are positively associated with mismatch which might be explained by insufficient skills of new entrants in the labour force, so that matching them with adequate positions is difficult. In contrast, a larger share of people without schooling leads to decreasing mismatch since these people seem to be hired in high-turnover and seasonal jobs. This possibility limits the conclusions that can be drawn from the estimated matching functions. These functions are dominated by fluctuations arising from short-term contracts, and do not necessarily reveal information about the matching efficiency of long-term contracts. In Europe, however, where workers change their jobs much less frequently and where the share of jobs with a short duration is much smaller than in the U.S., a large share of matches leading to *long-term* contracts is much more important for the reduction of overall unemployment than in the U.S. Evidently, matching functions do better suit the needs of the U.S labour market.

In order to be more instructive with respect to the role of particular occupational groups in the matching process, Section 3.6 analyses the process of occupational reallocation. A more general matching function based on search theory takes account of the fact that people change their professions. Among other results, the estimation of matching functions in which the pool of unemployed is enlarged by unemployed workers of other occupations reveals that unemployed workers from the shrinking primary sector are matched with vacant positions in the production and service sectors, that many unemployed service workers find jobs in the production sector and vice versa, and that technical workers seem to take jobs which were previosly occupied by less educated production workers (hence there is evidence of "job competition").

A neglected component in existing research of the labour market are school-leavers entering the labour market. Official figures of the German labour office show that this group represents a significant share of all job seekers: In 1992, for instance, there were 5.218 million persons looking for a job and there were 683,000 school-leavers which implies a share of 13 percent.[1] Thus, fluctuations in the labour market are highly affected by the successful or unsuccessful matching of this group. This phenomenon is reinforced by "time-to-build" problems, since an apprenticeship usually lasts three years. The choice of a profession has long-lasting consequences. The results of Section 3.7 suggest that apprentices and firms are backward looking when they forecast their future income streams (related to the probability of job separations) and future labour demand. Both groups extrapolate the recent labour market experience given by recent occupational unemployment figures and occupational vacancies. Thus, cyclical adjustment processes after a reallocation of the job market due to technical progress or changing tastes can be intensified by a myopic and backward-looking behaviour of school-leavers and hiring firms.

**1** Source: Amtliche Nachrichten der Bundesanstalt für Arbeit: Arbeitsstatistik 1992 - Jahreszahlen.

## Appendix A3.I: Data

$U$ = *Unemployment,* $V$ = *vacancies, and* $H$ = *hires, aggregate and at the occupational level*; Sources:

- Bundesanstalt für Arbeit, Amtliche Nachrichten der Bundesanstalt für Arbeit, various issues
- Ermann, K. (1984), *Arbeitsmarktstatistische Zahlen in Zeitreihenform,* Institut für Arbeitsmarkt- und Berufsforschung der Bundesanstalt für Arbeit, Beiträge zur Arbeitsmarkt- und Berufsforschung
- Ermann, K. (1988), *Arbeitsmarktstatistische Zahlen in Zeitreihenform,* Institut für Arbeitsmarkt- und Berufsforschung der Bundesanstalt für Arbeit, Beiträge zur Arbeitsmarkt- und Berufs- forschung
- Leupold, R. and K. Ermann (1973), *Arbeitsmarktstatistische Zahlen in Zeitreihenform,* Institut für Arbeitsmarkt- und Berufsforschung der Bundesanstalt für Arbeit, Beiträge zur Arbeitsmarkt- und Berufsforschung

$V_C$ = corrected vacancies; Corrections are made according to Franz, 1991a for the period 1960 to 1988. The corrections of the years 1989 to 1992 use the survey information of mediations performed by the labour office published in Reyer et al. (1990), assuming no change after 1989.

$DUC$ = *degree of capacity utilization* in manufacturing;
Source: Ifo ("Information und Forschung"-Institut, information and research institute, Munich)

$P$ = *output price* (GDP);
Source: German Statistical Yearbook (various issues)

$W_S$ = *Gross wage per week of skilled industrial workers* (Bruttowochenverdienste der Arbeiter der Leistungsgruppe 1 in der Industrie);
Source: German Statistical Yearbook (various issues)

$W_U$ = *Gross wage per week of unskilled industrial workers* (Bruttowochenverdienste der Arbeiter der Leistungsgruppe 3 in der Industrie);
Source: German Statistical Yearbook (various issues)

*POP* = *German labour force;*
Source: German Statistical Yearbook (various issues)

*RAT_M* = *Male participation rate* (male labour force / total male population);
Source: Institut der Deutschen Wirtschaft (1993), Zahlen zur Entwicklung der Bundesrepublik Deutschland, Köln: Deutscher Instituts-Verlag

*RAT_F = Female participation rate* (female labour force / total female population);
Source: Institut der Deutschen Wirtschaft (1993), Zahlen zur Entwicklung der Bundesrepublik Deutschland, Köln: Deutscher Instituts-Verlag
*SEARCH = Non-unemployed job seekers;*
Source: Amtliche Nachrichten der Bundesanstalt für Arbeit - Jahreszahlen, various issues
*MM_STOCK* = (cross section volatility of stock market performance); see text for construction; Source: sectoral stock market indices published by "Westdeutsche Landesbank"
*U_1YEAR = Share of unemployed workforce with unemployment duration of more than one year*;
Source: Amtliche Nachrichten der Bundesanstalt für Arbeit - Jahreszahlen, various issues
*STRUCT = Employment ratio "Manufacturing/Services";*
"Services" includes "Handel", "Kreditinstitute und Versicherungen", "Dienstleistungen" and "Verkehr und Nachrichtenübermittlung"; Source: Der Bundesminister für Arbeit und Sozialordnung (1993), Arbeits- und Sozialstatistik, Hauptergebnisse 1993
*NO_SCHOOL = Share of unemployed workforce without any school degree* ("ohne Hauptschulabschluß");
Source: Amtliche Nachrichten der Bundesanstalt für Arbeit - Jahreszahlen, various issues
*AGE_50 = Share of unemployed workforce with age >= 50;*
Source: Amtliche Nachrichten der Bundesanstalt für Arbeit - Jahreszahlen, various issues
*FOREIGN = Ratio "foreigners/population*;
Source: Statistical Yearbook, various issues.
*A = Number of apprentices in occupational groups;*
Source: Statistical Yearbook, various issues.

# Appendix A3.II: Spurious Regressions

## A3.II.1. Regressing two random walks with drifts

The usual practise when analysing regression models is to start by presuming the validity of an equation $y_t = \alpha + \beta x_t + u_t$, $t = 1,\ldots,T$, with adequate formulations of the time series variables $x_t$ and the disturbance $u_t$. In the particular case of time series regressions with a unit root, the contributions by Stock (1987), West (1988), Park and Phillips (1988, 1989), Sims et al. (1990), and others analyse the estimation of parameters of presumed models and of underlying data generation processes (DGP). All inference is based on the hypothesis that $y_t = \alpha + \beta x_t + u_t$ is the correct statistical model. A more conservative research strategy is to start by assuming that $y_t$ and $x_t$ are independent stochastic processes, as they are studied by Granger and Newbold (1974), Phillips (1986) and Durlauf and Phillips (1988). Whereas Durlauf and Phillips (1988) highlight the problem of spurious detrending, Phillips (1986) studied the phenomenon of spurious regression. In the case of random walks without drift, Phillips (1986) shows that the least squares regression

$$(B1) \qquad y_t = \hat{\alpha} + \hat{\beta} x_t + \hat{u}_t \quad , \quad t = 1,\ldots,T$$

leads to diverging OLS estimates of $\hat{\alpha}$ and to the convergence of $\hat{\beta}$ to a random variable, when $y_t$ and $x_t$ are generated as independent random walks *without* drift (i.e. equation $(B1)$ is a "nonsense regression" or "spurious regression" in the sense of Granger and Newbold, 1974; see also Yule, 1926, for an early example). Furthermore, Phillips (1986) shows that $R^2$ converges to a random variable, conventional *t*-values diverge with speed $T^{1/2}$ and the DW-statistic is $O_p(T^{-1})$. In the following, the corresponding properties of random walks with *non-zero* drifts are analysed. I define

$$(B2) \qquad y_t = \gamma_y + y_{t-1} + \epsilon_t, \quad x_t = \gamma_x + x_{t-1} + \nu_t, \quad t = 1,2,\ldots,$$

where $\nu_t$ is iid(0, $\sigma_x^2$) and $\epsilon_t$ is iid(0, $\sigma_y^2$). Under regularity assumptions made explicit in Phillips (1986) and Sims, Stock and Watson (1990), the following result can be obtained:

*Theorem B1: Suppose $(B1)$ is estimated by least squares regression. Then, as $T$ goes to infinity,*

(a) $$T^{1/2}\left(\hat{\beta}-\frac{\gamma_y}{\gamma_x}\right) \Rightarrow 12\left(\frac{\gamma_y}{\gamma_x}\right)\left(\frac{1}{\gamma_y}\xi_y-\frac{1}{\gamma_x}\xi_x\right) \equiv N\left(0,\frac{6}{5}\left(\frac{\gamma_y}{\gamma_x}\right)^2\left(\left(\frac{\sigma_y}{\gamma_y}\right)^2+\left(\frac{\sigma_x}{\gamma_x}\right)^2\right)\right),$$

*where*

$$\xi_y=\left(\int_0^1 t\sigma_y W_y(t)dt-\frac{1}{2}\int_0^1 \sigma_y W_y(t)dt\right), \xi_x=\left(\int_0^1 t\sigma_x W_x(t)dt-\frac{1}{2}\int_0^1 \sigma_x W_x(t)dt\right).$$

(b) $$\hat{\alpha}T^{-1/2} \Rightarrow 4\left(\sigma_y\int_0^1 W_y(t)dt-\frac{\gamma_y}{\gamma_x}\sigma_x\int_0^1 W_x(t)dt\right)+6\left(\frac{\gamma_y}{\gamma_x}\int_0^1 \sigma_x tW_x(t)dt-\int_0^1 \sigma_y tW_y(t)dt\right)$$
$$\equiv N\left(0,\frac{2}{15}\left(\sigma_y^2+\sigma_x^2\left(\frac{\gamma_y}{\gamma_x}\right)^2\right)\right),$$

*where $W_x(t)$ and $W_y(t)$ are independent Wiener processes on $C[0,1]$ and $\Rightarrow$ signifies convergence in distribution (weak convergence).*

*Furthermore, we obtain the following convergence properties for the Durbin-Watson statistic (DW) and for the coefficient of determination $R^2$*

*(c)* $DW = O_p(T^{-1})$,

*(d)* $(1-R^2) = O_p(T^{-1})$.

*Conventional t-ratios diverge as*

*(e)* $t_\beta = O_p(T)$,

*and*

*(f)* $t_\alpha = O_p(T^{1/2})$.

*Proofs:*

a) We write $x_t$ and $y_t$ as

$$x_t = t\gamma_x + S_t^x + x_0, \quad y_t = t\gamma_y + S_t^y + y_0,$$

where

$$S_t^x = \sum_{j=1}^{t} v_j, \quad S_t^y = \sum_{i=1}^{t} \epsilon_i$$

and $x_0 = v_0$ and $y_0 = \epsilon_0$ are (possibly non-zero) initial values.

The OLS estimator of $\beta$ can be written as

$$\hat{\beta} = \frac{\sum_{t=1}^{T}(x_t - \bar{x})(y_t - \bar{y})}{\sum_{t=1}^{T}(x_t - \bar{x})^2} = \frac{\frac{1}{T^3}\sum x_t y_t - \frac{1}{T^2}\bar{x}.\bar{y}}{\frac{1}{T^3}\sum x_t^2 - \frac{1}{T^2}\bar{x}^2}$$

We consider the convergence properties of individual sums, where we summarize terms of lower order if they do not play any role for subsequent proofs:

$$\sum_{t=1}^{T} y_t x_t = \Sigma(\gamma_y t + S_t^y + y_0)(\gamma_x t + S_t^x + x_0)$$

$$= \frac{T^3}{3}\gamma_y\gamma_x + T^{5/2}\left(\gamma_y\int_0^1 t\sigma_x W_x(t)dt + \gamma_x\int_0^1 t\sigma_y W_y(t)dt\right)$$

$$+ T^2\left(\int_0^1 \sigma_y\sigma_x W_y(t)W_x(t)dt + \frac{1}{2}\gamma_y\gamma_x + \frac{y_0\gamma_x + x_0\gamma_y}{2}\right) + O_p(T^{3/2})$$

$$T^2\bar{y}.\bar{x} = \left(\frac{T(T+1)}{2}\gamma_y + T^{3/2}\int_0^1 \sigma_y W_y(t)dt + Ty_0\right)\left(\frac{T(T+1)}{2}\gamma_x + T^{3/2}\int_0^1 \sigma_x W_x(t)dt + Tx_0\right)$$

$$= \frac{T^4}{4}\gamma_{yx} + T^{7/2}\left(\frac{\gamma_y}{2}\int_0^1 \sigma_x W_x(t)dt + \frac{\gamma_x}{2}\int_0^1 \sigma_y W_y(t)dt\right)$$

$$+ T^3\left(\int_0^1 \sigma_y W_y(t)dt\int_0^1 \sigma_x W_x(t)dt + \frac{1}{2}\gamma_y\gamma_x + \frac{x_0\gamma_y + y_0\gamma_x}{2}\right) + O_p(T^{5/2})$$

where we use the following results from Phillips (1986, Lemma 1) and Sims, Stock and Watson (1990, Lemma1):

$$\Sigma t S_t^x \Rightarrow T^{5/2}\int_0^1 t\sigma_x W_x(t)dt, \quad \Sigma t S_t^y \Rightarrow T^{5/2}\int_0^1 t\sigma_y W_y(t)dt$$

$$\Sigma S_t^x S_t^y \Rightarrow T^2\sigma_x\sigma_y\int_0^1 W_x(t)W_y(t)dt, \quad \sum_{t=1}^{T} S_t^x \Rightarrow T^{3/2}\sigma_x\int_0^1 V(t)dt.$$

Furthermore,

$$\Sigma t^2 = \frac{2T^3 + 3T^2 + T}{6}, \quad \Sigma t = \frac{T^2 + T}{2}.$$

Inserting into $\hat{\beta}$ as defined above, and collecting terms leads to

$$\hat{\beta} \Rightarrow \frac{\gamma_y\gamma_x\left(1 + 12T^{-1/2}\left(\frac{1}{\gamma_y}\xi_y + \frac{1}{\gamma_x}\xi_x\right) + 12T^{-1}\frac{1}{\gamma_y\gamma_x}B_{xy} + O_p(T^{-3/2})\right)}{(\gamma_x)^2\left(1 + 24T^{-1/2}\frac{1}{\gamma_x}\xi_x + 12T^{-1}\frac{1}{\gamma_x^2}B_{xx} + O_p(T^{-3/2})\right)},$$

where

$$\xi_y = \int_0^1 t\sigma_y W_y(t)dt - \frac{1}{2}\int_0^1 \sigma_y W_y(t)dt, \quad \xi_x = \int_0^1 t\sigma_x W_x(t)dt - \frac{1}{2}\int_0^1 \sigma_x W_x(t)dt,$$

$$B_{xy} = \int_0^1 \sigma_y \sigma_x W_y(t) W_x(t)dt - \int_0^1 \sigma_y W_y(t)dt \int_0^1 \sigma_x W_x(t)dt.$$

Applying the approximation $(1 + a(t))/(1 + b(t)) \to 1 + a(t) - b(t)$, with both $a(t)$ and $b(t)$ approaching zero for large $t$, we obtain

$$(B3) \qquad \hat{\beta} \Rightarrow \frac{\gamma_y}{\gamma_x}\left(1 + 12T^{-1/2}\left(\frac{1}{\gamma_y}\xi_y - \frac{1}{\gamma_x}\xi_x\right)\right) + 12T^{-1}\left(\frac{1}{\gamma_y\gamma_x}B_{xy} - \frac{1}{\gamma_x^2}B_{xx}\right) + O_p(T^{-3/2}).$$

$\xi_y$ and $\xi_x$ have normal distributions with mean zero (see, for instance, Durlauf and Phillips, 1988, Theorem 2.1). The variance of $\xi_z$, $z = x, y$, is given by

$$E\int_0^1\int_0^1\left(t-\frac{1}{2}\right)\left(s-\frac{1}{2}\right)\sigma_z^2 W_z(t)W_z(t)dtds$$

$$= \sigma_z^2\int_0^1\int_0^1\left(t-\frac{1}{2}\right)\left(s-\frac{1}{2}\right)\mathrm{Min}(t,s)dtds$$

$$= \sigma_z^2\int_0^1\left(t-\frac{1}{2}\right)dt\int_0^t s\left(s-\frac{1}{2}\right)ds = \sigma_z^2\frac{1}{120}$$

*q.e.d.*

b) Using $\hat{\alpha} = \bar{y} - \hat{\beta}\bar{x}$, inserting $\hat{\beta}$ from equation $(B3)$, and summarizing all terms containing $T$ and $T^{1/2}$ as highest exponents (terms of lower order do not play any role in the limit), we obtain

$$\hat{\alpha} \Rightarrow T^{1/2}\left(\int \sigma_y W_y(t)dt - \frac{\gamma_y}{\gamma_x}\left(6\gamma_x\left(\frac{1}{\gamma_y}\xi_y - \frac{1}{\gamma_x}\xi_x\right) + \int \sigma_x W_x(t)dt\right),\right.$$

where again highest order terms cancelled out. Replacing $\xi_y$ and $\xi_x$ leads to the expression in *Theorem B1.* Similar to the previous case, the new functionals $\int(4-6t)W_z(t)dt$ are normally distributed and the variance can be calculated in the same way:

$$E\int_0^1\int_0^1 (4-6t)(4-6s)W_z(t)W_z(s)\,dt\,ds=\frac{2}{15}$$

*q.e.d.*

Inserting $\hat{\beta}$ from $(B3)$ and using the convergence properties derived above, we obtain after summarizing terms of equal power

$$R^2=\frac{\hat{\beta}^2\Sigma(x_t-\bar{x})^2}{\Sigma(y_t-\bar{y})^2}$$

$$\Rightarrow\frac{T^3\frac{\gamma_y^2}{12}+T^{\frac{5}{2}}2\gamma_y\xi_y+T^2\left(\frac{\gamma_y}{\gamma_x}\right)^2\left(12\left(\frac{\xi_y}{\gamma_y}-\frac{\xi_x}{\gamma_x}\xi_x\right)(\gamma_x^2+4\gamma_x\xi_x)-B_{xx}+2B_{xy}\frac{\gamma_x}{\gamma_y}\right)+O_p\left(T^{\frac{3}{2}}\right)}{T^3\frac{\gamma_y^2}{12}+T^{\frac{5}{2}}2\gamma_y\xi_y+T^2B_{yy}+O_p\left(T^{\frac{3}{2}}\right)}$$

$$=\frac{\frac{\gamma_y^2}{12}(1+T^{-1/2}24\gamma_y\xi_y+O_p(T^{-1}))}{\frac{\gamma_y^2}{12}(1+T^{-1/2}24\gamma_y\xi_y+T^{-1}B_{yy})}$$

$$=1-T^{-1}(B_{yy}+O_p(1)),$$

thereby again employing $(1+a(t))/(1+b(t))=1+a(t)-b(t)$.

*q.e.d.*

c) The DW is

$$DW=\frac{\sum_{t=2}^{T}(\hat{u}-\hat{u}_{t-1})^2}{\sum_{t=1}^{T}\hat{u}_t^2}$$

We first consider

$$T^{-1}\Sigma(\hat{u}_t-\hat{u}_{t-1})=T^{-1}\Sigma(\gamma_y-\hat{\beta}\gamma_x+\epsilon-\hat{\beta}v_t)^2.$$

Applying the convergence of $\hat{\beta}$, we obtain for the numerator

$$T^{-1}\Sigma(\gamma_y-\hat{\beta}\gamma_x+\epsilon_t-\hat{\beta}v_t)^2\Rightarrow\Omega_{\epsilon 0}+\left(\frac{\gamma_y}{\gamma_x}\right)^2\Omega_{v0},$$

where

$$\Omega_{v0}=\lim_{T\to\infty}T^{-1}\sum_{t=1}^{T}E(v_t^2),\quad \Omega_{\epsilon 0}=\lim_{T\to\infty}T^{-1}\sum_{t=1}^{T}E(\epsilon_t^2).$$

The denominator can be written as

$$\sum_{t=1}^{T}\hat{u}_t^2=\Sigma(y_t-\bar{y})^2-\hat{\beta}^2\Sigma(x_t-\bar{x})^2.$$

Employing the results already derived for $R^2$, and dividing the numerator by $T^2$, the terms containing $T$ and $T^{1/2}$ cancel out so that we finally obtain $O_p(1)$ terms which do not vanish due to the single presence of, for example, $B_{xy}$.

$$T^{-2}\sum_{t=1}^{T}\hat{u}_t^2 \Rightarrow B_{yy} + \left(\frac{\gamma_y}{\gamma_x}\right)^2 B_{xx} - 2\frac{\gamma_y}{\gamma_x}B_{xy} + R,$$

where $R$ contains remaining $O_p(1)$ terms.

*q.e.d.*

d) The *t*-value can be written as

$$t_\beta = \frac{\hat{\beta}}{s_{\hat{\beta}}} = \frac{\hat{\beta}}{(T^{-1}(\Sigma(y_t-\bar{y})^2 - \Sigma\hat{\beta}^2(x_t-\bar{x})^2))^{1/2}(\Sigma(x_t-\bar{x})^2)^{-1/2}}.$$

Squaring the *t*-value, dividing the numerator by $T^3$ and the denominator by $T$ and replacing $s^2 = T^{-1}\Sigma(y_t-\bar{y})^2 - T^{-1}\hat{\beta}^2\Sigma(x_t-\bar{x})^2$, we obtain

$$\frac{t_\beta^2}{T^2} = \frac{T^{-3}\hat{\beta}^2\Sigma(x_t-\bar{x})^2}{T^{-2}\Sigma(y_t-\bar{y})^2 - T^{-2}\hat{\beta}^2\Sigma(x_t-\bar{x})^2}$$

$$\Rightarrow \frac{\frac{1}{12}\gamma_y^2 + O_p(T^{-1/2})}{O_p(1)},$$

as can be seen easily after inserting previous results.

*q.e.d.*

e) In squared values, the *t*-ratio of the constant is

$$t_\alpha^2 = \frac{\hat{\alpha}^2 T(\Sigma(x_t-\bar{x})^2)}{s^2\Sigma x_t^2}.$$

Studying the convergence properties of both numerator and denominator, we learn from previous results that the leading time trend of $\hat{\alpha}^2$ is $T$, multiplied by a sum of functionals of Wiener processes. This sum is multiplied by $T$ and a single term $(\gamma_x/12)T^3$, leading thus to nonvanishing terms of order $T^5$. In the denominator, we have a sum of functionals of order $T$ which replace $s^2$. This sum is multiplied by $(\gamma_x/12)T^3$, resulting in $T^4$. Finally, $s^2$ contains terms $B_{xy}$ which do not exist in the numerator and which exclude a further reduction of the ratio.

*q.e.d.*

*Remark: Theorem B1 only applies when there is a single I(1) regressor with drift. The presence of an additional regressor $z_t = \gamma_z + z_{t-1} + \omega_t$ would lead to asymptotic linear dependency of the deterministic trend terms. To see why, consider the asymptotic covariance of both time series written* *in terms of* $x_t = \gamma_x t + \Sigma v_\tau$ *and* $z_t = \gamma_z t + \Sigma \omega_\tau$. *The deterministic trends dominate the asymptotic behavior since stochastic trends are of lower order* $O_p(t^{1/2})$.[1]

Thus, contrary to spurious regressions without drift, OLS estimation of $\hat{\beta}$ does provide a consistent estimate of the ratio of the drift of the regressand and the drift of the regressor.[2] As in the standard asymptotic theory, we have asymptotic normality with the usual speed $T^{-1/2}$. This result is due to the fact that many functionals to which sample moments of I(1) processes converge can be expressed in terms of simple normal densities (see Banerjee and Hendry, 1992, for a discussion of this point). Note, however, the different speed of convergence when compared with "standard" I(1) regressions: If regressors in the standard regression $y_t = \alpha + \beta x_t + u_t$ are I(1) with drift, Park and Phillips (1988) prove the convergence of $T^{3/2}(\hat{\beta} - \beta)$ to a normal distribution. The result of the constant, $\hat{\alpha}$, is qualitatively the same as for random walks without drifts (see Phillips, 1986): The OLS estimate diverges with a rate $T^{1/2}$, but different from the zero-drift case, the asymptotic distribution and variances can be determined explicitly.

The DW-statistic approaches 0 with exactly the same speed as for random walks without drift. The same applies to the divergence of the $t$-ratio $t_\alpha$. Thus, conventional attempts to test potential stochastic dependency between $y_t$ and $x_t$ via the inspection of customary $t$-values fail even for small samples, since $t_\beta$ grows quickly with speed $T$. $R^2$ approaches unity with the same speed $T$.

Thus, the coefficient of determination is an important and useful diagnostic to distinguish nonsense regressions with drift from nonsense regressions without drift, in which case $R^2$ would converge to a nondegenerate random variable (see Phillips, 1986). An other promising indicator for the presence of drifts in spurious regressions is the $t$-ratio of $t_\beta$ which grows linearly in the presence of random walks with drift.

---

1 In the case of more than one I(1) spurious regressor with drift, the reduced rank of the explaining variables can be analysed following the proposals in Park and Phillips (1988) which would lead to a degeneracy similar to the one that occurs in the case of cointegration among processes which are integrated of order one.

2 Including an additional linear trend would be equivalent to run a regression with detrended $y_t$ and $x_t$; As for spurious regressions without drift, the slope estimator converges weakly to a nondegenerate random variable (see Durlauf and Phillips, 1988, and simulation experiments in Entorf, 1994).

## A3.II.2. Spurious fixed-effect models

A closely related result can be verified for the OLS estimation of a simple fixed effects model, if we consider the case of large $T$ and a finite number $N$ of individuals. As in the case of OLS, the asymptotic result is determined by the ratio of drifts.

*Theorem B2: If the least-squares dummy variable approach (see e.g. Hsiao, 1986, p. 29-32) is applied to a mistakenly conjectured (spurious) fixed-effect model*

$$(A4) \qquad y_{it} = \hat{\alpha}_i + \hat{\beta} x_{it} + \hat{u}_{it}, \quad i = 1 \ldots N, \quad t = 1, \ldots, T$$

*with* $N < \infty$, *where*

$$\hat{\beta} = T_{xx}^{-1} T_{xy}, \quad \hat{\alpha}_i = \bar{y}_i - \hat{\beta} \bar{x}_i,$$

*with*

$$T_{xx} = \sum_{i=1}^{N} \sum_{t=1}^{T} (x_{it} - \bar{x}_i)^2$$

$$T_{xy} = \sum_{i=1}^{N} \sum_{t=1}^{T} (x_{it} - \bar{x}_i)(y_{it} - \bar{y}_i)$$

$$\bar{y}_i = \frac{1}{T} \sum_{t=1}^{T} y_{it}, \quad \bar{x}_i = \frac{1}{T} \sum_{t=1}^{T} x_{it},$$

*when in fact the true data generating mechanism for* $x_{it}$ *and* $y_{it}$ *are independent random walks with drift,*

$$(B5) \qquad x_{it} = \gamma_{xi} + x_{i,t-1} + \nu_{it}$$

$$(B6) \qquad y_{it} = \gamma_{yi} + y_{i,t-1} + \epsilon_{it}, \quad i = 1, \ldots, N, \quad t = 1, \ldots, T,$$

*then we obtain the following asymptotic spurious fixed-effect estimation:*

*(a)*
$$T^{1/2}\left(\hat{\beta}-\frac{A}{B}\right) \Rightarrow 12\frac{A}{B}\sum_{i=1}^{N}\left(\frac{\gamma_{xi}}{A}\xi_{yi}+\left(\frac{\gamma_{yi}}{A}-2\frac{\gamma_{xi}}{B}\right)\xi_{xi}\right)$$

$$\equiv N\Big(0,\frac{6}{5B^2}\Big(\Sigma\gamma_{xi}^2\sigma_{yi}^2+\Sigma_i\left(\gamma_{yi}^2+\frac{4(A^2\gamma_{xi}^2-AB\gamma_{yi}\gamma_{xi})}{B^2}\right)\sigma_{xi}^2\Big)\Big),$$

*where*

$$A=\sum_{i=1}^{N}\gamma_{xi}\gamma_{yi}, \quad B=\sum_{i=1}^{N}\gamma_{xi}^2$$

$$\xi_{zi}=\int\sigma_{zi}tW_{zi}(t)dt-\frac{1}{2}\int\sigma_{zi}W_{zi}(t)dt, \quad z=x,y, \quad i=1,\ldots,N.$$

*(b) In case of individual random walks without drift,* $\hat{\beta}$ *converges weakly to a random variable.*

*(c) The estimate for the individual effect* $\hat{\alpha}_i=\bar{y}_i-\hat{\beta}\bar{x}_i$ *diverges with* $O(T^{1/2})$.

*Proof:*

As in Theorem B1, we divide both numerator and denominator by $T^3$, yielding

$$\beta=\frac{\sum_{i=1}^{N}\left(\frac{1}{T^3}\sum_{t=1}^{T}x_{it}y_{it}-\frac{1}{T^2}\overline{x}_i\cdot\overline{y}_i\right)}{\sum_{i=1}^{N}\left(\frac{1}{T^3}\sum_{t=1}^{T}x_{it}^2-\frac{1}{T^2}\overline{x}_i^2\right)}$$

Following along the lines of the proof of Theorem B1, we can write

$$\hat{\beta}\Rightarrow\frac{\Sigma_i\gamma_{xi}\gamma_{yi}+12T^{-1/2}\Sigma_i\gamma_{xi}\gamma_{yi}\left(\frac{1}{\gamma_{yi}}\xi_{yi}+\frac{1}{\gamma_{xi}}\xi_{xi}\right)}{\Sigma_i\gamma_{xi}^2+24T^{-1/2}\Sigma_i\gamma_{xi}^2\frac{1}{\gamma_{xi}}\xi_{xi}}$$

$$=\frac{A}{B}\frac{1+\frac{12}{A}T^{-1/2}\Sigma_i\gamma_{xi}\gamma_{yi}\left(\frac{1}{\gamma_{yi}}\xi_{yi}+\frac{1}{\gamma_{xi}}\xi_{xi}\right)}{1+\frac{24}{B}T^{-1/2}\Sigma_i\gamma_{xi}^2\frac{1}{\gamma_{xi}}\xi_{xi}}$$

Then, treating numerator and denominator in the same way as above leads to the convergence property stated in *Theorem B2*.

Furthermore, summing up *N* independent functionals ( $N < \infty$ ) instead of considering simple functionals in both the numerator and the denominator, the proof for the zero drift case follows directly from Phillips (1986, Theorem 1, p. 316).

Analogously, the divergence of the constant terms follows when we replace simple functionals by a finite sum of functionals (summation over $i$ ).

*q.e.d.*

This result is of importance even for researchers working with short panels and a large number of individuals and of high importance for macroeconomists working with long time series and a small number of individuals, for instance for multi-sectoral, multi-regional or multi-country studies. Note also that the "asymptotic" nature might already apply for reasonly small $T$, as subsequent simulation studies will show.

## A3.II.3. Simulated evidence

The different properties of spurious regressions with and without drift become evident by comparing time-dependent histograms of the OLS slope parameter $\hat{\beta}$. In a first simulation experiment we consider equations ($B1$) and ($B2$). The error terms are generated independently and normally distributed with means equal to zero. *Theorem B1, a)* reveals that the asymptotic distribution of $\hat{\beta}$ can be fully described by the *ratios* $\gamma_y/\gamma_x$ and the drift-noise ratios $\gamma_y/\sigma_y$ and $\gamma_x/\sigma_x$ which tie up the fourth ratio, $\sigma_y/\sigma_x$, Accordingly, simulation studies have to obey these ratios when parameterizing the simulation scenario. I assume identical variances $\sigma_x = \sigma_y = 1$ . Starting values $y_0$ and $x_0$ play almost no role in regression models since they "only" affect the (here less important) intercept term. This can be seen easily by inspecting the proofs of *Theorem B1* which all, except for the constant, depend on terms of the type $\Sigma(x_t - \bar{x})(y_t - \bar{y})$, where $x_0$ and $y_0$ cancel out. I choose $y_1 = \epsilon_1$ and $x_1 = \nu_1$ as random numbers according to presumed distributions and variances.[1] This avoids any spurious significance of the constant term arising from any arbitrarly large non-zero starting values.

Phillips (1986) shows the weak convergence of the OLS estimator to a random variable when random walks have no drift. Figure B1 reflects the nature of nonsense regressions without drift in terms of time-dependent

---

**1** This implies $y_0 = x_0 = 0$. The random numbers are generated applying the RNDN command of GAUSS.

histograms.[1] Irrespective of the length of the time series, we observe a symmetric and regular distribution. Figure B2 summarizes some interesting properties of this distribution to which the nonsense OLS slope estimator converges. The average estimate is about zero and the average 95%-fractile (5%-fractile) is slightly higher than unity (smaller than minus unity); average and median $t$-values diverge with decreasing growth rates (all reported $t$-values are in absolute values), leading to the wrong conclusion of a significant relationship (see the high percentage share of $t$-values larger than two).[2] As likewise shown by Phillips (1986), the distribution of the DW-statistic approaches zero for large samples.

*Figure B1:* Time-variant histogram of the OLS estimate: Random walks have no drift

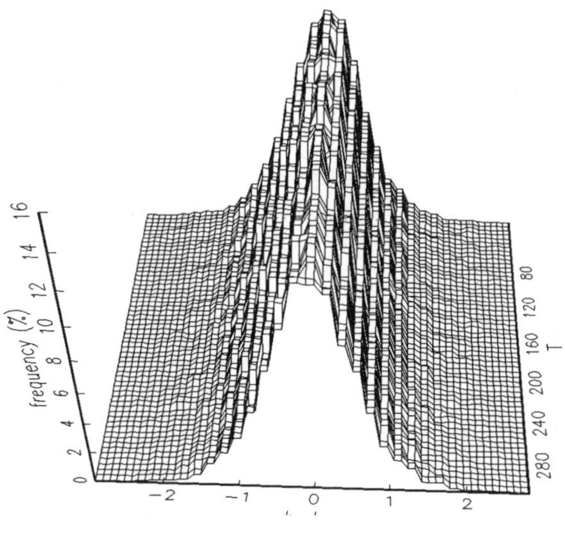


*Note:* Regressing two random walks as described in $(B1)$-$(B2)$ with zero drifts; the length of the simulated time series, T, is extended as follows: T = 20,30,...,300; 5000 replications of $(B2)$ and $(B3)$ are calculated for each T; the graphic displays the time-variant histogram (30 categories) of $\hat{\beta}$.79 outliers outside the range [-2.8, 2.8] are skipped; extreme values: -5.23, 3.94.

1 The three-dimensional histograms in the paper are constructed using GAUSS Puplication Quality Graphics. At each step (for instance time units), most of the individual simulations are replicated 5000 times and the results are captured using 30 different categories.

2 In their famous simulation experiment, Granger and Newbold (1974) report a rejection rate of 76 percent (50 observations, 100 replications).

*Figure B2:* Regressing random walks without drift: Summary graphics

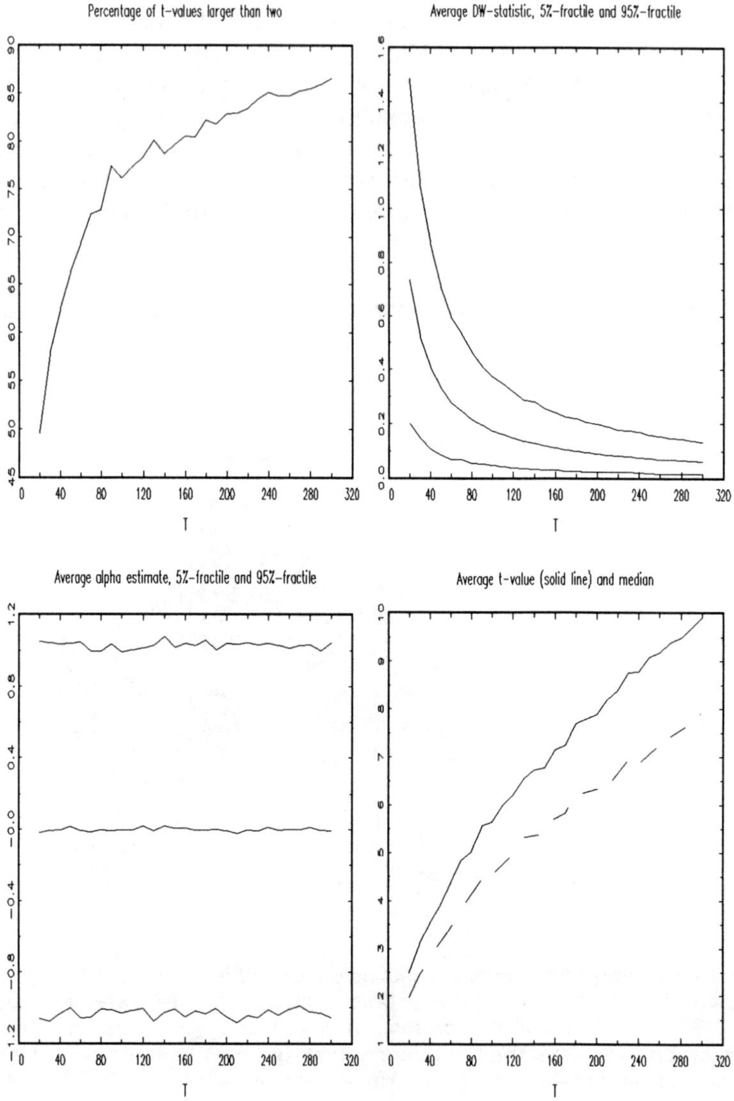


*Note:* The calculations are based on the simulation experiment described in Figure B1.

Contrary to the convergence to a random variable for spurious regressions without drift, Figure B3 displays the convergence to constants in the presence of drifts. Of course, the magnitude of imposed drifts is debatable. Hylleberg and Mizon (1989) estimate the magnitude of drifts for some macroeconomic time series ($\log(GNP)$, $\log(M1)$, $\log(u/1-u)$ ) and ( $\log(1+r)$, where $u$ = unemployment rate and $r$ = interest rate). The estimated ratios of drift and standard error range between -0.14 and 0.78.

To give a general impression of bivariate regressions with drift, I impose two drifts: the drift of the dependent variable is set to 0.5, the drift of the explaining regressor is 0.25, thus leading to a long-run parameter two; standard errors are kept as $\sigma_y = 1$ and $\sigma_x = 1$.

In small samples, we observe results very similar to those of random walks without drift: The distribution is flat and typical estimates are far away from the asymptotic pseudo true value. As Figure B3 displays, even with sample sizes of about 300 observations, we observe a skewed distribution and critical values still do not coincide with the asymptotic normal distribution. Using the result of *Theorem B1*, at $T = 300$ the upper 95%-fractile should be 2.93 and the 5%-fractile 1.07, whereas the simulation results are about 3.2 and 1.2, respectively. Furthermore, Figure B3 displays the linear increase of $t$-values of the slope parameter and the rapid decrease of DW, both properties shown in *Theorem B1*. As likewise mentioned before, the DW has the same limiting behavior as in the case of nonsense regressions without drift (due to vanishing drift terms, see the proofs of *Theorem B1*).

The (relative) magnitude of drifts plays an important role. The larger the drift is, the higher is the coefficient of a linear trend in a transformed formulation of equations $(B1)$ and $(B2)$. The proof of *Theorem B1* shows that the asymptotic behaviour of the OLS slope estimator boils down to the ratio of these trends, because the remaining terms reveal a slower rate of convergence. Thus, the larger the drifts are, the faster is the convergence of the trend-dominated terms, and the larger is the difference between the impact of the linear trend and the impact of the remaining terms which converge at a lower rate and which become less and less important when the sample size increases.

Figure B4 highlights the particular role of drifts. The simulation experiment compares the zero drift case with three non-zero situations. In all cases, the ratio of drifts is kept constant as $\gamma_y/\gamma_x = 2$, yielding the asymptotic OLS estimate 2. The ratio "drift" / "standard error" of the "explanatory" random walk is assumed to be 0.05, 0.25 and 0.75, thus the corresponding values of $\gamma_y$ have to be 0.1, 0.5 and 1.5, respectively. Resulting OLS estimates are compared with the regression of random walks without drift. Given the estimates by Hylleberg and Mizon (1989), the simulation results might cover the extreme range of possible speeds of convergence.

*Figure B3*: Regressing random walks with drift: Summary graphics

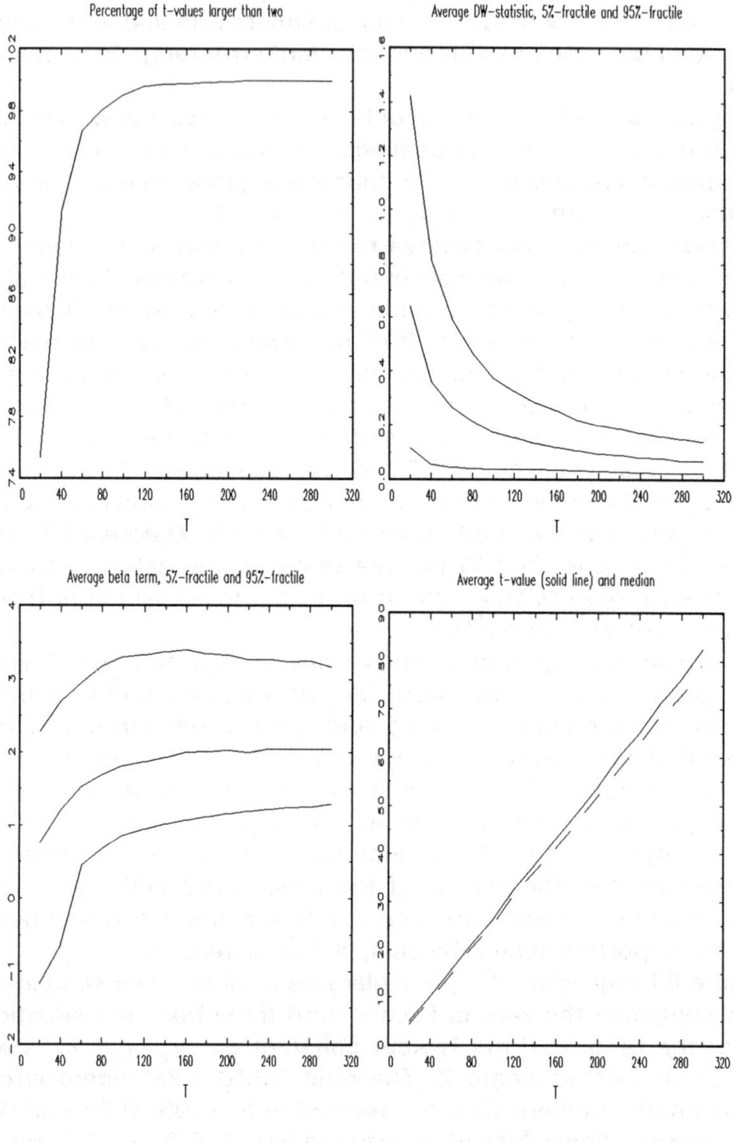


*Note:* Regression of two random walks as described in $(B1)$-$(B2)$; drifts are non-zero: $\gamma_y = 0.5$, $\gamma_x = 0.25$; the length of the simulated time series, $T$, is extended as $T = 20, 30, \ldots 300$; 5000... replications of $(B1)$ and $(B2)$ are calculated for each sample size $T$.

*Figure B4:* The impact of drift on the speed of convergence

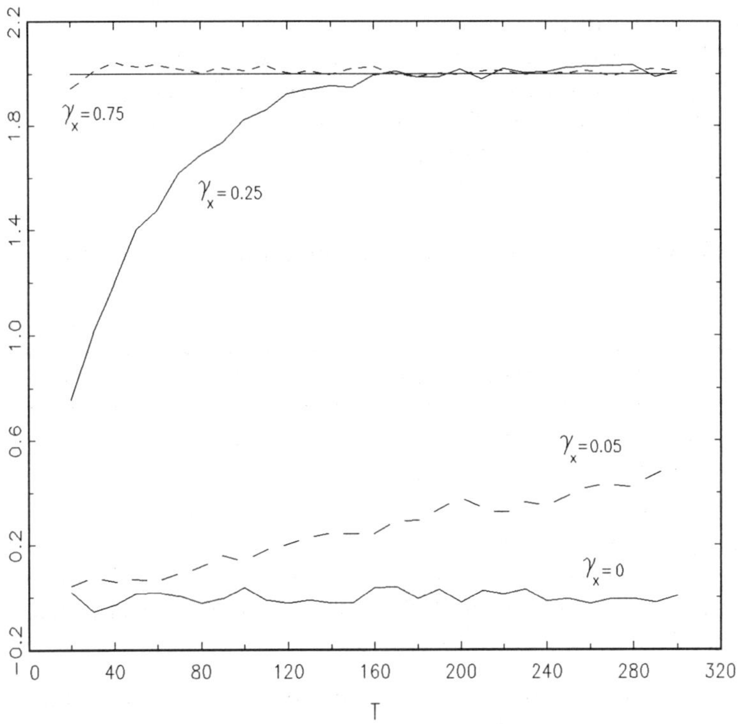


*Note:* Regression of two random walks as described in $(B1)$ and $(B2)$; sample sizes $T = 20.30,\ldots,300$ ; for each $T$ the model is replicated 1000 times; four alternative drifts are considered: $\gamma_x = 0,0.05,0.25,0.75$ , $\gamma_y = 2\gamma_x$ ; the graphic displays the average OLS estimator $\hat{\beta}$ depending on drift and T.

The estimates based on $\gamma_x = \gamma_y = 0$ fluctuate around zero, but - as already displayed in Figure B1 - no convergence to a constant value occurs. In small samples, for $\gamma_x = 0.05$ the estimate is substantially different from the asymptotic estimate (which is indicated by the upper solid line in Figure 4); even with $T = 300$ the average estimate remains below 0.5. If $\gamma_x = 0.25$ , the asymptotic result is approached for T larger than 170. For the largest drift under consideration, $\gamma_x = 0.75$ , even for very small samples of less than 30 observations observed estimates are close to the final result. Thus, given realistic sample sizes of less than 100 observations and ignorance about the true magnitude of drifts, OLS estimations can easily lead to wrong conclusions concerning the true nature of the data generation process - even when the convergence property towards the ratio of two drifts is known.

Different ratios of drift and standard error can produce quite different distribution functions, as can be seen in Table B1. Assuming $\gamma_y/\gamma_x = 1$, I analyse the 5%- and 95%-fractiles corresponding to $\gamma_x/\sigma_x = 0.25$ and $0.75$, respectively (keeping $\sigma_y = \sigma_x = 1$).

*Table B1:* Drift-noise ratio and the distribution of $\hat{\beta}$: Fractiles and means

a)

| | $\gamma_x/\sigma_x = 0.25$ | | | $\gamma_x/\sigma_x = 0.75$ | | |
|---|---|---|---|---|---|---|
| | 5% | Mean | 95% | 5% | Mean | 95% |
| $T = 30$ | -0.72 | 0.50 | 1.60 | 0.47 | 1.02 | 1.81 |
| $T = 90$ | 0.10 | 0.93 | 2.03 | 0.68 | 1.01 | 1.42 |
| $T = 150$ | 0.31 | 0.96 | 1.86 | 0.75 | 1.01 | 1.32 |
| $T = 210$ | 0.39 | 0.99 | 1.80 | 0.78 | 1.00 | 1.26 |

*Note:* Each entry is based on 1000 replications of the model described in equations ($B1$) and ($B2$); $\sigma_y = \sigma_x = 1$, $\gamma_y = \gamma_x$, $\gamma_x = 0.25$ and $\gamma_x = 0.75$.

b) Rising drifts and variances, holding $\gamma/\sigma$ constant

| | $\gamma_x/\sigma_x = 0.25$ | | | $\gamma_x/\sigma_x = 0.75$ | | |
|---|---|---|---|---|---|---|
| | 5% | Mean | 95% | 5% | Mean | 95% |
| $T = 30$ | -0.60 | 0.50 | 1.66 | 0.47 | 1.01 | 1.78 |
| $T = 90$ | 0.11 | 0.88 | 1.91 | 0.68 | 1.01 | 1.44 |
| $T = 150$ | 0.33 | 0.96 | 1.82 | 0.78 | 1.00 | 1.30 |
| $T = 210$ | 0.42 | 1.01 | 1.83 | 0.79 | 1.00 | 1.25 |

*Note:* Each entry is based on 1000 replications of the model described in equations ($B1$) and ($B2$); $\sigma_y = \sigma_x = 8$, $\gamma_y = \gamma_x$, $\gamma_x = 2$ and $\gamma_x = 6$.

Completing the conclusions drawn from Figure B4, Table B1 reveals that a detection of spurious regressions based on the fractiles of the distribution function of $\hat{\beta}$ is difficult for small $T$ and small drifts (small drift-noise ratios). Whereas for $T = 210$ and $\gamma_x/\sigma_x = 0.75$ the 90%-intervall is relatively small, $[0.78, 1.26]$, it is very large for $T = 30$ and $\gamma_x/\sigma_x = 0.25$, where it covers [-0.72, 1.60] (calculating the corresponding intervals according to the asymptotic normality in Theorem B1 would lead to [0.71, 1.29] and [-0.85, 2.85], respectively).

The possibility of wrong conclusions due to misleading t-values in panel estimations is usually ignored in applied economics. However, as can be seen from the *Theorem B2*, also panel data bear the problem of a spurious regression. Table B2 reveals that t-values can be much higher than conventional critical values if a spurious fixed-effects model is estimated. The table presents 5%-percentile, 95%-percentile and mean of the nonsense fixed-effects estimate as well as corresponding average t-values and the 90%-percentile of the t-value.

Panel a) shows that "spurious" conclusions even occur for random walks *without* drift. Conventional t-values (as they are presented in Hsiao, 1986, p.32, for example, using the OLS estimate for $\sigma_{\alpha}$, cf. p. 38) are above critical values.

Panel b) displays the role of $T$. Holding $N=20$ constant, we observe a slow convergence towards the asymptotic result which is approximately 1.083. Here, a simple inspection of t-values clearly is a misleading strategy: Spurious fixed-effects models with $T=30$ observations (and $N=20$ cross-sectional groups), for instance, have average (absolute) t-values of about 28.3.

Small-sample estimates are different from asymptotic results. In the particular case of identical variances of individual time series, the result of the *Theorem B2* boils down to

$$T^{1/2}\left(\hat{\beta}-\frac{A}{B}\right)\Rightarrow N\left(0,\frac{6\sigma^2}{5B^2}(B+\Sigma\gamma_{yi}^2)\right).$$

For instance, using this result and calculating the variance for $T=200$, we find asymptotic 5%- and 95%-fractiles of 1.00 and 1.16, while the simulated interval is [0.97, 1.13].

Looking for simple rule of thumbs, one might feel inclined to derive the rule that no spurious regression problem arises as long as $N$ is much larger than $T$. However, panel c) shows that this rule is wrong. In fact, increasing either $N$ or $T$ increases the probability of misleading t-values when drifts are included.

*Table B2:* Spurious fixed effect models

a) Individual time series have no drift

| | Distribution of $\hat{\beta}$ | | | Distribution of absolute t-values | |
|---|---|---|---|---|---|
| | Mean | 5% | 95% | Mean | 90% |
| T=20, N=20 | 0.00 | -0.23 | 0.24 | 2.3 | 4.6 |
| T=20, N=40 | 0.00 | -0.15 | 0.16 | 2.1 | 4.3 |
| T=100, N=5 | -0.01 | -0.48 | 0.44 | 5.2 | 11.1 |
| T=100, N=50 | 0.00 | -0.15 | 0.15 | 5.0 | 10.3 |

Assumptions: $\gamma_{yi} = \gamma_{xi} = 0$, $v_{it} \sim N(0,1)$, $\epsilon^y_{it} \sim N(0,1)$ for all i.

b) Spurious fixed effect models with drift: Increasing *T (N=20)*

| | Distribution of $\hat{\beta}$ | | | Distribution of absolute t-values | |
|---|---|---|---|---|---|
| | Mean | 5% | 95% | Mean | 90% |
| T=30 | 0.89 | 0.75 | 1.05 | 28.3 | 34.2 |
| T=100 | 1.02 | 0.91 | 1.13 | 71.2 | 81.5 |
| T=200 | 1.05 | 0.97 | 1.13 | 110.0 | 122.7 |
| T=1000 | 1.08 | 1.04 | 1.11 | 268.2 | 282.6 |

Assumptions: *N=20* and $\gamma_{yi} = 0.4 + i/40, \gamma_{xi} = 0.8 - i/40$, $i = 1,2,\ldots,20$; $v_{it} \sim N(0,1)$, $\epsilon^y_{it} \sim N(0,1)$. Thus, the asymptotic pseudo true value of $\hat{\beta}$ is *A/B* $\approx 1.083$.

c) Spurious fixed effect models with drift: Increasing *N* and *T*

| | Distribution of $\hat{\beta}$ | | | Distribution of absolute t-values | |
|---|---|---|---|---|---|
| | Mean | 5% | 95% | Mean | 90% |
| T=N=10 | 0.17 | -0.18 | 0.52 | 2.2 | 4.4 |
| T=N=30 | 0.37 | 0.19 | 0.55 | 12.0 | 16.6 |
| T=30, N=50 | 0.38 | 0.23 | 0.52 | 15.5 | 20.3 |
| T=50, N=30 | 0.50 | 0.34 | 0.66 | 22.3 | 28.4 |

Assumptions: $\gamma_{yi} = \gamma_{xi} = 0.2$, $v_{it} \sim N(0,1)$, $\epsilon^y_{it} \sim N(0,1)$.Thus, the asymptotic pseudo true value of $\hat{\beta}$ is *1.*

*Note:* All results are based on 1000 replications of the model (B4) - (B6). Starting values: $y_{i0} = x_{i0} = 0$.

## A3.II.4. Spurious regressions with a time regressor

*Theorem B3: The estimate* $\hat{\delta}$ *in the least squares regression*

$$(B7) \qquad y_t = \hat{\alpha} + \hat{\beta} x_t + \delta t + \hat{u}_t, \quad t = 1, \dots, T,$$

*converges to* $\gamma_y$. $y_t$ *and* $x_t$ *are independent random walks with drifts* $\gamma_y$ *and* $\gamma_x$ *and standard deviations* $\sigma_y$ *and* $\sigma_x$.

*Proof:*
After taking deviations from the mean value, the Frisch-Waugh theorem singles out the estimation of $\hat{\delta}$:

$$\hat{\delta} = ((\underline{t} - \bar{t})' M_1 (\underline{t} - \bar{t}))^{-1} (\underline{t} - \bar{t})' M_1 (y - \bar{y}),$$

where

$$\underline{t} = (1, 2, 3, \dots, T)', \quad M_1 = I - x^*(x^{*\prime} x^*) x^{*\prime},$$

and $x^* = x - \bar{x}$. Some basic algebra gives

$$\hat{\delta} = \frac{\left(\sum_{t=1}^{T} (x_t - \bar{x})(y_t - \bar{y})\right)\left(\sum_{t=1}^{T} (x_t - \bar{x})(t - \bar{t})\right) - \sum_{t=1}^{T} (y_t - \bar{y})(t - \bar{t})}{\left(\sum_{t=1}^{T} (x_t - \bar{x})(t - \bar{t})\right)^2 - \sum_{t=1}^{T} (t - \bar{t})^2}$$

After dividing numerator and denominator by $\Sigma(x_t - \bar{x})(t - \bar{t})$, we obtain

$$(B8) \qquad \hat{\delta} = \frac{\Sigma(x_t - \bar{x})(y_t - \bar{y}) - A_t}{\Sigma(x_t - \bar{x})(t - \bar{t}) - B_t},$$

where

$$A_t = \frac{\Sigma(y_t - \bar{y})(t - \bar{t})}{\Sigma(x_t - \bar{x})(t - \bar{t})}, \quad B_t = \frac{\Sigma(t - \bar{t})^2}{\Sigma(x_t - \bar{x})(t - \bar{t})}.$$

$A_t$ *and* $B_t$ are of order $O_p(1)$. The convergence of $\Sigma(x_t - \bar{x})(y_t - \bar{y})$ of the numerator in (B8) has been analysed in the proof of *Theorem B1*:

$$\Sigma(x_t - \bar{x})(y_t - \bar{y}) \Rightarrow \gamma_y \gamma_x \left( \frac{1}{12} T^3 + T^{5/2} \left( \frac{1}{\gamma_y} \xi_y + \frac{1}{\gamma_x} \xi_x \right) + O_p(T^2) \right).$$

The denominator is dominated by $\Sigma(x_t - \bar{x})(t - \bar{t})$, which may be written as $\Sigma x_t t - T\bar{x}\bar{t}$. It follows

$$\Sigma x_t t = \Sigma(\gamma_x t + S_t^x)t \Rightarrow \gamma_x \frac{T^3}{3} + T^{5/2} \int_0^1 t\sigma_x W_x(t)dt + O_p(T^2)$$

$$T\bar{x}\bar{t} = \Sigma(\gamma_x t + S_t^x)\frac{T+1}{2} \Rightarrow \gamma_x \frac{T^3}{4} + \frac{T^{5/2}}{2} \int_0^1 \sigma_x W_x(t)dt + O_p(T^2).$$

Collecting terms and dividing both numerator and denominator by $12T^3$ leads to

$$\hat{\delta} \Rightarrow \frac{\gamma_y \gamma_x (1 + O_p(T^{-1/2}))}{\gamma_x (1 + O_p(T^{-1/2}))}.$$

*q.e.d.*

## Appendix A3.III: List of occupational groups

1) Farmer, Animal Breeder, Fisher ("Pflanzenbauer, Tierzüchter, Fischereiberufe")

2) Forester, Hunter Careers ("Forst- und Jagdberufe")

3) Miner ("Bergleute, Mineralgewinner")

4) Quarryman, Construction Material Producer ("Steinbearbeiter, Baustoffhersteller")

5) Potter, Glassmaker ("Keramiker, Glasmacher")

6) Chemical Worker, Synthetic Material Processer ("Chemiearbeiter, Kunststoffverarbeiter")

7) Paper Fabrication, Paper Processer ("Papierhersteller, -verarbeiter")

8) Printer ("Drucker")

9) Wood Restorater, Wood Worker ("Holzaufbereiter, Holzwarenfertiger")

10) Metal Production, Metal Processer ("Metallerzeuger, -bearbeiter")

11) Locksmith, Mechanic, associated Careers ("Schlosser, Mechaniker und zugeordnete Berufe")

12) Electrician ("Elektriker")

13) Installater, Metal Careers ("Montierer und Metallberufe, a.n.g.")

14) Textile, Clothing Careers ("Textil- und Bekleidungsberufe")

15) Leather Refiner, Furrier ("Lederhersteller, Leder- und Fellverarbeiter")

16) Nutritionist ("Ernährungsberufe")

17) Construction Careers ("Bauberufe")

18) Construction Supplier, Furniture Supplier, Upholsterer ("Bau-, Raumausstatter und Polsterer")

19) Carpenter, Modeller ("Tischler, Modellbauer")

20) Painter-Decorater, Laquer and associated Careers ("Maler, Lackierer und verwandte Berufe")

21) Qualitywarrent Testing, Distribution Packer ("Warenprüfer, Versandfertigmacher")

22) Unskilled Worker ("Hilfsarbeiter ohne nähere Tätigkeitsangabe")

23) Machinist and associated Careers ("Maschinisten und zugehörige Berufe")

24) Engineer, Chemist, Physicist, Mathematician ("Ingenieure, Chemiker, Physiker, Mathematiker")

25) Technician ("Techniker")

26) Technical Specialist ("Technische Sonderkräfte")

27) Merchandise Manager ("Warenkaufleute")

28) Service Manager ("Dienstleistungskaufleute")

29) Transportation Careers ("Verkehrsberufe")

30) Warehouse Manager, Warehouse and Transport Worker ("Lagerverwalter, Lager- und Transportarbeiter")

31) Organization, Management, Office Careers ("Organisations-, Verwaltungs- und Büroberufe")

32) Security Service Careers ("Ordnungs- und Sicherheitsberufe")

33) Publication, Translater, Librarian ("Publizisten, Dolmetscher, Bibliothekare")

34) Artist and associated Careers ("Künstler und zugeordnete Berufe")

35) Health Care Careers ("Gesundheitsdienstberufe")

36) Social Work, Pedagogy, Science Careers ("Sozial- und Erziehungsberufe, geistes- und naturwissenschaftliche Berufe a.n.g.")

37) Beauty Culture ("Körperpfleger")

38) Guest Assistant ("Gästebetreuer")

39) Domestic Economy, Housekeeping ("Hauswirtschafliche Berufe")

40) Cleaning Industry ("Reinigungsberufe")

Summary of main groups:
*PRIM*: 1) - 3)
*PROD*: 4) - 23)
*TECH*: 24) - 26)
*SERV*: 27) - 34), 37) - 40)
*SOCU*: 35) - 36)

## Appendix A3.IV: Panel data modelling

Several panel estimation techniques have been followed (see a) to k)). The basic model for the panel of occupational groups is
a)

$$(B9) \qquad \ln(H_{it}) = \beta \ln(V_{it}) + \gamma \ln(U_{it}) + \alpha_i + \omega_t + \epsilon_{it},$$

where $t = 1,\ldots, T$ are the number of periods, and $i = 1,\ldots, K$ are the number of groups. In the "one way fixed-effects" model, the term $u_{it} = \alpha_i + \omega_t + \epsilon_{it}$ is treated the same as in the classical regression analysis: $\alpha_i$ is treated as a regressor (i.e. not necessarily independent of *ln(U)* and *ln(V)*) and it is estimated as an individual (occupational group specific) constant. The time effects are covered by a linear time trend. The error term has the usual "white noise" properties:

$$(B10) \qquad \ln(H_{it}) = \alpha_i + \beta \ln(V_{it}) + \gamma \ln(U_{it}) + \delta t + \epsilon_{it},$$

where

$$E(\epsilon_{it}) = 0, \quad Var(\epsilon_{it}) = \sigma_\epsilon^2.$$

b) The most restriced model is the constrained (pooled) regression, where we assume that all individual constants are identical :

$$(B11) \qquad \ln(H_{it}) = \alpha + \beta \ln(V_{it}) + \gamma \ln(U_{it}) + \delta t + \epsilon_{it}.$$

c) Instead of treating individual effects as a constant, "random-effects models" (REM, Balestra and Nerlove, 1966) exploit the complete structure of a composed error $\psi_{it} = u_i + \epsilon_{it}$. The "one-way-random effects" model is

$$(B12) \qquad \ln(H_{it}) = \alpha + \beta \ln(V_{it}) + \gamma \ln(U_{it}) + \delta t + (u_i + \epsilon_{it}),$$

where

$$E(u_i) = 0, \quad Var(u_i) = \sigma_u^2, \quad E(\epsilon_{it} u_i) = 0.$$

The variance-covariance matrix is determined by

$$Var(\epsilon_{it} + u_i) = \sigma_\epsilon^2 + \sigma_u^2,$$

implying that the model is a generalized regression model. It is efficiently estimated in a two step procedure.[1] The variance components are first estimated using the residuals from ordinary least squares. Then feasible "generalized least squares" (GLS) obeys the error structure given in $(B12)$ using the estimated variances from the first step (see Hsiao, 1986, for further details).

In random-effects models, disturbances in different periods are correlated because of their common component:

$$\rho_u \equiv Corr(\epsilon_{it} + u_i, \epsilon_{is} + u_i) = \frac{\sigma_u^2}{\sigma_\epsilon^2 + \sigma_u^2}.$$

Disturbances of different groups are uncorrelated:

$$\rho_w \equiv Corr(\epsilon_{it} + u_i, \epsilon_{jt} + u_j) = 0.$$

d) "Two-way-fixed-effects models" have an overall constant as well as a group effect for each occupational group and a time effect for each period from 1971 to 1992:

$$(B13) \qquad \ln(H_{it}) = \alpha_0 + \alpha_i + \psi_t + \beta \ln(V_{it}) + \gamma \ln(U_{it}) + \epsilon_{it}.$$

The problem of multicollinearity is avoided by the restriction $\Sigma\alpha_i = \Sigma\psi_t = 0$.

e) The "two-way-random effects" model is

$$(B14) \qquad \ln(H)_{it} = \alpha + \beta \ln(V_{it}) + \gamma \ln(U_{it}) + (u_i + \omega_t + \epsilon_{it}),$$

where

$$E(u_i) = 0, \quad E(\omega_t) = 0, \quad E(\epsilon_{it}) = 0, \quad E(\epsilon_{it}\omega_t) = 0, \quad E(u_i\omega_t) = 0,$$

$$E(u_i^2) = \sigma_u^2, \quad E(\omega_t^2) = \sigma_\omega^2, \quad E(\epsilon_{it}^2) = \sigma_\epsilon^2.$$

For a given $t$, disturbances of different groups are correlated by virtue of their common period effect:

$$\rho_\omega = Corr(u_i + \omega_t + \epsilon_{it}, u_j + \omega_t + \epsilon_{jt}) = \sigma_\omega^2 / (\sigma_u^2 + \sigma_\omega^2 + \sigma_\epsilon^2).$$

As before, disturbances in different periods are correlated due to their common group effect:

$$\rho_u = Corr(u_i + \omega_t + \epsilon_{it}, u_i + \omega_s + \epsilon_{is}) = \sigma_u^2 / (\sigma_u^2 + \sigma_\omega^2 + \sigma_\epsilon^2).$$

---

**1** All estimations use LIMDEP (6.0).

f) A further specification provides a dynamic approach to panel econometrics. Assuming a one-way-fixed-effects model with an autoregressive structure $\epsilon_{it} = \rho \epsilon_{i,t-1} + \nu_{it}$, where $\nu_{it}$ is a "white noise" process, we can follow Durbin's (1960) procedure to correct for serial correlation (see Hsiao, 1986, 55-57): Subtracting $\rho \ln(H_{i,t-1})$ from $\ln(H_{it})$ yields

$$(B15) \qquad \ln(H_{it}) = \alpha_i(1-\rho) + \beta \ln(V_{it}) - \rho\beta \ln(V_{i,t-1}) + \gamma \ln(U_{it}) - \rho\gamma \ln(U_{i,t-1}) + \rho \ln(H_{i,t-1}) + \delta(1-\rho)t + \nu_{it},$$

which can be estimated by using fixed effects (here fixed effects represent $\alpha_i^* = (1-\rho)\alpha_i$). The estimated parameter on $\ln(H_{i,t-1})$ is a consistent estimate ($T \to \infty$) of $\rho$. This estimate can be used in a second step, where the variance-covariance matrix of the autocorrelated error structure is estimated using estimated parameters of the first step (see, Hsiao, 1986, p. 56, for details). Then, in a third step, GLS estimation provides an asymptotically efficient estimator if $T \to \infty$. Estimates of the first step as well as GLS estimates of the final step are presented in Table 3.4; the results of the GLS step are indicated as *AR1*.

g) Alternative dynamic representations follow the two- way-fixed-effects model. Note that here Durbin's procedure implies a difference $\ln(H_{it}) - \rho \ln(H_{i,t-1})$, which adds a differenced periods effect $\omega_t - \rho\omega_{t-1}$ to the transformed model $(B15)$.

h) Furthermore, a dynamic *AR1* version of a one way random-effects model is based on a consistent estimate of $\rho$ in the first step, and uses GLS estimation of the error structure $u_i^* + \nu_{it}$ in the second step, where $u_i^* = (1-\rho)u_i$.

i) Unemployment and, in particular, vacancies may have errors of measurement. Hsiao (1986, p. 63-65) presents a procedure to correct additive errors in a fixed-effects model. In terms of logs of vacancies, the presumed error structure is

$$(B16) \qquad \ln(V_{it}^*) = \ln(V_{it}) + \tau_{it}.$$

$\ln(V_{it})$ is the true value. The additive log-structure leads to multiplicative errors in the original dimension of the data that seems to be more realistic and is more in line with the observation that the error resembles the degree of capacity utilization (assuming that "error" = "corrected vacancies" minus "observed vacancies" in the sense of Figure 2.3). The error $\tau_{it}$ is uncorrelated with explanatory variables, group effects and residuals of the fixed-effects model $y_{it} = \alpha_i + \beta' x_{it}' + \epsilon_{it}$:

$$cov(x_{it}, \tau_{is}) = cov(\alpha_i, \tau_{it}) = cov(u_{it}, \tau_{is}) = 0,$$

$$Var(\tau_{it}) = \sigma_\tau^2, \quad cov(\tau_{it}, \tau_{is}) = 0.$$

The inconsistency of the least-squares estimator can be alleviated by first differencing the data and then using instrumental variable techniques. If the measurement error $\tau_{it}$ is independently identically distributed across *i* and *t*, we can use $\ln(V^*_{i,t-2})$ as instruments for $\ln(V^*_{it}) - \ln(V^*_{i,t-1})$. Even though *T* may be finite, the resulting IV estimator is consistent when *K* tends to infinity (Aigner et al., 1984). In Table 3.4. both unemployment and vacancies are treated as variables with errors of measurement.

j) Instrumental variable techniques are used to avoid a potential endogeneity bias. Vacancies and unemployment are instrumented by lagged unemployment and vacancies, as well as by several aggregate macroeconomic variables. Besides the degree of capacity utilization, *DUC* (see also the estimation of aggregate matching function), *SEARCH* (non-unemployed job seekers), *W/P* (real wage costs) and *RAT_F* (female participation rate) are used as instrumental variables of unemployment and vacancies.

k) Anderson and Hsiao (1981) have shown that panel-data models with lagged endogenous variables lead to biased estimates when *T* is small. This can be seen by a subsequent substitution of the lagged endogenous variable so that parameter estimates depend on initial values (see Hsiao, 1986, p. 73). This problem is less severe in the present case where *T* is considerably high, but it is more important for usual panel-data modelling where *T* is small. Nevertheless, equation $(B15)$ is reconsidered using the instrumental variable technique proposed by Anderson and Hsiao (1981, see Keane and Runkle, 1992, for a recent discussion) which provides a consistent estimate when *T* is fixed and $K \to \infty$. The estimation is based on first differencing the data in order to eliminate the fixed effect. Consistent estimates are achieved by instrumenting $\Delta\ln(H_{i,t-1})$ with $\ln(H_{i,t-2})$.

# 4. Matching and new technologies: Does unmeasured ability explain the higher wages of new-technology workers?[1]

## 4.1. Introduction

In the U.S., low-skilled, low-educated workers have experienced a falling wage gap with respect to the better educated work force. The increasing wage differential between high-school and college graduates during the last 20 years is by now well documented (see, among others, Bound and Johnson, 1992, Murphy and Welch, 1992). Several recent studies find a similar increase in earnings inequality in other industrialized countries (Davis, 1992, Katz, Loveman and Blanchflower, 1995, Freeman and Katz, 1995) but not in Germany (Abraham and Houseman, 1994). One prominent explanation of these changes of the wage structure is the emergence of new technologies that have induced an increased demand for skilled labour because of changes in relative productivities or in relative complementarities with respect to the capital in use (Bound and Johnson, 1992, Katz and Murphy, 1992, Davis and Haltiwanger, 1991). Indeed, Krueger (1993) shows that U.S. "*workers are rewarded more highly if they use computers at work*". Krueger shows that there are large and persistent wage differentials (10% - 15%) between computer users and non-users, even after controlling for a wide variety of worker and job characteristics.

Using data of the French labour force survey, this chapter analyses whether the prevalence of wage differentials holds for a larger group of "new technologies" (including robots, computer-assisted machine tools, computers etc.), and whether the differential can be explained in a matching model with unmeasured and time-variant abilities. The existence of a persistent wage differential is confirmed only for a subgroup of new technologies that consists of computer-related and "intelligent" new technologies (NT, henceforth), whereas jobs using new technologies with a low autonomy (such as "assemby line" and "robot") are not rewarded higher than observationally equivalent conventional jobs.

---

**1** The econometric analysis of the wage equation in this chapter draws on joint work with Francis Kramarz: "The impact of new technologies on wages: Lessons from matching panels on employees and on their firms" (INSEE Discussion paper, 1994). I am grateful to INSEE, Paris, and in particular to Francis Kramarz for the opportunity to work with the INSEE data sources "Enquête Emploi" and "Enquête sur la Technique et l'Organisation du Travail auprès des Travailleurs Occupés" while I was visiting CREST.

The model in Section 4.2. explains the persistent wage differential among observationally equivalent workers by differences in workers' productive abilities that are not observable by the econometrician: Through a learning and matching process, high-ability workers find their position in new-technology jobs, where they are better paid than elsewhere, while low-ability workers are employed in conventional jobs. Alternative explanations include wage differentials arising in models of compensating differences (Rosen, 1986), rent sharing (Katz and Summers, 1989, Nickell and Wadwhani, 1990), and efficiency wages (Katz, 1986).[1]

The matching model deviates from standard explanations of unmeasured ability in which ability is time-invariant and equally valued in all firms. Learning causes the firm's evaluation of a potential match between a worker's ability and the firms's technology to vary over time. Thus, unlike standard unmeasured-ability models, the model predicts that those who switch from conventional (new-technology) jobs to NT jobs (conventional) jobs experience a positive (negative) wage change. Moreover, standard unmeasured-ability models fail to explain why the wage differential between different groups grows with experience. The model in Section 4.2. predicts that the wage differential between high-ability workers in new-technology jobs and low-ability workers in conventional jobs grows with the duration of employment in new-technology jobs. Moreover, the model predicts that the mobility of mismatched workers improves both wages and match of NT workers. Hence, perceived mismatch of new-technology workers should be lower in high-wage groups. These hypotheses will be tested in Section 4.4..

The data is presented in Section 4.3. I will use a unique panel that matches data on individuals with data on their firms (for a similar U.S. dataset without the panel information, see Troske, 1993). The 1987 supplement of the French labour force survey gives detailed information about the use of new technologies by more than 17,000 wage earners of which 3930 have a firm identification number which can be matched with an unbalanced panel of firms which have been followed between 1978 and 1987 (see Abowd and Kramarz, 1993, for a description of this data set). Furthermore, workers surveyed in 1987 on new technologies can be followed from 1985 to 1987 by using retrospective information of the labour force survey.

---

**1** Both hypotheses (unmeasured ability versus true wage differentials) have become popular as explanations for the phenomenon of inter-industry wage differentials. The unmeasured-ability hypothesis is confirmed by Murphy and Topel (1987). A summary of the evidence is given by Gibbons and Katz (1992).

Based on the matching framework described in Section 4.2., Section 4.4. presents cross-sectional estimates of wage differentials between new-technology and conventional jobs. The results demonstrate that the use of computer-related NT with high autonomy and high training requirements yields a wage advantage between 4% and 5% for a worker with zero NT experience. Computed at the average level of the population, experience with NT adds another 5%. The analysis by occupations (by wage levels) shows that the higher the skill (wage) level is, the lower is the bonus. In accordance with the predictions in Section 4.2., mismatch due to new-technologies is less important for high-wage groups. A by-product of the analysis is that perceived mismatch is lower for female new-technology workers than for male colleagues.

Krueger (1993) did not answer the question of whether higher wages of computer users arise due to unmeasured ability or due to true wage differentials. Section 4.5 tries to answer the question according to the model presented in Section 4.3. Fixed-effects panel estimations support the hypothesis of unmeasured ability. There is ambigous evidence for the hypothesis that unmeasured ability is differently valued in NT and non-NT jobs: Wage differentials of NT-workers disappear, but experience with NT remains significant. Section 4.6 concludes.

## 4.2. Matching, mobility, and unmeasured ability

An important explanation of wage differences among observationally similar workers in competitive labour markets is that workers have productive abilities that cannot be captured in the data set of the econometrician. The unmeasured-ability hypothesis is based on the observation that measurable dimensions of human capital (education, experience) are associated with employment in high-wage industries (Dickens and Katz, 1987). Furthermore, it is conjectured that unmeasured ability is correlated with observable human capital so that forces that cause the sorting of workers across firms by measured productive abilities cause similar sorting by unmeasured human capital.

The standard unmeasured-ability model assumes that unmeasured workers' productive abilities are time-invariant and equally valued in all firms. Wage equations can be written as

$$\ln w_{it} = X_{it}\beta + u_{it}, \qquad (4.1)$$

where $u_{it} = \theta_i + \epsilon_{it}$. $X_{it}$ is a vector of individual characteristics, $u_{it}$ is an unobservable error term in which $\theta_i$ is the productive ability of the worker and $\epsilon_{it}$ is white noise. Thus, if workers are sorted across new-technology jobs and conventional jobs by unmeasured abilities, cross-sectional estimates reveal higher wages for NT-jobs in competitive labour markets:

$$(4.2) \qquad \ln w_i = const. + \alpha T_i + X_i\beta + \nu_i,$$

where $T_i = 1$ if the worker is working with NT, and $T_i = 0$ if not. $\alpha > 0$ captures the difference between NT-wages and conventional wages.

Fixed-effects estimation or first differencing eliminate individual time-invariant effects, so that the estimate

$$(4.3) \qquad \Delta \ln w_{it} = \gamma \Delta T_{it} + \Delta X_{it}\beta + \Delta u_{it}$$

would yield $\gamma = 0$.

The framework changes when a particular ability is higher valued in a NT job (knowing the UNIX system is of small value in the professional world of a carpenter but of high value in a computer-related job). Switching from a conventional job to a NT work place would yield a better match and higher wages so that $\gamma > 0$: workers' unmeasured productive ability ceases to be time-invariant.

The appealing idea of time-variant productive abilities which may be of different values for NT and conventional jobs is that there are incentives to move. The motivation of mobility remains unclear in the standard unmeasured-mobility explanation. Mobility decisions are endogeneous in the following framework, which applies a more general framework by Gibbons and Katz (1992). They are based on incomplete information about workers productive abilities. Learning, however, improves information and leads to a better matching of abilities and jobs over time. At the time of hiring, the market observes a noisy signal about each worker's ability, thereafter, high-ability workers are attracted by ability-sensitive new-technology jobs. Since the econometrician can only observe the wages and the technology of the work place, wage equations such as (4.3) (or fixed-effects estimates) would yield a *positive* wage effect from changing.

More formally, there are two abilities, $\eta_H$ and $\eta_L$ (high and low), that lead to the following ranking of productivies of NT-workers *(T)* and conventional jobs *(C)*:

$$(4.4) \qquad y_{TH} > y_{CH} > y_{CL} > y_{TL},$$

where $y_{xy}$ represents output in a job with technology $x$ and ability $y$. The ranking reveals the assumption that new-technology jobs are more sensitive to ability than conventional jobs. Low-ability workers in new-technology jobs are of lower value than in conventional jobs, whereas high-ability workers are best rewarded in a new-technology position. The lowest productivity is the one of a (mis-matched) low-ability worker in a NT-position.[1]

Furthermore, there is a noisy signal $s$ before hiring occurs. $s$ takes two values, $s \in (s_a, s_b)$, where $p(s)$ is the probability that the worker is of high quality. $s_a$ indicates a high-ability worker with higher certainty than the signal $s_b$: $1 > p(s_a) > p(s_b) > 0$. It is assumed that the signal $s_a$ is accurate enough ($p(s_a)$ is sufficiently close to one) that the expected productivity of new-technology jobs is higher than for conventional positions:[2]

$$(4.5) \qquad \begin{aligned} E_{T|a} &\equiv p(s_a)y_{TH} + (1 - p(s_a))y_{TL} \\ > E_{C|a} &\equiv p(s_a)y_{CH} + (1 - p(s_a))y_{CL}, \end{aligned}$$

where $E_{T|a}$ and $E_{C|a}$ denote expected productivity conditional on signal $s_a$. The reverse argument leads to the assumption $E_{T|b} < E_{C|b}$, i.e.

$$p(s_b)y_{TH} + (1 - p(s_b))y_{TL} < p(s_b)y_{CH} + (1 - p(s_b))y_{CL}.$$

Thus, in the first period after the signal occurs, workers with the appearance of high-ability workers (i.e. workers with signal $s_a$), and who in fact are high-ability workers with a relatively high probablity ( $p(s_a) > p(s_b)$), start their employment in a NT-position, workers with a less favourable signal $s_b$ start in a conventional job.

In competitive labour markets, firms are able to pay wages up to expected productivity. Thus, in the first period, NT-workers earn

$$(4.6) \qquad w_{T1} \equiv E_{T|a} = p(S_a)y_{TH} + (1 - p(s_a))y_{TL},$$

while workers in conventional jobs receive

---

1 Spence (1976) provides an early example of introducing productivities depending on both individual skills and jobs. As in (4.4), it is assumed that the less skilled are always more productive in the low-skilled job than they are in the high-skilled one.

2 In a competitive labour market of perfect information, high-ability workers would work in new-technologies where their higher productivity is higher rewarded than in conventional positions, whereas low-ability workers remain in conventional jobs.

$$(4.7) \qquad w_{C1} \equiv E_{C|b} = p(S_b)y_{CH} + (1 - p(s_b))y_{CL}.$$

From (4.5) and because $p(s_a) > p(s_b)$, it follows that $w_{T1} > w_{C1}$:

$$w_{T1} = p(s_a)y_{TH} + (1 - p(s_a))y_{TL} > p(s_a)y_{CH} + (1 - p(s_a))y_{CL}$$

$$= p(s_a)(y_{CH} - y_{CL}) + y_{CL} > p(s_b)(y_{CH} - y_{CL}) + y_{CL} = w_{C1}.$$

After the first period, actual production reveals true ability and the information becomes perfect. Hence, mismatched workers change positions, which leads to a better allocation of workers to technologies: Remaining high-ability workers in conventional jobs switch to NT-jobs where they earn $w_{T2} = y_{TH}$, while low-ability workers have to leave their previous NT-position, and they are employed in conventional jobs in period two, where they earn low-ability wages $w_{C2} = y_{CL}$.

Three important conclusions can be drawn:

- I) The general wage-level of NT-jobs is higher than that of conventional jobs: $w_{T1} > w_{C1} > w_{C2}$, $w_{T2} > w_{C1} > w_{C2}$. Hence, even the simultaneous existence of both cohorts, "period 1" ("noisy-signal") and "period 2" ("complete information"), in observed data sets would lead to higher wages of NT-workers in a cross-sectional analysis.
- II) Workers moving from a conventional job to a NT-job experience a wage increase $(w_{C1} \rightarrow w_{T2})$, whereas workers who start in a NT-Job and are employed in a conventional job are paid less in period two when true ability becomes obvious $(w_{T1} \rightarrow w_{C2})$.
- III) The wage differential between new-technology workers and conventional jobs grows with increased work experience: $(w_{T2} - w_{T1}) > (w_{C2} - w_{C1})$.

Moreover, the theory predicts that the presence of new technologies leads to mismatched workers and that mobility will improve the match.[1] This, in turn, causes the wages of adequately matched NT-workers to be higher than comparable wages of mismatched NT-workers. Thus, it can be argued that in general[2]

- IV) workers in high-wage groups should have a better match with NT-job requirements than in low-wage groups.

All predictions lead to easily testable hypotheses in both cross-sectional and panel data analysis.

---

**1** Note that the meaning of "match" and "mismatch" is generalized in Chapter 4. Until now mismatch has meant a discrepancy between *U* and *V*, now mismatch is discrepancy between *U* and *V and* between expected and true ability.

**2** Assuming that a majority of workers can be characterized as "period 2" workers.

## 4.3. The micro datasets: Presentation and descriptive analysis

### 4.3.1. INSEE data sources

The data used in this chapter comes from 5 different INSEE ("Institut National de la Statistique et des Etudes Economiques", National Institute for Statistics and Economic Studies) sources. The two basic sources are "Enquête Emploi, 1985-1987", the French labour force survey, and "Enquête sur la Technique et l'Organisation du Travail auprès des Travailleurs Occupés, 1987" (TOTTO). TOTTO is an appendix to the labour force survey which asks questions about the diffusion of new technologies and the organisation of the work place. Besides the usual questions from labour force surveys (salary, tenure, age, education, etc.), the appendix contains a rich source of information on the use (e.g.intensity, experience, sectoral affiliation, required training) of microcomputers, terminals, text processing, robots and other well specified groups of "new technology" labour. Likewise, questions concerning the hierarchy of labour and working-time schedules help in drawing more detailed conclusions concerning the impact of new technologies than would be possible by the analysis of standard labour force surveys.

Employing firms in both data sets, "Enquête Emploi 1987" and TOTTO, can be followed by so-called SIREN identification numbers. Each number represents the enterprise at which the individual is employed in 1987. This feature of the French INSEE classification system enables me to employ information from corresponding firm-level surveys (such as profits and share of sales going to exports, for instance) over the period 1985-1987. Three additional sources have been added: "Bénéfices Industriel et Commerciaux" (BIC) and "Enquête sur la Structure de l'Emploi" (ESE) and "Enquête Annuelle sur L'Emploi" (EAE). A detailed description of BIC, ESE and EAE and the question of merging can be found in Abowd and Kramarz (1993).

The survey "Enquête sur la Technique et l'Organisation du Travail auprès des Travailleurs Occupés" (TOTTO) was performed in March 1987. It represents a total of about 20 million individuals of civilian employment. The probability of being selected is 1/1000; thus the survey contains about 20000 workers. Questions concerning the organisation of labour were only presented to wage-earners and salaried employees. Questions concerning the use of "New Technologies" were presented to all members (including civil-servants) of the civilian work-force (according to the definition of the OECD). In this paper, the sample (based on TOTTO) used for estimating purposes consists of 17184 wage-earners and salaried employees.

### 4.3.2. The definition of "new technology" categories

When the employment division of INSEE and the Ministry of labour envisaged the TOTTO questionnaire, experts in the field of modern machines and techniques were part of the survey design team. Because no simple classification of NT existed, it was necessary to create a classification system as a part of the survey.

The list of NTs included in the questionnaire is rather long (see Tables C3 to C10, Appendix A4.I). Thus, to keep the analysis tractable, NTs are grouped into categories. The first principle, used also by firms themselves, distinguishes between office automation and industrial automation. However, as can be seen from the descriptive analysis, computer-related techniques are also used on the production line by blue-collar workers (400,000 in 1987). On the other hand, sociologists show that efficient use of modern NTs and the amount of autonomy involved in operating a NT are closely related (Berry, 1988). They also show that autonomy in a NT-job is related to the amount of information that is exchanged with the machine (Cézard, Dussert and Gollac, 1992). Hence, the amount of training that is necessary to operate the respective new technology seems to be a natural indicator for grouping.

The following principles are separated into three categories which divide workers according to their relation to computers *and* according to the amount of autonomy left to the worker:

- $T1$: "*Computer-related NT with high autonomy*". $T1 = 1$ if she or he is a "regular user" (see below) of at least one of the following techniques: microcomputer, text processing, Minitel (the French videotext), terminal (emission and reception), computer listings, data entry, video control (supervising) and laser technique, $T1 = 0$ if not.
- $T2$: "*Computer-related NT with average autonomy*". $T2 = 1$ if she or he is a regular user of at least one of the following techniques: "terminal, reception only", "terminal, emission only" , machine-tool with numerical command and the category "other NT" of the questionnaire, $T2 = 0$ if not.
- $T3$: "*Computer-related NT with low autonomy*". $T3 = 1$ if she or he is a regular user of at least one of the techniques robot, assembly line and automatic transportation (operating automates), $T3 = 0$ if not.

The definition of "regular users" in *T1, T2,* and *T3* is based on the survey category "Use of NT as a main task". Table 4.1. reveals that 36% of all workers have a NT-job. The alternative category "Use of NT as a supplementary task" (less than one hour per day on average) is disregarded.[1] Descriptive statistics in Table C1 (Appendix A4.I) reveal that 28.7% of all workers have at least one task belonging to *T1*, 8.0% have a job in *T2* and 4.5% have a job with low autonomy (*T3*).[2] Note that these values are representative for the group of *all* workers (incl. civil-servants, services, etc), the *industrial* average of *T3* would be higher, for instance.

The categories are homogeneous with the possible exception of video control and laser techniques which are in the first group of high autonomy. However, both techniques are rare (see Table 4.2.), rely on electronic techniques and leave a lot of autonomy to their users. In these respects, they could not be classified with the other two groups and were not important enough to be summarized in a specific group.

Moreover, as can be seen from Table 4.2., self-reported training requirements of NT-workers confirm the grouping into *T1, T2* and *T3.* Only between 2.6% and 6.1% of NT-workers belonging to *T1* do not need any training for their jobs, whereas these shares are much larger for the NTs in the low-autonomy group *T3;* they range between 20.2% and 42.1%. The corresponding shares of *T2* are between 8.0% and 16.0%.

Table 4.1.: New technologies: Global figures

Percentage of workforce working with new technologies by gender and overall:

| | "Used as main task" | "Only used supplementary" | Subtotal of part-time workers: "Used as main task" |
|---|---|---|---|
| Men (56.3%) | 35.1 | 7.9 | 19.7 (14.3%) |
| Women (43.7%) | 37.3 | 7.6 | 18.7 (85.7%) |
| Total (100%) | 36.0 | 7.8 | 18.9 (100%) |

*Note:* The figures are based on answers of 17184 employed workers; 1379 of them are part-time workers. Source: INSEE, Enquête Emploi, 1987 (French labour force survey, 1987). The numbers in parentheses give the percentage share of men and women in the respective totals.

1 Casual users of NT are rare: Only 10% of NT users use them less than one hour per week (Dussert, 1992).

2 Note that this sum is larger than the entry 36.0% in Table 4.1., since double-counting allows that the same worker can be both a regular member of *T1* and *T2*, for instance.

*Table 4.2.:* New technologies: Importance and required training

| | Percentage of workforce working with NT | | Proportion in each NT reporting "no training needed" 1) |
|---|---|---|---|
| | "Used as main task" | "Supplementary use" | |
| New technology | | | |
| Micro | 9.8 | 3.7 | 2.6 |
| Text processing | 3.1 | 2.0 | 2.6 |
| Minitel | 5.9 | 5.7 | 4.2 |
| Video (supervising) | 3.1 | 1.3 | 3.7 |
| Terminal | 10.1 | 2.7 | 5.0 |
| Use of listings | 14.6 | 4.2 | 5.1 |
| Data entry | 10.4 | 3.4 | 6.0 |
| Laser technique | 0.4 | 0.3 | 6.1 |
| Terminal: Reception only | 1.8 | 0.8 | 8.0 |
| Terminal: Emission only | 1.2 | 0.4 | 11.3 |
| Other modern technology | 4.3 | 0.9 | 14.0 |
| Machine-tool (with numerical command) | 1.2 | 0.5 | 16.0 |
| Automatic transportation | 1.9 | 0.3 | 42.1 |
| Robot | 1.0 | 0.4 | 20.2 |
| Assembly line | 2.2 | 0.3 | 33.5 |
| Use of conventional techniques only | - | - | 30.5 |

*Note:* The figures are based on a sample of 17184 employed workers, of which 1379 are part-time workers. Source: INSEE, Enquête Emploi, 1987 (French labour force survey, 1987).
1) Percentage share responding with "no training is needed" to the survey question "Does your job correspond with your training?"

The use of computers is covered in more detail in this data set than in other surveys (see Krueger, 1993, for instance). The questionaire provides explicit categories for using text processing only, data entry and the use of listings. "Terminal" even covers a distinction between "reception only", "emission only" and both, reception and emission ("terminal"). Using a more general meaning of the word "computers" (collecting micros, terminals, data entry, listings, but excluding text processing and including supplementary use), Gollac (1989, 1990) calculates that about 25% of all civilian employees (4,540,000) use "computers".[1] On the other hand, robots and other computer aided automates (cf. *T3*) are of minor importance: Only 400,000 were counted in 1987 (Gollac, 1989). The inclusion of these techniques, sometimes considered as "stupid" NT when compared to the "intelligent" use of microcomputers, allows for comparisons between both groups of workers.

### 4.3.3. "New technologies" and "organization of the work place"

This subsection describes NT in relation to other economic variables.

A description of the key variables can be found in Tables 4.1. and 4.2. as well as in Table C1 - Table C10 of Appendix A4.I. Table 4.1. reveals that the decomposition of NT by gender results in almost identical figures: 35.1% of all men and 37.3% of all women are NT-workers. Working part-time leads to a substantial reduction of NT (18.9%). The lower demand for part-time workers might arise from the prohibitively high costs of job-specific training per working-hour necessary to run most of the more "intelligent" new techniques. On the supply side, workers with high investments in human capital would have high opportunity costs when they only work part-time.

The most popular NT is the use of listings: 14.6% according to Table 4.2. Other categories related to computer use are almost of the same size: Data entry (10.4%), terminal (10.1%) and microcomputer (9.8%). 3.1% of all NT users apply text processing (this category means using computers *exclusively* for text processing).[2] Specifying the low value of *T3* in Table C1 of the Appendix, Table 4.2. reveals that only 2.2% (440,000) use assembly lines and 1.0% operate a robot. Thus, in terms of employment (perhaps not in terms of sales or in terms of other size variables) the new wave of "new technologies" is in fact very much related to "intelligent computer" use ("computer" in a broad sense).

Hence, it is not surprising that computing mainly affects the professional world of service industries. As can be seen from the entry "at least one NT" in Table C3 (Appendix), the banking sector is the one with the highest proportion of NT users (82.9% of all workers in the sector; see in particular "listings" and "terminal"). Somewhat surprising, however, is the high percentage of NT for industrial sectors: 79% for the small (in terms of employment) but capital-intensive "petroleum and natural gas" sector,

---

1 According to some more recent figures from the French Ministery for Employment and Professional Formation ("Enquête Conditions de Travail, 1991"), Gollac (1993) reports an increase towards 30% in 1991.

2 Note the possibility of double counting if the same worker uses more than one NT as "main task".

58.6% for the big "electrics and electronics" sector. Industrial sectors also include techniques with low autonomy (low training requirements, as defined in *T3*). New technologies of any kind are almost non-existent in the building industry (12.7%) and in agriculture, fishery (10.8%).

The distribution of wages (Table C4, Appendix) reveals that the wage structure of "NT with low autonomy" (assembly line, automatic transportation and robot) is almost identical to the one without NT (see "No NT", respectively "conventional technology"). Apparently, wages for NT users are higher, with "micro" ranging above the average. More generally, computer users (micro, listings, terminal) as well as Minitel and laser-technique users have the highest shares in the category of top salaries (15000 FF and more).[1] The next chapters will analyse whether these wage differentials are due to better education and other individual characteristics of *T1*-workers or due to the unobservable abilities associated with new technologies.

It is interesting to note that, despite the apparently higher wages for "NT with high autonomy", only workers for "NT with low autonomy" confirm receiving a premium for their work with NT: Table C5 reports a premium for 10%-12% of all workers belonging to *T3*, but e.g. only 3% of micro users receive an extra bonus and only 0.8% of listings users report a premium. Evidently, better educated people have to accept new technologies as a usual part of their work assignments.

Taking all NT-workers as 100%, Table C6 shows that among this group clerks represent the biggest group: 20.6% of all workers using at least one NT belong to this socio-professional category. Surprisingly enough, the second biggest group is skilled blue collar workers, representing 12.0% of all NT-workers (note, however, that skilled blue collar workers represent 20.5% of all civilian employees, whereas the share of clerks amounts to only 10.5%). Table C6 reveals that skilled blue collar workers mainly operate machine-tools and robots.

However, considering all workers belonging to one socio-professional group as 100 percent, Gollac (1993) reports that 10% of all skilled blue collar workers also use a "computer" in a more general sense (based on a broader definition: micro, listing, terminal and data entry, see also above) which represents about 400,000 workers. The same author reports the use of computers for 60% of all managers, engineers and professionals, 47% for the group of middle-level professionals, 36% for the clerks and 5% for unskilled blue collar workers (Gollac, 1993).

---

**1** It should be noted that the French labour force survey only provides categorical information on wages, with a very detailed classification for low wages. The categories are (in 1000 FF): 1 and less, 1-1.5, 1.5-2, 2-2.5, 2.5-3, 3-3.5, 3.5-4, 4-4.5, 4.5-5, 5-6, 6-7, 7-8, 8-9, 9-10, 10-15, 15-20, 20-25, 25-30, 30 and more.

New technologies are concentrated in large firms (see Table C7). This holds a fortiori for NT with low autonomy (*T3*: assembly line, robots, automatic transportation) and terminals.

The high proportion of workers reporting "no training needed" (Table 4.2.) for NT within *T3* is confirmed by the general level of education: Table C8 reveals that for each *T3* the schooling outcome "no educational degree" represents the largest group. Working in conventional jobs (respectively working without NT) seems to be similar to "NT with low autonomy". 31.6 percent of workers falling into the category "No NT" have no educational degree, which is significantly more than the share of this group in total civilian employment (23.1%). Micro users mainly consist of workers who left school with a degree from a junior high school (19.8%) or a high school (19.2%).[1] More generally, the majority of NT users grouped as *T1* (high autonomy) have a degree from a junior high school (see listings, data entry, Minitel, micro, terminal).

Table C9 considers each educational degree as 100%. The entry "at least one NT" reveals that 58.7% of the graduates of technical colleges and 57.3% of the university graduates work with NT, wheras only 19.5% of the workers without a degree work with NT. The categories "assembly line" and "robots" reveal that a substantial part of this share belongs to *T3*. Thus, "no education" most likely leads to some work without NT or to the operation of machines with "low autonomy". On the other hand, graduating with a degree superior or equal to high school would lead, with more than 50% probability, to the use of NT.

Working with "NT with high autonomy" allows more flexibility with respect to working time. Table C10 shows a concentration of workers in the category "fixed schedule every day" for "No NT". Listings, Minitel, laser technique and micro, but also data entry and text processing are more likely subsumed under "variable time schedules", being determined by the worker themselves.[2] Shift work (two or three shifts) mainly concerns *T3* (assembly lines, automates, robots) and machine-tools.

Some other variables worth mentioning that deal with NT and organization of labour are summarized in Table C1. The questionnaire TOTTO asks for each NT the number of years of experience with exactly this particular technique. This information is very important with respect to the theoretical prediction that the wage differential between NT users and conventional workers grows with experience (see Section 4.2.). The individual answers are used to construct ANNT, "years of experience with NT". If someone works with more than one NT, I calculate average values.

---

**1** See Appendix A4.II for the definition of English expressions for French educational degrees.

**2** Some items of the question in the questionaire remain unclear, but the variable will mostly be used as a control variable in the econometric analysis.

Thus, three types of "experience" can be distinguished: Tenure (ANCA1), age (in fact, AGE1 = age - minimum age of workers in the sample = age - 14, sometimes refered to as experience) and ANNT. Moreover, in order to measure some potential gender-specific divergencies arising from the experience with NT, I define ANT_M and ANT_F which indicate if the person is a male or a female worker with long NT experience.

CAD_1 - CAD_4 capture effects caused by production norms: CAD_1 is an indicator showing whether the mode of operation follows the dictates of installed machines. CAD_2 and CAD_3 concern the existence of allowable production delays, and CAD_4 equals one if no such norms exist. For 59% of all workers, there are no norms, whereas some 14.5% have to respect quality norms (see QUAL).

### 4.3.4. Variables representing the firm-level background of individual workers

In addition to the sample described in Tables 4.1., 4.2. and in tables of Appendix A4.I, a second sample is used that keeps all individuals of the first sample if corresponding firm-level information of the worker is available. Additional firm-level variables of individual workers are presented in Table C2 (Appendix A4.I). They are based on a panel of firms covering the years 1978 to 1987 (see Abowd and Kramarz, 1993). The firm level information comes from an exhaustive sample for large firms (more than 500 employees) and an INSEE probability sample for smaller firms. The sample plan provides a weighting variable which is used in subsequent estimations in order to estimate a variance-covariance matrix that is representative for the population of individuals (such that the bias arising from the higher probablity of large firms to be in the sample can be offset). Due to missing small firms and due to missing observations for certain firm-level variables, the merged sample contains only 3930 individual observations for the cross-sectional analysis and 8118 (pooled) individual observations on the three year panel (see Section 4.5.).

The other main difference between the initial sample and the merged sample is that only privately-owned firms appear in the merged sample, whereas public firms as well as administration (civil servants) were included in the initial sample.

To provide some background of the firms' average situation, firm-level data are introduced as the means of the years 1978 until 1987. Capital is based on the sum of "Dettes" (debt) and "Fonds propres à l'entreprise" (owners equity). The measure is equal to "Actif total" (Total assets) in French accounting systems. Moreover, the sector-by-sector, time varying index of the cost of capital (KAPP) is used, which is designed such that the mean of the index values across sectors in the year 1980 is 100, to deflate capital yielding CAPITR. MCAPITR is the corresponding mean value.

As for MCAPITR, BIC provides the "Excédent brut d'exploitation" (operating income), or EBE (the formula used to calculate EBE, consisting of 14 different terms, is shown, for instance, in Abowd, Kramarz and Margolis, 1993). EBE is then divided by 1000 and deflated by the "prix de valeur ajoutée" (industry specific value added price) to yield EBER, or real operating income, in thousands of 1980 FF. EBER is finally divided by CAPITR to yield EBERC, or real operating income per unit of capital, in 1980 FF. Taking the mean yields MEBERC.

MING is the mean share of the workforce that is comprised of supervisors and above, and MOQA is the mean share of skilled labour. The remaining part (1 - MING -MOQA) is the firm's mean share of unskilled workers. MEFFEC is the mean of the size of the workforce and MTEXP is the mean share of sales sold abroad.

## 4.4. Cross-sectional results

### 4.4.1. Specifying the wage equation

In order to study the influence of NT on wages, different models are estimated. I distinguish between NT techniques according to the three groups ("high autonomy", "average autonomy", "low autonomy") described in the preceding section.

The wage variable is discrete. The French labour force survey uses a classification with cell widths of 500 francs for low and intermediate wages, and widths of 1000 francs for high salaries. Thus, the estimating strategy is constrained by the available type of information. Subsequent results are based on ordered logit, a maximum likelihood approach with exogenous thresholds (instead of taking the average of each wage group, for instance).[1] Note that the standard error of the equation is identified and thus the estimated coefficients can be interpreted as in the OLS case.[2]

At this stage the approach is simililar to Krueger's (1993) testing strategy. The log of monthly wage $\ln(w_i)$ is regressed on a vector of characteristics of the individual $X_i$, an indicator variable for workers belonging to one (or more) of the NT groups, *T1, T2* or *T3* (hence the reference group is "No NT", respectively "conventional technology"). In

1 All estimations are performed at CREST, INSEE (Paris) using SAS. I would like to thank Stephane Lollivier for his help with the maximum-likelihood implementation, and Françis Kramarz for the access to INSEE firm-level data.

2 Using the average of each wage group only leads to minor changes of estimated parameters.

addition to Krueger (1993), these variables are complemented by firm-level characteristics $F_{ij}$ from the supplement of the labour force survey (working time schedules, sector, size) and from our firm-level panel dataset (size, assets, profits, skill structure, export ratio).[1] $F_{ij}$ also includes elements of the work organization of the firm - namely the hierarchical structure within each worker is embeded, number of workers sharing the same superior and norms of production demanded of individual workers.

Thus, in addition to the worker-specific estimation

$$(4.8.a) \qquad \ln w_i = const. + \alpha_1 T1_i + \alpha_2 T2_i + \alpha_3 T3_i + X_i\beta' + \nu_i,$$

$$(4.8.b) \quad \ln w_{ij} = const. + \alpha_1 T1_i + \alpha_2 T2_i + \alpha_3 T3_i + X_i\beta' + F_{ij}\gamma' + \nu_{ij}$$

depends on associated firms $j$. $\nu_{i(j)}$ is normally distributed with a zero mean and a variance $\sigma_\nu^2$.

## 4.4.2. Some theoretical and empirical reasons to include firm level variables

Standard wage equations do not include variables providing information about the worker's employer, since these data are not part of usual labour force surveys. However, adding firm-level variables to standard variables of wage equations might cover some part of the "unobserved heterogeneity" which leads to the wage differentials for computer users (in the sense of Krueger, 1993, here: "new-technology users").

For example, it is possible to implement the "gift exchange" hypothesis which induces workers to perform better. This efficiency wage argument is based on the assumption that workers' willingness to co-operate depends on the motto "I treat you well and you treat me well" (Akerlof, 1982, 1984). A variable used in this sense is "profits/assets" which is included in the data set.

The same variable represents an indicator for "profit-sharing" or "rent-sharing". "*...wages of similar workers do vary positively with the profitability of the enterprise. In the absence of collective bargaining, the obvious explanation for this is that workers expect to be paid more if the firm is profitable and to slack off if they are not paid more - they feel hard done by*" (Layard et al, 1991, p. 161, reproducing arguments by Kahneman et al., 1986, and Frank, 1985). Note that in France profit-sharing is (almost) mandatory since firms have to propose a "participation" arrangement to their workers (for a description, see Cahuc-Dormont, 1992).

---

1 For exact comparisons with Krueger's results, note that no information about race is available in French surveys, and that no information on individual union membership is asked.

Related arguments refer to the inclusion of "profits/assets" because of "fair wages". If more profits can be extracted, workers expect a fair distribution of profits between shareholders and workers, i.e higher wages.

The "fair wage" is also influenced by "reference groups": The expected wage involves a mixture of what people actually forecast for themselves and what they feel entitled to (Layard, 1980). If one occupational group is highly paid, then *all* categories of workers tend to be highly paid (see Dickens and Katz, 1987, for some evidence based on sectoral wage equations). Hence, since the workers' perception of the "fair wage" is influenced by the wage of their colleagues, variables on the skill structure (share of skilled workers, for instance) are introduced in the wage regression. Moreover, the skill structure may reflect the complexity of tasks in a given firm or industry. Spillover effects may also play a role close to the one they play in endogenous growth theories: Firms with many engineers, managers, as well as educated employees, possess an amount of knowledge (technical as well as organizational) that benefits everybody thus making every other employee more productive (see also Groshen, 1991).

As the skill structure, also the export share might reflect some ability which is difficult to measure in real data. A relatively high export share captures a knowledge of techniques which meets the needs of competitive international markets. This complexity of tasks (knowledge of foreign languages, for instance, and other "unmeasured abilities") is rewarded by higher wages.

There is by now a rich amount of literature on the influence of size on wage determination. Reproducing hypotheses found in the literature[1], it is argued that size is a proxy for a multiplicity of variables:

(i) Compensating differentials are larger in large firms because of unpleasant working conditions;

(ii) large firms have higher profits, of which organized labour captures a high share;

(iii) technology is more complex, requiring higher quality workers in large firms; and

(iv) productivity is more sensitive to wages in large firms because of high turnover or monitoring costs.

Since there will be at least one variable directly related to each of the preceding hypotheses, the basic question will be: Do size effects remain or disappear after introducing such controls?

---

**1** See Strand (1987), Barron-Black-Loewenstein (1987), Brown-Medoff (1989), Schmidt-Zimmermann (1991), Currie-McConnel (1992). See also Groshen (1991) for her survey on the variation of wages among employers.

For instance, since large firms are more capital-intensive, and find it more difficult to monitor the efforts of workers, they pay more. In the present sample, however, the size of groups sharing the same superior and variables on potential production norms provide a direct test of monitoring arguments in efficiency wage theories.

Finally, following Currie and McConnell (1992), it is possible to justify the introduction of variables such as the rate of profits (profit/assets), the rate of exports and total assets in the wage equation, since these factors can be viewed as proxies of the cost of a strike for a firm. For instance, the higher the export ratio, the higher is the size of inventories needed in case of strike, or the higher are the delays due to transportation (distance from the markets) in the event of a strike. Thus the higher the cost of a strike, the higher is the wage. Note that due to legal arrangements, in France strikes can occur at almost any time rather than just during the bargaining process as in the US or in Germany.

### 4.4.3. The impact of new technologies on wages: Global results

Table 4.3., columns (1) - (3), present overall cross-sectional results for NT/conventional workers. NT effects are captured by the NT-indicator variables and by experience with NT (as well as by the latter variable squared). Column (1) presents the result based on the labour force survey, columns (2)-(7) present estimates for the matched employer-employee data set.

The results show that the classification significantly affects the wage determination process: Workers who use "computer-based NT with high autonomy" earn more, other things equal, than their colleagues using other types of NT or a conventional technique. This result is very stable across all cross-sectional estimations irrespective of whether firm-specific variables are included or not. For a NT-workers with zero NT experience, the unmatched sample (column (1) in Table 4.3.) reveals a premium of about 5.0% (exp(0.049)-1) of the wage. Without controlling for individual and firm characteristics, the effect would be 43.3 % (see Table C11, Appendix A4.III).

Including firm-level variables[1] accounts for a small part of "unobserved

---

**1** Note that the reduction of sample size is controlled using a weighted variance-covariance matrix based on the known INSEE sampling plan, making the merged sample representative for individuals working in privately owned firms (see also Abowd and Kramarz, 1993). Alternatively, an indicator of match was computed (equal to 1 when present in the sample, 0 if not). The indicator-variable was modelled as a Probit depending upon the following variables: Sex, education, marital status, age and age-squared, size of the firm, sector of the firm. Mill's ratio is then used as additional regressor (Heckman, 1979). Both results are very similar so that I only present the results of the first method.

ability", as can be seen from Table 4.3., column (3)[1]: The premium is reduced to 4.3%. Note, however, that both samples are not perfectly compatible since the merged sample only covers privately owned firms.

Another source of NT wage differentials is experience with new technologies. It provides an immediate test for the presence of returns which might arise in addition to the usual variables age (experience) and tenure. Moreover, experience with NT, *ANNT*, has the advantage that it captures experience not only with the same employer but even with the same machine. Table 4.3., column (3), confirms the theoretical result of a positive (concave) effect from experience with NT derived in Section 4.2.:

$$0.021\ ANNT - 0.00108\ ANNT\text{-}squared.$$

Computed at the average experience with NT (3.6 years), the effect adds another 4.8% to the basic NT effect of an average NT-worker, yielding a total average premium of 9.1% for NT-workers. The concave shape of the NT wage differential suggests a rapidly growing premium for NT users. The maximum occurs after 11 years where experience with NT yields additional 10.7% when compared to NT users with zero experience. However the strong quadratic term suggests that knowledge associated with NT becomes obsolete faster than experience (age) or tenure (where the quadratic terms are -0.00041 and -0.00016, respectively).[2]

The statistical significance of the firm-specific variables introduced in Section 4.4.2. underlines the importance of these variables in the wage equations. For instance, the higher the general skill structure of a firm, the higher is the individual wage (other things equal). This effect is particularly strong for firms that have a large share of managers, professionals and technicians. A straightforward interpretation is that the individual quality and productivity of a worker varies with the general skill structure because of knowledge spillovers and the complexity of the used production techniques. A different interpretation is that a higher skill structure causes better individual training: For French manufacturing industries, Delame and Kramarz (1993) show that firms' individual training expenses (training expenses/wage bill) are mainly explained by the proportion of engineers and technicians.

---

**1** Column (2) deviates from column (3) by the missing experience (age) variable.

**2** Note, however, that calulating the impact of experience with NT is based on observations which mainly range between 0 and 10 years, so that reasoning about experience for more than (say) 10 years is based on pure extrapolation, not on direct statistical inference.

*Table 4.3.:* New technologies and wages in a cross-section

Dependent variable: ln (monthly wage)

| Independent Variable | (1) Total | (2) Total | (3) Total | (4) Skilled blue collar workers | (5) Un-skilled blue collar workers | (6) Clerks | (7) Middle-level professional |
|---|---|---|---|---|---|---|---|
| Intercept | 8.141<br>(0.053) | 8.421<br>(0.097) | 8.222<br>(0.096) | 8.336<br>(0.184) | 7.919<br>(0.193) | 8.306<br>(0.240) | 7.696<br>(0.348) |
| Uses new technologies (NT) at work (1 = yes): | | | | | | | |
| Computer-based NT with high autonomy | 0.049<br>(0.006) | 0.043<br>(0.009) | 0.042<br>(0.009) | 0.074<br>(0.017) | 0.128<br>(0.030) | 0.029<br>(0.021) | -0.021<br>(0.036) |
| Computer-based NT with average autonomy | -0.013<br>(0.008) | -0.025<br>(0.011) | -0.028<br>(0.011) | 0.031<br>(0.018) | -0.026<br>(0.023) | -0.034<br>(0.031) | 0.046<br>(0.051) |
| Production-based NT with low autonomy | 0.003<br>(0.012) | -0.034<br>(0.015) | -0.027<br>(0.015) | 0.008<br>(0.018) | -0.027<br>(0.016) | -0.042<br>(0.099) | -0.294<br>(0.172) |
| Number of workers sharing the same superior: (1 = yes) | | | | | | | |
| 1-4 | -0.027<br>(0.005) | -0.016<br>(0.008) | -0.013<br>(0.008) | -0.026<br>(0.013) | 0.044<br>(0.015) | -0.015<br>(0.018) | 0.061<br>(0.036) |
| More than 49 | 0.020<br>(0.007) | 0.038<br>(0.010) | 0.038<br>(0.010) | -0.017<br>(0.016) | 0.014<br>(0.016) | 0.059<br>(0.032) | 0.196<br>(0.056) |
| Sex (1 = male) | 0.149<br>(0.006) | 0.158<br>(0.009) | 0.158<br>(0.009) | 0.109<br>(0.018) | 0.159<br>(0.014) | 0.127<br>(0.021) | 0.239<br>(0.033) |
| Tenure | 0.010<br>(0.001) | 0.020<br>(0.001) | 0.010<br>(0.001) | 0.006<br>(0.002) | 0.023<br>(0.002) | 0.006<br>(0.004) | 0.026<br>(0.006) |
| Tenure-squared *100 | -0.011<br>(0.002) | -0.038<br>(0.004) | -0.016<br>(0.004) | -0.003<br>(0.006) | -0.059<br>(0.008) | 0.009<br>(0.012) | -0.041<br>(0.016) |
| Experience with NT | 0.013<br>(0.002) | 0.021<br>(0.003) | 0.021<br>(0.003) | 0.005<br>(0.005) | 0.020<br>(0.005) | 0.038<br>(0.008) | -0.018<br>(0.014) |
| (Experience with NT)-squared *100 | -0.058<br>(0.010) | -0.106<br>(0.019) | -0.108<br>(0.018) | -0.046<br>(0.036) | -0.113<br>(0.034) | -0.184<br>(0.063) | 0.306<br>(0.106) |
| Experience | 0.032<br>(0.001) | - | 0.024<br>(0.002) | 0.017<br>(0.003) | 0.013<br>(0.003) | 0.033<br>(0.005) | 0.050<br>(0.009) |
| Experience-squared *100 | -0.053<br>(0.002) | - | -0.041<br>(0.003) | -0.032<br>(0.005) | -0.023<br>(0.006) | -0.056<br>(0.009) | -0.084<br>(0.017) |

*Table 4.3.* (continued)

| Independent Variable | Total a) | Total b) | Total c) | Skilled blue collar workers | Un-skilled blue collar workers | Clerks | Middle-level professional |
|---|---|---|---|---|---|---|---|
| **Norms of production (1 = yes):** | | | | | | | |
| Norms induced by used machines | 0.003 (0.013) | 0.021 (0.015) | 0.024 (0.014) | 0.003 (0.018) | 0.061 (0.018) | -0.005 (0.061) | -0.391 (0.134) |
| Tolerated delay: 1 hour - 1 day | -0.007 (0.006) | 0.003 (0.008) | 0.006 (0.008) | -0.004 (0.012) | 0.017 (0.014) | -0.081 (0.022) | -0.011 (0.042) |
| Tolerated delay: more than one day | 0.028 (0.007) | 0.039 (0.009) | 0.038 (0.009) | 0.036 (0.015) | 0.060 (0.022) | -0.003 (0.024) | 0.033 (0.035) |
| Quality norms | 0.011 (0.007) | 0.013 (0.008) | 0.013 (0.008) | 0.024 (0.011) | 0.021 (0.014) | -0.029 (0.033) | -0.058 (0.040) |
| **Working-time schedule (1 = yes):** | | | | | | | |
| 1 shift (1 x 8 hours) | - | - | - | -0.050 (0.014) | -0.038 (0.018) | - | - |
| 2 shifts (2 x 8 hours) | 0.039 (0.011) | 0.005 (0.012) | 0.012 (0.012) | -0.053 (0.018) | -0.048 (0.022) | - | - |
| 3 shifts (3 x 8 hours) | 0.095 (0.014) | 0.114 (0.017) | 0.110 (0.016) | 0.072 (0.024) | 0.003 (0.027) | - | - |
| Varying, firm determined | 0.035 (0.006) | 0.056 (0.012) | 0.067 (0.012) | - | - | 0.032 (0.036) | 0.245 (0.068) |
| A la carte | 0.028 (0.010) | 0.024 (0.013) | 0.025 (0.013) | - | - | -0.001 (0.023) | 0.041 (0.042) |
| Varying, individual choice | 0.088 (0.008) | 0.155 (0.011) | 0.140 (0.011) | - | - | 0.127 (0.042) | 0.280 (0.038) |
| Firm characteristics: | | | | | | | |
| Number of workers *100 | - | 0.066 (0.032) | 0.056 (0.032) | 0.210 (0.058) | 0.017 (0.060) | -0.050 (0.100) | -0.082 (0.164) |
| Share of skilled workers | - | 0.086 (0.022) | 0.091 (0.022) | 0.412 (0.036) | 0.031 (0.040) | -0.065 (0.072) | -0.006 (0.148) |
| Share of managers, technicians and professionals | - | 0.378 (0.025) | 0.367 (0.024) | 0.295 (0.042) | 0.313 (0.062) | 0.108 (0.065) | 0.599 (0.122) |
| Profits/assets | - | 0.192 (0.030) | 0.193 (0.029) | 0.143 (0.040) | 0.134 (0.051) | 0.412 (0.094) | 0.330 (0.144) |
| Total assets $*10^6$ | - | -0.234 (0.146) | -0.225 (0.143) | -2.481 (1.234) | -0.086 (0.441) | -0.265 (0.221) | -0.465 (0.400) |
| Export ratio | - | 0.042 (0.020) | 0.041 (0.019) | 0.060 (0.034) | 0.059 (0.030) | 0.299 (0.042) | 0.089 (0.087) |

*Table 4.3.* (continued)

| Independent Variable | Total a) | Total b) | Total c) | Skilled blue collar workers | Unskilled blue collar workers | Clerks | Middle-level professional |
|---|---|---|---|---|---|---|---|
| Number of observations | 15384 | 3648 | 3648 | 974 | 720 | 480 | 288 |
| Number of occupational groups | 9 | 7 | 7 | - | - | - | - |
| Number of sectoral groups | 38 | 14 | 14 | 11 | 11 | 11 | 11 |
| Number of educational groups | 7 | 7 | 7 | 5 | 5 | 5 | 7 |
| McFadden's Pseudo-$R^2$ | 0.238 | 0.309 | 0.316 | 0.299 | 0.161 | 0.249 | 0.258 |

*Notes*: Standard errors are presented in parentheses. All regressions include marital status, a regional dummy ("Ile de France") and a dummy for part-time work.
*Sources:* Total, a): French Labor Force Survey 1987, INSEE (Enquête Emploi 1987); all other columns: merged samples with BIC-EAE and ESE.

Other interesting results are given by the positive influence of profits (profits/assets) and exports. These effects are stable across cross-sectional estimates. Thus, firms that are confronted with international competition in their markets may have to reward their workers in order to improve quality, for instance. The positive impact of the rate of profit can be seen as an efficiency wage argument: Pay more to improve profits - or in terms of a profit-sharing device - profits are shared with workers through a "participation" or "intéressement" procedure (see Cahuc-Dormont (1992)) that is well developed in France.

Table 4.3. (columns (1), (2) and (3)) show the global impact of supervision and norms of production on pay. When many workers (50 and more) share the same superior, they get paid better. On the contrary, when this number is less than 5, the impact is strongly negative. If monitoring costs are high when many workers have only one superior, the result shows that firms implement efficiency wages.

The effect of production do not give rise to clearcut interpretations. Workers with long delays of production are better paid other things equal. When delays are long, norms cannot be precise, and monitoring costs (for effort) are likely to be high. This confirms efficiency-wage arguments. Another interpretation goes along other lines: Long delays are proofs of task complexity that must be rewarded rewarded. In contrast, paying attention to quality norms and norms induced by used machines does not yield any bonus.

Remaining standard variables produce standard results. Working more than one regular shift causes a premium, experience and tenure have concave time profiles, and the size of the firm maintains its positive influence on wages despite several variables which are potential substitutes of the size effect.

### 4.4.4. The impact of new technologies on occupational wages

The same type of analysis has been performed by main occupational groups (Table 4.3., columns (4) - (7)). More detailed results can be found in Appendix A4.III.

Even though very few individuals receive explicit premia or bonuses when they use modern NT (see Table C5, Appendix), blue-collar (skilled or unskilled) workers receive a particularly high bonus if they work with *T1*. The bonus vanishes (becomes insignificant) for clerks and professionals at an intermediate level. Evidently, the use of new technologies is part of today's normal definition of these jobs. Appendix A4.III, Tables C12 and C13 confirm the same result for the occupational groups "managers, engineers, professionals" and technicians. One may conclude that use of computer-related NT with high autonmy (*T1)* leads to a bonus (other things equal) for occupational groups with a relatively *low* level of education, where NT abilities are still rare and demand for a higher wage.

Put differently, the advantage of using NT leaving high autonomy to their users decreases when pay increases with general education (from unskilled blue collar workers to clerks and to managers, engineers and professionals). Low-skilled workers using NT are very distinguished from their fellow low-skilled workers. Furthermore, unskilled workers and clerks receive an additional wage premium related to *experience* with NT. In contrast, employees who are high in the hierarchy do not get any extra advantage from NT use; it is part of their job.

Most effects of firm-specific variables observed at the aggregate level are confirmed at the occupational level. However, it appears that clerks benefit the most from high rates of profit or export and that unskilled blue-collar workers benefit the least from good performances of their firms. These two results seem to show that the bargaining interpretation (Currie and McConnel ,1992) is not the preferred explanation especially if one believes that negotiations are active mostly in manufacturing industries (where most unskilled workers are employed). On the other hand, the dataset includes many banks and insurance companies where unions are sometimes more active than in manufacturing companies.

In general, results are in accordance with efficiency wage theories, at least for the groups of skilled and unskilled workers. Table 4.3. shows the distinctive role of norms of production and hierarchy of skilled versus unskilled blue collar workers. Only unskilled workers benefit from norms induced by machines. From what is known of work organization, such norms and corresponding rewards must be seen in the context with piece-rate (or easy monitoring) contracts (see Brown, 1992). On the other hand, both types of workers benefit from long delays, cases where efficiency wages may be useful.

Influence of hierarchy offers another source of different wage determination for skilled and unskilled blue collar workers: Smaller groups of skilled blue collar workers sharing the same superior receive lower wages than workers organized in large groups (which again confirms the monitoring argument of efficiency wage theory), whereas the opposite is true for unskilled blue collar workers.[1] Evidently, it makes no sense to pay efficiency wages for unskilled blue collar workers. If they work in large groups, monitoring is relatively inexpensive since they work in terms of piece-rates (which is rewarded via extra payments for quality norms and for norms dictated by machines, see above).

## 4.4.5. Mismatch related to new-technology use

Economic theory predicts that the presence of new technologies leads to mismatched workers so that mobility will improve the match. This, in turn, causes wages of well matched NT-workers to exceed those of mismatched NT-workers. Thus, it can be argued that workers in high-wage groups should have a better match (lower mismatch) with NT-job requirements than low-wage groups (see Section 4.2.).

In the following, this hypothesis is analysed using the Appendix of the French labour force survey (TOTTO). "Mismatch" is defined as an indicator variable based on the survey question "Does your job correspond with your training?" ("Votre emploi correspond-il à votre formation?"). If people respond "yes" with respect to the survey categories "other training/education needed" or "better training/education needed", then "mismatch" is 1, if not, "mismatch" is 0.

Table 4.4. presents a Probit estimation, where "mismatch" is related to the use of new technologies (*T1* - *T3*), education, working-time schedule, region, sex, experience, tenure, experience with NT, occupation, size and sectoral affiliation. Corresponding to the mismatch-wage hypothesis of Section 4.2., two relatively homogeneous low and high salary groups are considered: a) 4500-5000 FF (1878 observations), b) 9000-10,000 FF (785 observations).

---

1 The monitoring argument also holds for clerks: Larger groups are better paid than small groups (see Table 4.3., column (6)).

As predicted, low-wage groups reveal a mismatch when workers work with new technologies. This also holds for NT with low autonomy (*T3*), where the sign is positive though only weakly significant. On the contrary, mismatch in the high-wage group (columns (3) and (4)) does not reveal any significant difference between new-technology jobs and conventional positions.

If one goes further into detail, some interesting observations can be made. Women seem to be better matched than men. Moreover, column (4) shows that experienced male NT-workers ($ANNT > 3$) reveal a higher mismatch than experienced female NT-workers. These observations lead us to perform separate estimations for men and women (see columns (5) and (6)). The results will be explained below. With respect to occupational groups, salespersons (only considered in the low-wage group, there are too few observed salespersons in the high-wage group) are significantly lower matched than skilled blue-collar workers (which is the reference group), whereas a good match can be observed for direct personal service.[1] Finally, there is no evidence that mismatch is related to the size of the firm (as wages are).

Separating the sample into men and women reveals some interesting differences. Though both men and women share the result that computer-related use of NT with high autonomy is accompanied by higher mismatch than in the case of conventional jobs, the gap between *T1* jobs and conventional jobs is higher for men (using the result of the constant, for instance, we obtain 0.21/0.743=0.28 versus 0.13/596=0.22). Moreover, there is an additional source of mismatch that grows with the duration of NT use, and it grows more quickly for men: The coefficient of "experience with NT" is higher for men. Evidently, women accept the use of new technologies more easily as men. One may argue that this simply reflects the fact that our sample focuses on "light" new technologies that are more widely used in workplaces typically hold by women, such as secretary jobs. However, a look at the *high-wage* category in Table 4.4., column (4), forbids this kind of reasoning: Here, experienced male NT workers report a higher mismatch than experienced female NT workers.

---

1 Additional results for different occupational groups and overall samples can be found in Appendix A4.III, Table C15. Blue-collar workers (both skilled and unskilled) have high and significant contributions to mismatch, whereas "middle-level professionals" have a non-significant impact. These results confirm the high-wage/low-wage comparison made in Table 4.4.

*Table 4.4.:* Explaining mismatch for selected subsamples: Salary groups, women and men

Dependent variable: "*Mismatch*" (1 = yes)

| Independent variable | (1) Salary: 4500-5000 (FF per month) | (2) Salary: 4500-5000 (FF per month) | (3) Salary: 9000-10000 (FF per month) | (4) Salary: 9000-10000 (FF per month) | (5) Women | (6) Men |
|---|---|---|---|---|---|---|
| Intercept | -0.939<br>(0.193) | -0.935<br>(0.194) | -1.047<br>(0.339) | -1.045<br>(0.342) | -0.569<br>(0.115) | -0.743<br>(0.068) |
| Computer-based NT use with high autonomy (1 = yes) | 0.308<br>(0.113) | 0.301<br>(0.101) | 0.084<br>(0.131) | 0.081<br>(0.120) | 0.126<br>(0.048) | 0.212<br>(0.040) |
| Use of NT with average autonomy (1 = yes) | 0.084<br>(0.139) | 0.069<br>(0.133) | -0.122<br>(0.185) | -0.126<br>(0.184) | 0.020<br>(0.064) | -0.049<br>(0.050) |
| Use of NT with low autonomy (1 = yes) | 0.286<br>(0.151) | 0.277<br>(0.149) | -0.210<br>(0.338) | -0.256<br>(0.339) | -0.024<br>(0.104) | 0.095<br>(0.062) |
| Educational degree (1 = yes): | | | | | | |
| None | -0.161<br>(0.126) | -0.159<br>(0.126) | 0.122<br>(0.248) | 0.134<br>(0.247) | -0.035<br>(0.065) | 0.063<br>(0.054) |
| Elementary school | 0.085<br>(0.139) | 0.084<br>(0.128) | 0.395<br>(0.206) | 0.401<br>(0.206) | 0.043<br>(0.062) | 0.167<br>(0.056) |
| Vocational technical school | -0.031<br>(0.113) | -0.030<br>(0.113) | 0.287<br>(0.169) | 0.306<br>(0.168) | 0.114<br>(0.052) | 0.168<br>(0.047) |
| Junior high school | 0.441<br>(0.152) | 0.440<br>(0.152) | 0.308<br>(0.218) | 0.348<br>(0.217) | 0.282<br>(0.066) | 0.236<br>(0.064) |
| Technical college | -0.427<br>(0.285) | -0.434<br>(0.286) | -0.701<br>(0.219) | -0.714<br>(0.219) | -0.374<br>(0.083) | -0.388<br>(0.072) |
| University | -0.243<br>(0.316) | -0.217<br>(0.316) | -0.448<br>(0.225) | -0.431<br>(0.225) | -0.355<br>(0.101) | -0.552<br>(0.079) |
| Working-time dummies (1 = yes): | | | | | | |
| Fixed, all day | - | - | - | - | - | - |
| 2 shifts (2 x 8 hours) | 0.150<br>(0.131) | 0.148<br>(0.131) | -0.090<br>(0.314) | -0.068<br>(0.314) | 0.151<br>(0.080) | 0.113<br>(0.060) |
| 3 shifts (3 x 8 hours) | 0.120<br>(0.203) | 0.111<br>(0.203) | 0.718<br>(0.286) | 0.743<br>(0.287) | -0.079<br>(0.179) | 0.266<br>(0.069) |
| Varying, firm determined | -0.007<br>(0.103) | -0.009<br>(0.103) | 0.253<br>(0.161) | 0.276<br>(0.161) | 0.060<br>(0.050) | 0.213<br>(0.042) |
| A la carte | 0.207<br>(0.189) | 0.191<br>(0.190) | 0.563<br>(0.198) | 0.557<br>(0.200) | 0.111<br>(0.067) | 0.222<br>(0.069) |
| Varying, individual choice | 0.153<br>(0.167) | 0.147<br>(0.167) | 0.334<br>(0.248) | 0.317<br>(0.248) | 0.105<br>(0.066) | 0.220<br>(0.048) |

Table 4.4. (continued)

| Independent variable | (1) Salary: 4500-5000 (FF per month) | (2) Salary: 4500-5000 (FF per month) | (3) Salary: 9000-10000 (FF per month) | (4) Salary: 9000-10000 (FF per month) | (5) Women | (6) Men |
|---|---|---|---|---|---|---|
| Lives in "Ile de France" (1 = yes) | 0.147 (0.088) | 0.147 (0.088) | 0.371 (0.117) | 0.381 (0.118) | 0.132 (0.040) | 0.094 (0.034) |
| Sex (1 = male) | 0.299 (0.087) | 0.295 (0.089) | 0.365 (0.146) | 0.304 (0.172) | - | - |
| Single (1 = yes) | -0.080 (0.107) | -0.082 (0.128) | -0.222 (0.182) | -0.217 (0.182) | -0.068 (0.053) | -0.131 (0.050) |
| Part-time (1 = yes) | 0.461 (0.228) | 0.452 (0.228) | - | - | -0.088 (0.050) | -0.108 (0.103) |
| Experience | 0.001 (0.013) | 0.002 (0.013) | -0.020 (0.019) | -0.020 (0.019) | -0.012 (0.006) | -0.005 (0.005) |
| $(\text{Experience})^2$ *100 | -0.049 (0.047) | -0.051 (0.047) | 0.035 (0.051) | 0.038 (0.051) | 0.033 (0.018) | -0.006 (0.014) |
| Experience with NT | -0.021 (0.041) | - | -0.002 (0.041) | - | 0.028 (0.016) | 0.022 (0.011) |
| $(\text{Experience with NT})^2$ *100 | -0.030 (0.328) | - | 0.287 (0.263) | | -0.158 (0.116) | -0.082 (0.066) |
| Experienced male NT worker (1 = yes) | - | -0.163 (0.175) | - | 0.288 (0.147) | - | - |
| Experienced female NT worker (1 = yes) | - | -0.186 (0.157) | - | 0.125 (0.235) | - | - |
| Occupation: | | | | | | |
| Managers, engineers, professionals | - | - | 0.331 (0.248) | 0.317 (0.248) | 0.047 (0.138) | 0.351 (0.071) |
| Managers, engineers, professionals / CS | - | - | -0.346 (0.296) | -0.382 (0.297) | -0.546 (0.155) | -0.283 (0.098) |
| Middle level professionals | -0.146 (0.243) | -0.154 (0.243) | 0.182 (0.233) | 0.173 (0.233) | 0.085 (0.109) | 0.472 (0.068) |
| Middle level professionals / CS | 0.027 (0.193) | 0.028 (0.193) | -0.265 (0.254) | -0.264 (0.253) | -0.576 (0.107) | 0.003 (0.070) |
| Technicians | -0.180 (0.324) | -0.172 (0.324) | -0.031 (0.232) | -0.027 (0.232) | -0.077 (0.165) | 0.162 (0.062) |
| Technical foremen | 0.656 (0.587) | 0.663 (0.587) | 0.098 (0.224) | 0.113 (0.224) | 0.434 (0.236) | 0.148 (0.064) |

Table 4.4. (continued)

| Independent variable | (1) Salary: 4500-5000 (FF per month) | (2) Salary: 4500-5000 (FF per month) | (3) Salary: 9000-10000 (FF per month) | (4) Salary: 9000-10000 (FF per month) | (5) Women | (6) Men |
|---|---|---|---|---|---|---|
| Clerks | -0.001 (0.142) | -0.005 (0.142) | 0.040 (0.277) | 0.031 (0.278) | -0.128 (0.094) | 0.138 (0.085) |
| Clerks / CS | 0.033 (0.133) | 0.033 (0.132) | 0.342 (0.289) | 0.331 (0.289) | -0.230 (0.097) | 0.411 (0.056) |
| Sales workers | 0.601 (0.176) | 0.603 (0.176) | - | - | 0.152 (0.112) | 0.339 (0.119) |
| Direct personal service | -0.622 (0.250) | -0.625 (0.250) | - | - | -0.524 (0.106) | -0.134 (0.127) |
| Unskilled blue collar workers | -0.036 (0.092) | -0.038 (0.092) | 0.847 (0.840) | 0.838 (0.840) | -0.369 (0.092) | -0.032 (0.043) |
| Size dummies (number of workers; 1 = yes): | | | | | | |
| 0-49 | -0.006 (0.093) | -0.011 (0.093) | -0.023 (0.148) | -0.034 (0.147) | -0.010 (0.049) | -0.097 (0.040) |
| 50-499 | 0.059 (0.106) | 0.054 (0.106) | -0.117 (0.179) | -0.138 (0.179) | 0.004 (0.057) | -0.062 (0.045) |
| Number of sectoral groups | 11 | 11 | 11 | 11 | 12 | 12 |
| Number of observations | 1878 | 1878 | 785 | 785 | 7493 | 9691 |
| Number of cases with "event = 1" | 532 | 532 | 260 | 260 | 1805 | 3110 |
| McFadden's Pseudo $R^2$ | 0.053 | 0.053 | 0.167 | 0.165 | 0.068 | 0.059 |

*Notes*: Probit estimates; standard errors are presented in parentheses.
CS = civil servants.
*Source:* French Labour Force Survey 1987, INSEE (Enquête Emploi 1987).

# 4.5. Wages and new technologies: Evidence from panel data

## 4.5.1. Construction of panel data

Relying on the data sources described in Section 4.3., I construct a panel data set. It is based on the longitudinal version of the French labour force survey, the panel of related firms for the construction of a merged panel data set for which each individual is surveyed in 1985, 1986 and 1987, and the supplement of the 1987 labour force survey on the use of a well defined NT (a precisely defined machine). The latter is only available for 1987. From the backward looking information about "experience with NT", the first year of NT use can be calculated, and, hence, a change from conventional techniques to NT can be detected. However, back-casting *T1, T2* and *T3* of preceding years in this way cannot be perfectly correct, since there is no information about potential switches from NT to conventional techniques (in 1987, there is no survey question such as "experience with No-NT").

Note that this is a problem with respect to a direct test of the matching model derived in Section 4.2., which predicts that low-ability workers in NT jobs have to change to conventional jobs. Again, in terms of the theoretical model, the panel constructed in the way described above only contains information about the change of high-ability workers from conventional jobs to new technology positions. What happens to the "NT versus No-NT" wage differential? Some (unknown) number of workers changed from NT jobs to conventional jobs (they are surveyed as conventional workers in 1987), hence they might have received (higher) NT wages in 1985 and 1986.[1] However, during these years they are counted as conventional workers. This might render the conventional wage too high. The wage differential would be underestimated.

The potential bias of "experience with NT" is difficult to predict in the sense of theoretical reasoning. On the one hand, since the true conventional-job wage of the panel data might be smaller than conjectured in 1985/86, true wage increases due to changes to NT and subsequent NT experience might be larger than estimated. On the other hand, the true contribution of general experience and tenure on conventional-job wages might be underestimated, since potentially unobserved changes from a NT job to a No-NT job cause falling wages, that are mistakenly related to No-NT wage changes, since these workers are counted as No-NT throughout 1985 to 1987. Hence, *if* the impact from global experience

---

**1** Note that the matching model predicts a NT-wage in the first period (see equation (4.6) ) which is higher than conventional wages in the first and second period.

and tenure are underestimated, then a growing differential between wage growth due to conventional experience and wage growth due to NT experience might be an artifact of the underestimated parameter on conventional experience.

## 4.5.2. The impact of new technologies on wages: Fixed-effect modelling

Since the number of NT-users is growing, it is reasonable to presume that most switches are from No-NT to NT, so that mobility in this direction may be the dominating one in the data set. Taking into account all the problems addressed in Section 4.5.1., Table 4.5. presents the estimates of a fixed-effect model. These estimates are based on ordinary least-squares, where the ordered wage level of cross-sectional regressions is replaced by the average of (the very detailed) wage categories. Comparisons of the two types of regression techniques ordered logit and OLS show that these methods produce almost identical results.

Fixed-effect estimation identifies changing realizations of modelled variables. Before discussing results in detail, one may wonder whether identification of the effect of NT is possible. The answer is affirmative at least for *T1* of the original panel, where 5.8% of the workers change their status from "No-NT" (in 1985 or 1986) to NT (in 1987). The answer is less clear for the remaining categories, where only smaller percentages are observable (2.2% change from No-NT to *T2*, for instance). The merged panel provides 5.3% changes from No-NT to *T1*, 2.5% changes from No-NT to *T2* and 2.0% changes from No-NT to *T3*. Due to smaller samples in the merged panel case, it should be noted that these percentages represent a relatively small number of observations: 144, 69 and 54, respectively.

At a glance, both panels, with and without firm-specific variables, confirm the result of time-*invariant* unobserved abilities which have led to significant NT effects in cross-sectional results: All parameter estimates on *T1, T2* and *T3* become insignificant. This would partly contradict the matching model in 4.2., that allows for some unobserved ability, but predicts that unobserved ability is time-*variant*, which would lead to a positive NT-parameter in fixed-effect estimations (see Section 4.2. for details). Unfortunately, however, the conclusion can only be ambigous. On the one hand, the missing impact of NT might be due to a truely time-invariant, unmeasured ability, on the other hand it might be the result of underestimation as described above.

Results concerning "experience with NT" are in accordance with the predicted result that improved matching leads to a growing wage differential between NT-workers and workers at conventional work-places. "Experience with NT" remains significant (and concave) for the original (non-merged) panel, whereas the effect is insignificant in the merged panel. Note, however, that the original sample seems to be more reliable due to a larger (relative and absolute) number of mobility events. Moreover, the probability of overestimating the true effect of "experience with NT" due to underestimating wage changes due to general experience seems to be small, since the estimated parameter of general experience is even higher than for the cross-sectional result in Table 4.3. (in fact, the now higher impact of "experience" compensates the vanishing influence of "tenure"). Hence, a wage differential which might be even higher than estimated is in fact very likely since the second potential bias arising from underestimation (see above) cannot be excluded.

*Table 4.5.:* New technologies and wages in fixed-effect panel estimations

Dependent variable: ln (monthly wage)

| Independent Variable | Original panel | Merged panel |
|---|---|---|
| Uses new technologies (NT) at work (1 = yes): | | |
| Computer-based NT with high autonomy | 0.006<br>(0.008) | 0.002<br>(0.015) |
| Computer-based NT with average autonomy | 0.006<br>(0.013) | 0.007<br>(0.022) |
| Production-based NT with low autonomy | -0.047<br>(0.025) | 0.012<br>(0.037) |
| Lives "Ile de France" | 0.004<br>(0.024) | 0.045<br>(0.037) |
| Part-time | -0.265<br>(0.009) | -0.403<br>(0.028) |
| Tenure | 0.0003<br>(0.001) | 0.005<br>(0.002) |
| Tenure-squared *100 | 0.004<br>(0.003) | -0.015<br>(0.007) |
| Experience with NT | 0.007<br>(0.003) | -0.003<br>(0.005) |
| (Experience with NT)-squared *100 | -0.042<br>(0.021) | 0.010<br>(0.035) |
| Experience | 0.039<br>(0.009) | 0.046<br>(0.011) |
| Experience-squared *100 | -0.060<br>(0.005) | -0.076<br>(0.010) |

*Table 4.5.* (continued)

| Dependent variable: ln (monthly wage) | | |
|---|---|---|
| Independent Variable | Original panel | Merged panel |
| **Size of enterprise** | | |
| 0-49 | 0.006<br>(0.007) | - |
| 50-499 | 0.022<br>(0.009) | - |
| **Firm characteristics:** | | |
| Number of workers *100 | - | 0.344<br>(0.189) |
| Share of skilled workers | - | -0.126<br>(0.055) |
| Share of managers, technicians and professionals | - | -0.087<br>(0.068) |
| Profits/assets | - | -0.017<br>(0.023) |
| Total assets *$10^6$ | - | 0.404<br>(0.211) |
| Export ratio | - | 0.00005<br>(0.00002) |
| Number of observations | 30228 | 8118 |
| Number of occupational groups | 12 | 9 |
| Number of sectoral groups | 38 | 14 |
| Number of educational groups | 7 | - |
| $R^2$ | 0.942 | 0.943 |

*Notes*: Standard errors are presented in parentheses. The fixed-effect model is based on least-squares estimators.
*Sources:* French Labor Force Survey 1987, INSEE (Enquête Emploi 1987), BIC-EAE and ESE.

Finally, firm-specific variables have very little impact on the individual wage once fixed effects are introduced. Most of the coefficients are not significantly different from zero. In particular, the influence of the share of managers, technicians and professionals disappears. This is reasonable because such a variable does not change much during a three year period. The same type of arguments can be made for almost all the variables that were significant in Table 4.3 and become insignificant in Table 4.5. However, increases in the export ratio maintain their positive, though small, influence on individual wages.

## 4.6. Concluding remarks

This chapter analyses the matching of new-technology related abilities with new-technology jobs. The theoretical framework provides a matching model with time-variant unmeasured abilities. It predicts higher wages for new-technology jobs, wage increases (decreases) of workers who change from conventional (new-technology) jobs to new-technology (conventional) jobs, a match of workers' abilities with new-technology requirements that is better in high-wage groups than in low-wage groups, and a wage-differential between conventional jobs and new-technology jobs that grows with the duration of new-technology experience.

The econometric test of these hypotheses is based on a unique data-set which combines data on worker's individual characteristics with corresponding information about the worker's employer. These data allow testing additional hypotheses related to efficiency wages, gift-exchange, profit sharing and other wage determinants more directly than in standard wage equations.

The empirical results confirm the existence of a positive wage premium for NT use paid to low-skilled (low-wage) workers and the better quality of matching in high-wage groups. Results based on panel data reveal evidence in favour of a wage gap between conventional and new-technology workers that grows with new-technology experience. The predicted wage change of people who change their job cannot be found in the data. Though the latter result would be evidence in favour of simple (time-invariant) unmeasured ability models, all other results confirm the view that workers with unmeasured high abilities will be allocated in better paid new-technology positions, while workers with poor abilities will be matched with conventional work places.

Regarding Krueger's (1993) widely discussed result that computer-related jobs are better paid than comparable jobs done conventionally, the chapter gives an affirmative answer only for a subgroup of workers. After analyzing a broader and more general group of new technologies, two main conclusions can be drawn: A positive and significant wage differential exists for workers with relatively low skills (blue-collar workers), and it exists for workers who operate computer-related new technologies with high autonomy. The use of computer-related technologies within the group of managers, professionals etc., however, seems to be taken for granted.

## Appendix A4.I.: Descriptive statistics

*Table C1:* Descriptive statistics of the French labour-force survey

| Variable Name | Variable description | Mean (Std. Dev.) |
|---|---|---|
| T1 | Dummy for workers using computer-based NT with high autonomy ("use as a main task")[1] | 0.287 (0.453) |
| T2 | Dummy for workers using computer-based NT with average autonomy ("use as a main task")[1] | 0.080 (0.272) |
| T3 | Dummy for workers using production-based NT with low autonomy ("use as a main task")[1] | 0.045 (0.207) |
| ILE | Living in "Ile de France" (Paris and surroundings), dummy variable, 1 =yes | 0.225 (0.418) |
| SEX | Sex, 1 = male, 0 = female | 0.563 (0.496) |
| PARTIEL | Part-time working, dummy, 1 =yes | 0.080 (0.271) |
| SINGLE | Marital status = single, dummy, 1 =yes | 0.101 (0.301) |
| ANCA1 | Tenure, in years | 10.26 (8.75) |
| ANCA2 | ANCA1-squared | 181.01 (274.2) |
| ANNT | Experiencc of working with NT, in years | 3.64 (3.54) |
| ANNT2 | ANNT-squared | 25.88 (68.11) |
| AGE1 | Experience: Age-14 | 22.28 (10.87) |
| AGE2 | AGE1-squared | 612.01 (539.01) |
| CAD_1 | Imposed production norms: induced by machines (1 =yes) | 0.045 (0.207) |
| CAD_2 | Imposed production norms: Tolerated production delay = one hour - one day (1 =yes) | 0.218 (0.413) |
| CAD_3 | Imposed production norms: Tolerated production delay = more than one day (1 =yes) | 0.148 (0.355) |
| CAD_4 | No well defined production norm (1 =yes) | 0.590 (0.492) |
| QUAL | Quality norms demanded (1 =yes) | 0.145 (0.352) |
| ANT_M | Experienced male NT worker; dummy=1, if ANNT > 3 and SEX = 1 | 0.098 (0.297) |
| ANT_F | Experienced male NT worker; dummy=1, if ANNT > 3 and SEX = 0 | 0.069 (0.253) |

*Table C1:* (continued)

| Variable Name | Variable description | Mean (Std. Dev.) |
|---|---|---|
| TAI1 | Size of enterprise (number of workers): 0 - 49, dummy | 0.601 (0.489) |
| TAI2 | Size of enterprise (number of workers): 50 - 499, dummy | 0.149 (0.356) |
| TAI3 | Size of enterprise (number of workers): 500 or more, dummy | 0.244 (0.430) |

*Notes:* Source: INSEE, Enquête Emploi, 1987 (French labour force survey, 1987). The data set of the year 1987 includes questions concerning the use of new technologies (NT) and the organisation of labour ("questionnaire complémentaire sur les techniques et l'orgainsation du travail"). The descriptive statistics are based on the responses of 17184 workers. More descriptions of the data set (educational degree, working-time schedules, occupational groups, sectoral groups, salary groups, detailed decomposition of NT groups) can be found in Tables C3 - C10.
1) Note that the grouping T1 - T3 allows for double counting: The same worker can be captured in more than one category, e.g. if he responds affirmatively both with repect to the use of micro (T1) and with respect to terminal reception (T2) as "main tasks".

*Table C2:* Descriptive statistics of workers' firm-level background.

| Variable Name | Variable description | Mean (Std. Dev.) |
|---|---|---|
| MCAPITR | Mean real capital stock (in 1,000,000 FF, 1980) | 82.20 (359.22) |
| MEBERC | Mean real operating income per unit of capital (in FF, 1980) | 0.090 (0.115) |
| MING | Mean share of workforce comprised of technicians, engineers and managers | 0.296 (0.172) |
| MOQA | Mean share of workforce comprised of skilled labour | 0.485 (0.171) |
| MEFFEC | Mean size of workforce | 735.3 (1605.19) |
| MTEXP | Mean share of sales going to exports | 0.168 (0.210) |

*Notes:* Sources: MCAPITR, MEBERC, MEFFEC and MTEXP come from merging BIC-EAE (Bénéfices Industriel et Commerciaux, Enquête Annuelle sur l'Emploi), MING and MOQA from ESE (Enquête sur la Structure de l'Emploi). They are implemented as means of the years 1978-1987. See also Abowd and Kramarz (1993). 3930 observations are available.

*Table C3:* The sectoral distribution of new technologies

| New technology | Share of NT-worker in sectors |
|---|---|
| Assembly line | Rubber, plastic materials (1.4): 15.1, meat and milk industries (0.9): 13.7, basic chemical products (1.0): 10.8 |
| Terminal: reception (no emission) | Petroleum, natural gas (0.2): 15.8* |
| Terminal: emission (no reception) | Food retailing (2.9): 5.7 |
| Use of listings | Financial units (2.4): 55.2, insurance companies (0.9): 37.9, petroleum, natural gas (0.2): 36.8, electrical and electronic industries (3.1): 32.2 |
| Data entry | Financial units (2.4): 35.5, insurance companies (0.9): 27.3, petroleum, natural gas (0.2): 21.1* |
| Video (supervising) | Petroleum, natural gas (0.2): 13.2* |
| Automatic transportation | Glass industry (0.4): 23.0, milk and meat industries (0.9): 17.2, paper, carton (0.7): 10.4 |
| Text processing | Petroleum, natural gas (0.2): 13.2*, financial units (2.4): 10.4, insurance companies (0.9): 10.6 |
| Minitel | Financial units (2.4): 24.8, telecommunication and mailing (2.8): 19.0, petroleum, natural gas (0.2): 15.8* |
| Micro | Petroleum, natural gas (0.2): 39.5, financial units (2.4): 25.4, electrical and electronic industries (3.1): 23.2 |
| Terminal | Financial units (2.4): 53.3, insurance companies (0.9): 43.5, petroleum, natural gas (0.2): 34.2 |
| Machine tool (with numerical command) | Foundery, metal industry (2.3): 7.5 |
| Robot | Fuel production (0.3): 5.3*, foundery, metal industry (2.3): 4.5; |
| Laser technique | Foundery, metal industry (2.3): 1.3* |
| At least one NT | Financial units (2.4): 82.9, petroleum, natural gas (0.2): 79.0, insurance companies (0.9): 72.1, electrical and electronic industries (3.1): 58.6, parachemical and pharmaceutical industries (1.1): 58.6, telecommunication and mailing (2.8): 54.6,... building industry (7.0): 12.7, agriculture, fishery (1.0): 10.8 |

*Notes:* The table presents sectors which are top ranked with respect to the use of new technologies. The figures (percentage points) are based on "use NT as a main task" (17184 observations); they represent the share of workers of the respective sector working with NT. * denotes entries based on less than 10 observations. In parentheses: the relative size of sector (share of total employment). Source: INSEE, Enquête Emploi, 1987 (French labour force survey, 1987).

*Table C4:* The distribution of wages: A comparison of "new technology" wages and "conventional technology" wages

| New technology | Categories in terms of monthly wages (Francs). <5000 | [5000,8000) | [8000, 15000) | ≥15000 |
|---|---|---|---|---|
| Assembly line | 41.8 | 46.2 | 9.4 | 0.6 |
| Terminal: reception (no emission) | 13.8 | 45.3 | 35.1 | 3.6 |
| Use of listings | 12.5 | 43.5 | 35.0 | 7.5 |
| Terminal: emission (no reception) | 17.4 | 53.4 | 23.6 | 3.9 |
| Data entry | 15.4 | 48.4 | 30.9 | 3.9 |
| Video (supervising) | 6.2 | 40.7 | 46.5 | 4.4 |
| Automatic transportation | 42.1 | 47.3 | 7.4 | 0.0 |
| Text processing | 17.3 | 45.5 | 29.9 | 5.5 |
| Minitel | 14.3 | 41.9 | 33.0 | 7.8 |
| Micro | 10.4 | 43.7 | 35.9 | 8.2 |
| Terminal | 11.7 | 44.8 | 35.7 | 6.4 |
| Machine-tool (with numerical command) | 26.4 | 52.8 | 18.3 | 1.0 |
| Robot | 30.2 | 51.6 | 15.7 | 1.9 |
| Laser technique | 19.3 | 36.8 | 35.1 | 8.8 |
| Other modern technology | 6.2 | 40.7 | 46.5 | 4.4 |
| At least one NT | 19.7 | 46.0 | 27.6 | 4.9 |
| No NT (conventional technology only) | 44.1 | 43.2 | 9.8 | 0.8 |
| Total | 32.9 | 44.3 | 18.1 | 2.8 |

*Notes:* The entries are based on 14622 respondents who can be identified as full time workers. The numbers do not sum to 100 per cent due to some non-respondents (total sample: 2.4% missing values). The calculation is based on responses refering to "use NT as main task". Source: INSEE, Enquête Emploi, 1987 (French labour force survey, 1987).

*Table C5*: Percentage share of workers receiving a premium for working with NT

| | |
|---|---|
| Assembly line: 12.1 | Minitel: 0.8 |
| Terminal reception: 2.5 | Micro: 3.0 |
| Terminal emission: 2.5 | Terminal: 4.6 |
| Use of listings: 0.8 | Machine-tool: 11.1 |
| Data entry: 1.4 | Robot: 9.5 |
| Video (supervising): 2.8 | Laser technique: 5.3[1] |
| Text processing: 3.3 | Other modern technology: 3.8 |

*Notes:* 1) The percentage share is based on 6 affirmative responses only. The figures are based on "use NT as a main task" (17184 observations). Source: INSEE, Enquête Emploi, 1987 (French labour force survey, 1987).

*Table C6:* Who is working with "new technologies"? The main socio-professional characteristics.

| New technology | Decomposition of workers using the same NT |
|---|---|
| Assembly line | Unskilled blue collar workers: 41.7, skilled blue collar workers: 36.0 |
| Terminal: Reception only | Clerks: 22.2 |
| Terminal: Emission only | Clerks: 19.7 |
| Use of listings | Clerks: 25.6 |
| Data entry | Clerks: 30.1 |
| Video (supervising) | Medium-level professionals / civil servants:[1] 31.9 |
| Automatic transportation | Unskilled blue collar workers: 50.6, skilled blue collar workers: 36.8 |
| Text processing | Clerks: 42.1 |
| Minitel | Clerks: 23.7<br>Medium-level professionals: 16.9 |
| Micro | Clerks: 23.7, managers, engineers, professionals: 14.6 |
| Terminal | Clerks: 30.9, managers, engineers, professionals: 15.2 |
| Machine-tool (with numerical command) | Skilled blue collar workers: 52.4, unskilled blue collar workers: 23.6 |
| Robot | Skilled blue collar workers: 45.7, unskilled blue collar workers: 22.5 |
| Laser technique | Skilled blue collar workers: 22.7, technicians: 19.7 |
| At least one NT | Clerks: 20.6, skilled blue collar workers: 12.0, medium-ranked professionals / civil servants:[1] 10.7 |
| No NT (conventional technology only) | Skilled blue collar workers: 27.2, unskilled blue collar workers: 18.1 |
| Total | Skilled blue collar workers: 20.5, unskilled blue collar workers: 13.6,<br>clerks / civil servants : 12.7, clerks: 10.5, medium-level professionals / civil servants:[1] 10.2 |

*Notes:* The table reads as follows: For each group of NT-workers given in the first column, x% belong to the socio-professional group y (subset of workers using the same NT = 100%). The figures (percentage points) are based on "use NT as a main task" (17184 observations).

1) The exact phrasing is "intermediate positions in schooling, health care, public sector, and related professional groups"; though some unknown part of the group is non-public, I nevertheless consider "civil servant" to be the most adequate characterization.

Source: INSEE, Enquête Emploi, 1987 (French labour force survey, 1987).

*Table C7:* New technologies and size of enterprises.

| New technology | Size category (number of workers) [0, 99] | [100, 999] | >=1000 |
|---|---|---|---|
| Assembly line | 35.8 | 27.7 | 36.5 |
| Terminal: Reception only | 26.9 | 22.3 | 50.8 |
| Terminal: Emission only | 38.9 | 20.8 | 40.3 |
| Use of listings | 33.5 | 22.5 | 40.0 |
| Data entry | 39.7 | 22.6 | 37.7 |
| Video (supervising) | 38.9 | 17.0 | 44.1 |
| Automatic transportation | 24.9 | 32.8 | 42.3 |
| Text processing | 45.8 | 20.1 | 34.1 |
| Minitel | 50.7 | 17.2 | 32.1 |
| Micro | 43.1 | 19.1 | 37.8 |
| Terminal | 30.1 | 21.7 | 48.2 |
| Machine-tool (with numerical command) | 34.8 | 25.3 | 39.9 |
| Robot | 35.1 | 23.8 | 41.1 |
| Laser technique | 51.1 | 20.0 | 28.9 |
| At least one NT | 40.9 | 21.1 | 38.1 |
| No NT (conventional technology only) | 60.6 | 18.0 | 21.5 |
| Total | 51.9 | 19.2 | 29.0 |

*Notes:* The table presents percentage shares of the size categories in the total number of people using the respective new technology. The figures (percentage points) are based on "use NT as a main task" (12338 observations). Source: INSEE, Enquête Emploi, 1987 (French labour force survey, 1987).

*Table C8:* New-technology workers and their education

| New technology | The decomposition of NT groups with respect to their degree |
|---|---|
| Assembly line | None: 32.3, elementary school: 23.6 |
| Terminal: Reception only | Junior high school: 24.1, vocational technical school: 23.1 |
| Terminal: Emission only | Vocational technical school: 22.7, junior high school: 19.7 |
| Use of listings | Junior high school: 20.9, high school: 20.5, vocational technical school: 18.9 |
| Data entry | Junior high school: 22.9, high school: 22.2 |
| Video (supervising) | University: 24.0, technical college: 17.1 |
| Automatic transportation | None: 36.5, vocational technical school: 25.0 |
| Text processing | Junior high school: 25.2, high school: 20.3 |
| Minitel | Junior high school: 22.9, high school: 20.9 |
| Micro | Junior high school: 19.8, high school: 19.2, vocational technical school: 16.1, university 16.0 |
| Terminal | Junior high school: 23.3, high school: 20.7, vocational technical school: 18.9, university: 12.0 |
| Machine-tool (with numerical command) | Vocational technical school: 36.3, none: 28.3 |

*Table C8:* (continued)

| New technology | The decomposition of NT groups with respect to their degree |
|---|---|
| Robot | None: 32.4, vocational technical school: 31.8 |
| Laser technique | University: 22.7, vocational technical school: 22.7 |
| At least one NT | Vocational technical school: 20.1, junior high school: 19.6, high school: 16.5, none: 12.5, elementary school: 11.4 technical college: 10.1, university: 9.9 |
| No NT (conventional technology only) | None: 31.6, vocational technical school: 23.0, elementary school: 19.2, junior high school: 13.0, high school: 7.0, technical university: 3.1, university: 3.1 |
| Total | None: 23.1, vocational technical school: 21.8, junior high school: 15.9, elementary school: 15.7, high school: 11.2, university: 6.2, technical college: 6.2 |

*Notes:* The table presents percentage the NT workers holding the reported (maximal) degree as a percentage of workers using the same NT (each row = 100%). The figures are based on "use NT as a main task" (17184 observations). Appendix A4.II. gives the exact French titles of reported educational degrees. Source: INSEE, Enquête Emploi, 1987 (French labour force survey, 1987).

*Table C9:* The relative importance of new technologies for different educational groups (decomposition of educational groups)

| New technology | (# NT workers with degree XY)/(all workers with degree XY) |
|---|---|
| Assembly line | Elementary school: 3.2, none: 3.0 |
| Terminal: Reception only | High school: 2.9 |
| Terminal: Emission only | High school: 1.8 |
| Use of listings | Technical college: 29.2, university: 28.5, high school: 26.8 |
| Data entry | High school: 20.7, junior high school: 15.8 |
| Video (supervising) | University: 12.1, technical college: 8.7 |
| Automatic transportation | None: 3.1 |
| Text processing | Technical college: 6.4, high school: 5.6 |
| Minitel | University: 12.4, high school: 11.2 |
| Micro | University: 25.2, technical college: 24.9, high school: 16.7 |
| Terminal | University: 19.5, technical college: 18.9, high school: 18.8 |
| Machine-tool | Vocational technical school: 2.1 |
| Robot | Vocational technical school: 1.5 |
| Laser technique | University: 1.4 |
| At least one NT | Technical college: 58.7, university: 57.3, high school: 53.4 junior high school: 44.7, vocational technical school: 33.3, elementary school: 26.3, none: 19.5 |

*Notes:* The table presents shares of NT workers holding the reported degree in the total number of workers with the respective degree (number of workers having the same degree = 100 %). The figures (percentages shares) are based on "use NT as a main task" (17184 observations). Source: INSEE, Enquête Emploi, 1987 (French labour force survey, 1987).

*Table C10:* The working-time schedule depending on the choice of NT

| New technology | fix, all day[a] | changing: 2 altern.[b] | changing: 3 altern.[c] | changing: n altern.[d] | changing: *à la carte*[e] | changing: ind. choice[f] |
|---|---|---|---|---|---|---|
| Assembly line | 45.1 | 22.3 | 16.3 | 12.5 | 0.8 | 3.0 |
| Terminal reception | 50.5 | 6.4 | 7.1 | 8.7 | 13.5 | 13.8 |
| Terminal emission | 51.7 | 5.4 | 4.9 | 16.3 | 7.9 | 13.8 |
| Use of listings | 54.1 | 2.7 | 1.3 | 7.6 | 14.8 | 20.0 |
| Data entry | 55.7 | 2.7 | 1.1 | 9.4 | 13.6 | 17.5 |
| Video (supervising) | 31.7 | 3.0 | 9.4 | 34.1 | 3.7 | 18.1 |
| Automatic transportation | 48.5 | 27.1 | 14.8 | 6.9 | 1.8 | 0.9 |
| Text processing | 61.5 | 1.1 | 0.9 | 6.0 | 15.3 | 15.1 |
| Minitel | 53.7 | 2.4 | 0.9 | 8.0 | 9.4 | 25.7 |
| Micro | 54.7 | 2.9 | 2.4 | 11.7 | 10.8 | 17.5 |
| Terminal | 53.2 | 3.8 | 2.6 | 8.8 | 17.1 | 14.6 |
| Machine-tool | 48.1 | 25.0 | 10.9 | 9.0 | 4.3 | 2.8 |
| Robot | 52.6 | 14.5 | 16.2 | 9.3 | 0.6 | 6.9 |
| Laser technique | 47.0 | 1.5 | 1.5 | 19.7 | 7.6 | 22.7 |
| At least one NT | 54.3 | 6.1 | 3.9 | 12.2 | 9.8 | 13.8 |
| No NT | 66.9 | 5.2 | 2.3 | 16.3 | 1.9 | 7.3 |
| Total | 61.3 | 5.5 | 3.0 | 14.7 | 5.3 | 10.2 |

*Notes:* a) Always identical time schedule, b) Alternating time schedule: 2x8 hours, 2 teams, etc., c) alternating time schedule: 3x8 hours, 3 teams, etc., d) changing daily, determined by the enterprise, e) individual choice according to a system "*à la carte*", f) variable time schedule, determined by the worker.
The table presents percentage shares of NT workers working according to the reported time schedule in the total number of respective NT workers. The figures are based on "use NT as a main task" (17184 observations). Source: INSEE, Enquête Emploi, 1987 (French labour force survey, 1987).

## Appendix A4.II.: Definition of educational degrees

| Degree | Exact French classification (highest degrees): |
|---|---|
| "Elementary School" | CEP |
| "Vocational technical school" | (CAP, BEP) or (BP, BEI, BEC, BEA) |
| "Junior high school" | BEPC |
| "High school" | "Baccalauréat de technicien" or "baccalauréat général" or "paramédical ou social avec/sans baccalauréat général" or "baccalauréat général et diplôme technique secondaire" |
| "Technical college" | "1er cycle universitaire" or BTS,DUT |
| "University" | "2ème ou 3ème cycle universitaire" or "grande école" or "diplôme d'ingenieur" |

*Notes:* BTS= brevet de technicien superieur, DUT= diplôme universitaire de technologie, BP= brevet professionnel, BEI= brevet d'enseignement industriel, BEC= brevet d'enseignement commercial, BEA= brevet d'enseignement agricole, CAP= certification d'aptitude professionelle, BEP= brevet d'enseignement professionel, BEPC= brevet d'études du premier cycle, CEP= certificat d'études primaires.

## Appendix A4.III: Additional cross-sectional results

*Table C11:* Ordered logit estimates of the effect of new-technology use on pay

Dependent variable: ln (monthly wage)

| Independent Variable | (1) | (2) | (3) | (4) | (5) | (6) |
|---|---|---|---|---|---|---|
| Intercept | 8.689<br>(0.051) | 8.112<br>(0.050) | 8.111<br>(0.050) | 8.396<br>(0.051) | 8.396<br>(0.051) | 8.401<br>(0.051) |
| Uses new technologies (NT) at work (1 = yes) | | | | | | |
| NT with high autonomy | 0.361<br>(0.009) | 0.052<br>(0.006) | 0.064<br>(0.006) | 0.049<br>(0.007) | 0.062<br>(0.006) | (Table C14) |
| NT with average autonomy | 0.055<br>(0.015) | -0.012<br>(0.008) | -0.003<br>(0.008) | -0.013<br>(0.009) | -0.003<br>(0.009) | (Table C14) |
| NT with low autonomy | -0.031<br>(0.024) | 0.007<br>(0.012) | 0.015<br>(0.012) | -0.002<br>(0.013) | 0.006<br>(0.013) | (Table C14) |
| Educational degree (1 = yes) | | | | | | |
| None | - | -0.094<br>(0.008) | -0.095<br>(0.008) | -0.063<br>(0.008) | -0.064<br>(0.008) | -0.065<br>(0.008) |
| Elementary school | - | -0.072<br>(0.009) | -0.073<br>(0.009) | -0.020<br>(0.008) | -0.021<br>(0.008) | -0.021<br>(0.008) |
| Vocational technical school | - | -0.006<br>(0.008) | -0.007<br>(0.008) | 0.015<br>(0.007) | 0.014<br>(0.007) | 0.014<br>(0.007) |
| Junior high school | - | 0.016<br>(0.008) | 0.017<br>(0.008) | 0.026<br>(0.010) | 0.026<br>(0.010) | 0.025<br>(0.010) |
| Technical college | - | 0.098<br>(0.011) | 0.100<br>(0.011) | 0.107<br>(0.011) | 0.109<br>(0.011) | 0.105<br>(0.011) |
| University | - | 0.172<br>(0.011) | 0.172<br>(0.011) | 0.196<br>(0.011) | 0.196<br>(0.011) | 0.194<br>(0.011) |
| Lives in "Ile de France" (1 = yes) | | 0.110<br>(0.005) | 0.110<br>(0.005) | 0.115<br>(0.006) | 0.114<br>(0.006) | 0.114<br>(0.006) |
| Sex (1 = male) | - | 0.157<br>(0.006) | 0.157<br>(0.006) | 0.155<br>(0.006) | 0.156<br>(0.006) | 0.154<br>(0.006) |
| Single (1 = yes) | - | -0.004<br>(0.007) | -0.004<br>(0.007) | -0.018<br>(0.007) | -0.018<br>(0.007) | -0.018<br>(0.007) |
| Part-time (1 = yes) | - | -0.698<br>(0.008) | -0.698<br>(0.008) | -0.697<br>(0.008) | -0.697<br>(0.008) | -0.699<br>(0.008) |
| Tenure | - | 0.011<br>(0.001) | 0.011<br>(0.001) | 0.024<br>(0.001) | 0.024<br>(0.001) | 0.024<br>(0.001) |
| Tenure-squared *100 | - | -0.011<br>(0.002) | -0.012<br>(0.002) | -0.042<br>(0.002) | -0.043<br>(0.002) | -0.041<br>(0.002) |
| Experience | - | 0.032<br>(0.001) | 0.032<br>(0.001) | - | - | - |
| Experience-squared *100 | | -0.055<br>(0.002) | -0.055<br>(0.002) | - | - | - |

Table C11: (continued)

| Independent Variable | (1) | (2) | (3) | (4) | (5) | (6) |
|---|---|---|---|---|---|---|
| Experience with NT | - | 0.015 (0.002) | - | 0.016 (0.002) | - | 0.019 (0.002) |
| (Experience with NT)-squared *100 | - | -0.063 (0.010) | - | -0.066 (0.010) | - | -0.080 (0.010) |
| Experienced male NT worker (1=yes) | - | - | 0.044 (0.008) | - | 0.049 (0.008) | - |
| Experienced female NT worker (1=yes) | - | - | 0.051 (0.010) | - | 0.056 (0.011) | - |
| Size of enterprise | | | | | | |
| 0-49 | - | -0.031 (0.007) | -0.032 (0.007) | -0.030 (0.007) | -0.031 (0.007) | -0.031 (0.007) |
| 50-499 | - | -0.024 (0.008) | -0.025 (0.008) | -0.024 (0.008) | -0.024 (0.008) | -0.025 (0.008) |
| Working-time schedule (1=yes) | | | | | | |
| 2 shifts (2 x 8 hours) | - | 0.038 (0.011) | 0.038 (0.011) | 0.028 (0.012) | 0.028 (0.012) | 0.027 (0.012) |
| 3 shifts (3 x 8 hours) | - | 0.094 (0.014) | 0.096 (0.014) | 0.089 (0.015) | 0.091 (0.015) | 0.088 (0.015) |
| Varying, firm determined | - | 0.029 (0.006) | 0.029 (0.006) | 0.028 (0.006) | 0.028 (0.006) | 0.029 (0.006) |
| A la carte | - | 0.028 (0.010) | 0.031 (0.010) | 0.030 (0.011) | 0.033 (0.011) | 0.030 (0.011) |
| Varying, individual choice | - | 0.078 (0.007) | 0.078 (0.007) | 0.091 (0.008) | 0.091 (0.008) | 0.091 (0.008) |
| 15 new-technology groups | - | No | No | No | No | Yes[1] |
| 12 occupational groups | - | Yes | Yes | Yes | Yes | Yes |
| 38 sectoral groups | - | Yes | Yes | Yes | Yes | Yes |
| McFadden's Pseudo-$R^2$ | 0.022 | 0.242 | 0.241 | 0.229 | 0.229 | 0.229 |

*Notes*: Standard errors are presented in parentheses. The figures are based on a maximum likelihood approach using ordered logit with exogenous thresholds. The sample size is 17184.

1) See Table C14 for a detailed list of NT parameters.

*Source:* French Labor Force Survey 1987, INSEE (Enquête Emploi 1987).

*Table C12*: Ordered logit estimate of the effect of new-technology use on pay: By occupation

| Independent variable | Skilled blue collar workers | Unskilled blue collar workers | Clerks | Managers, engineers, professionals |
|---|---|---|---|---|
| Intercept | 8.252<br>(0.103) | 7.765<br>(0.129) | 8.290<br>(0.156) | 8.606<br>(0.273) |
| NT with high autonomy (1 = yes) | 0.090<br>(0.014) | 0.120<br>(0.028) | 0.028<br>(0.014) | 0.040<br>(0.026) |
| NT with average autonomy (1 = yes) | 0.024<br>(0.016) | 0.004<br>(0.024) | -0.019<br>(0.020) | 0.032<br>(0.046) |
| NT with low autonomy (1 = yes) | 0.005<br>(0.015) | 0.030<br>(0.019) | 0.085<br>(0.070) | -0.044<br>(0.188) |
| Sex (1 = male) | 0.158<br>(0.014) | 0.148<br>(0.013) | 0.092<br>(0.016) | 0.184<br>(0.028) |
| Tenure | 0.004<br>(0.001) | 0.011<br>(0.002) | 0.013<br>(0.003) | -0.007<br>(0.004) |
| Tenure-squared *100 | -0.001<br>(0.005) | -0.027<br>(0.006) | -0.013<br>(0.008) | 0.023<br>(0.012) |
| Experience with NT | -0.001<br>(0.003) | 0.008<br>(0.006) | 0.026<br>(0.006) | 0.021<br>(0.009) |
| (Experience with NT)-squared *100 | -0.005<br>(0.020) | -0.049<br>(0.042) | -0.133<br>(0.045) | -0.066<br>(0.053) |
| Experience | 0.025<br>(0.002) | 0.032<br>(0.002) | 0.025<br>(0.003) | 0.058<br>(0.007) |
| Experience-squared*100 | -0.043<br>(0.003) | -0.057<br>(0.004) | -0.038<br>(0.006) | -0.083<br>(0.013) |
| Additional variables | 4 educational groups, 11 sectoral dummies, one regional dummy, 3 size dummies, partial-time, 5 work-time groups, marital status | 4 educational groups, 11 sectoral dummies, one regional dummy, 3 size dummies, partial-time, 5 work-time groups, marital status | 6 educational groups, 11 sectoral dummies, one regional dummy, 3 size dummies, partial-time, marital status | 6 educational groups, 5 sectoral dummies, one regional dummy, 3 size dummies, partial-time, marital status |
| Number of observations | 3543 | 2505 | 1808 | 884 |
| McFadden's Pseudo-$R^2$ | 0.110 | 0.187 | 0.172 | 0.108 |

Table C12: (continued)

| Independent variable | Skilled blue collar workers | Unskilled blue collar workers | Clerks | Clerks/ civil servants |
|---|---|---|---|---|
| Intercept | 8.491<br>(0.105) | 7.964<br>(0.128) | 8.469<br>(0.160) | 8.475<br>(0.137) |
| NT with high autonomy (1 =yes) | 0.086<br>(0.015) | 0.118<br>(0.030) | 0.022<br>(0.015) | 0.058<br>(0.016) |
| NT with average autonomy (1 =yes) | 0.026<br>(0.015) | 0.013<br>(0.026) | -0.010<br>(0.021) | -0.063<br>(0.024) |
| NT with low autonomy (1 =yes) | -0.001<br>(0.016) | 0.024<br>(0.020) | 0.046<br>(0.077) | -0.008<br>(0.053) |
| Sex (1 =male) | 0.168<br>(0.015) | 0.127<br>(0.014) | 0.091<br>(0.016) | 0.193<br>(0.012) |
| Tenure | 0.013<br>(0.001) | 0.025<br>(0.002) | 0.026<br>(0.002) | 0.030<br>(0.002) |
| Tenure-squared *100 | -0.020<br>(0.005) | -0.058<br>(0.006) | -0.037<br>(0.008) | -0.054<br>(0.006) |
| Experience with NT | -0.000<br>(0.004) | 0.009<br>(0.007) | 0.024<br>(0.006) | 0.014<br>(0.006) |
| (Experience with NT)-squared *100 | -0.005<br>(0.025) | -0.060<br>(0.044) | -0.116<br>(0.046) | -0.067<br>(0.043) |
| Experienced male NT worker (1 =yes)[1] | -0.014<br>(0.016) | 0.019<br>(0.030) | 0.075<br>(0.029) | 0.044<br>(0.024) |
| Experienced female NT worker (1 =yes)[1] | 0.020<br>(0.055) | 0.020<br>(0.038) | 0.052<br>(0.016) | 0.018<br>(0.026) |
| Additional variables | 4 educational groups, 11 sectoral dummies, one regional dummy, 3 size dummies, partial-time, 5 work-time groups, marital status | 4 educational groups, 11 sectoral dummies, one regional dummy, 3 size dummies, partial-time, 5 work-time groups, marital status | 6 educational groups, 11 sectoral dummies, one regional dummy, 3 size dummies, partial-time, marital status | 6 educational groups, 5 sectoral dummies, one regional dummy, 3 size dummies, partial-time, marital status |
| Number of observations | 3543 | 2505 | 1808 | 2199 |
| McFadden's Pseudo-$R^2$ | 0.094 | 0.167 | 0.159 | 0.235 |

*Table C12:* (continued)

| Independent variable | Direct personal services | Salesmen | Technicians | Technical foremen |
|---|---|---|---|---|
| Intercept | 7.896<br>(0.284) | 8.068<br>(0.263) | 8.487<br>(0.285) | 8.559<br>(0.414) |
| NT with high autonomy (1 = yes) | 0.073<br>(0.143) | 0.042<br>(0.036) | 0.029<br>(0.027) | 0.099<br>(0.032) |
| NT with average autonomy (1 = yes) | 0.115<br>(0.136) | -0.031<br>(0.044) | -0.009<br>(0.030) | -0.065<br>(0.041) |
| NT with low autonomy (1 = yes) | -0.145<br>(0.180) | 0.079<br>(0.132) | -0.022<br>(0.052) | -0.084<br>(0.066) |
| Sex (1 = male) | 0.265<br>(0.044) | 0.180<br>(0.026) | 0.145<br>(0.037) | 0.239<br>(0.071) |
| Tenure | 0.020<br>(0.006) | 0.033<br>(0.005) | 0.032<br>(0.004) | 0.014<br>(0.005) |
| Tenure-squared *100 | -0.033<br>(0.021) | -0.074<br>(0.014) | -0.056<br>(0.011) | -0.019<br>(0.011) |
| Experience with NT | 0.079<br>(0.044) | 0.030<br>(0.015) | 0.049<br>(0.011) | -0.003<br>(0.010) |
| (Experience with NT)-squared *100 | -0.689<br>(0.435) | -0.195<br>(0.149) | -0.286<br>(0.098) | 0.003<br>(0.060) |
| Experienced male NT worker (1 = yes)[1] | 0.175<br>(0.224) | -0.077<br>(0.134) | 0.102<br>(0.027) | 0.018<br>(0.033) |
| Experienced female NT worker (1 = yes)[1] | 0.184<br>(0.133) | 0.084<br>(0.049) | 0.211<br>(0.068) | -0.059<br>(0.166) |
| Additional variables | 5 educational groups, 3 sectoral dummies, one regional dummy, 3 size dummies, partial-time, marital status | 6 educational groups, 3 sectoral dummies, one regional dummy, 3 size dummies, partial-time, marital status | 6 educational groups, 11 sectoral dummies, one regional dummy, 3 size dummies, partial-time, marital status | 6 educational groups, 9 sectoral dummies, one regional dummy, 3 size dummies, partial-time, marital status |
| Number of observations | 906 | 647 | 737 | 568 |
| McFadden's Pseudo-$R^2$ | 0.150 | 0.147 | 0.103 | 0.089 |

*Table C12:* (continued)

| Independent variable | Managers, engineers, professionals | Managers, engineers, professionals / civil servants | Middle-level professionals | Middle-level professionals / civil servants |
|---|---|---|---|---|
| Intercept | 9.300<br>(0.288) | 8.897<br>(0.297) | 8.613<br>(0.268) | 8.672<br>(0.146) |
| NT with high autonomy (1 = yes) | 0.010<br>(0.027) | 0.024<br>(0.037) | 0.058<br>(0.029) | 0.017<br>(0.018) |
| NT with average autonomy (1 = yes) | 0.044<br>(0.049) | -0.003<br>(0.053) | -0.044<br>(0.047) | -0.004<br>(0.029) |
| NT with low autonomy (1 = yes) | -0.012<br>(0.152) | 0.114<br>(0.126) | -0.185<br>(0.218) | -0.026<br>(0.061) |
| Sex (1 = male) | 0.209<br>(0.030) | 0.204<br>(0.035) | 0.217<br>(0.028) | 0.110<br>(0.016) |
| Tenure | 0.008<br>(0.004) | 0.036<br>(0.005) | 0.025<br>(0.004) | 0.036<br>(0.002) |
| Tenure-squared *100 | -0.004<br>(0.012) | -0.052<br>(0.016) | -0.040<br>(0.013) | -0.066<br>(0.006) |
| Experience with NT | 0.024<br>(0.009) | 0.019<br>(0.014) | 0.008<br>(0.012) | 0.017<br>(0.005) |
| (Experience with NT)-squared *100 | -0.056<br>(0.053) | -0.061<br>(0.109) | 0.118<br>(0.092) | -0.066<br>(0.023) |
| Experienced male NT worker (1 = yes)[1] | 0.089<br>(0.031) | 0.072<br>(0.047) | 0.140<br>(0.037) | 0.075<br>(0.032) |
| Experienced female NT worker (1 = yes)[1] | 0.177<br>(0.056) | 0.061<br>(0.071) | 0.048<br>(0.051) | 0.029<br>(0.027) |
| Additional variables | 6 educational groups, 11 sectoral dummies, one regional dummy, 3 size dummies, partial-time, marital status | 6 educational groups, 5 sectoral dummies, one regional dummy, 3 size dummies, partial-time, marital status | 6 educational groups, 11 sectoral dummies, one regional dummy, 3 size dummies, partial-time, marital status | 6 educational groups, 5 sectoral dummies, one regional dummy, 3 size dummies, partial-time, marital status |
| Number of observations | 884 | 663 | 957 | 1767 |
| McFadden's Pseudo-$R^2$ | 0.077 | 0.147 | 0.072 | 0.146 |

*Table C12:* (continued)

*Notes*: Standard errors are presented in parentheses. The figures are based on a maximum likelihood approach using ordered logit with exogenous thresholds.
1) Two rows contain two parameters estimated from a slightly deviating specification: Instead of "experience with NT" and "experience-squared with NT", these two variables are replaced by "experienced male NT worker" and "experienced female NT worker", all other remaining variables are kept. Re-running the regression yields the presented alternative parameter estimates.
*Source:* French Labor Force Survey 1987, INSEE (Enquête Emploi 1987).

*Table C13:* Ordered logit estimates of the effect of new-technology use on pay: Controlling for firm-specific abilities

Dependent variable: ln (monthly wage)

| Independent Variable | Total sample: | Skilled blue collar workers | Un-skilled blue collar workers | Clerks | Managers, engineers, professionals |
|---|---|---|---|---|---|
| Intercept | 8.199 (0.090) | 8.245 (0.174) | 7.933 (0.186) | 8.277 (0.237) | 8.581 (0.354) |
| **Uses new technologies (NT) at work (1 = yes)** | | | | | |
| NT with high autonomy | 0.051 (0.009) | 0.071 (0.017) | 0.138 (0.030) | 0.042 (0.021) | 0.033 (0.031) |
| NT with average autonomy | -0.015 (0.011) | 0.041 (0.018) | -0.012 (0.024) | 0.000 (0.027) | 0.023 (0.049) |
| NT with low autonomy | -0.017 (0.014) | 0.016 (0.017) | -0.001 (0.015) | - | - |
| **Educational degree (1 = yes)** | | | | | |
| None | -0.107 (0.012) | -0.071 (0.022) | 0.052 (0.026) | -0.186 (0.040) | -0.022 (0.060) |
| Elementary school | -0.079 (0.013) | -0.005 (0.023) | 0.090 (0.027) | -0.108 (0.031) | -0.028 (0.077) |
| Vocational technical school | -0.034 (0.010) | 0.025 (0.022) | 0.121 (0.026) | -0.087 (0.023) | 0.052 (0.045) |
| Junior high school | -0.030 (0.015) | 0.063 (0.032) | 0.127 (0.033) | -0.035 (0.027) | -0.290 (0.050) |
| Technical college | 0.091 (0.016) | - | - | - | 0.097 (0.044) |
| University | 0.192 (0.016) | - | - | - | 0.189 (0.040) |
| Lives in "Ile de France" (1 = yes) | 0.094 (0.008) | 0.136 (0.014) | 0.105 (0.016) | 0.100 (0.018) | 0.046 (0.028) |

*Table C13:* (continued)

| Independent Variable | Total sample | Skilled blue collar workers | Un-skilled blue collar workers | Clerks | Managers, engineers, professionals |
|---|---|---|---|---|---|
| Sex (1 =male) | 0.165 (0.008) | 0.114 (0.018) | 0.151 (0.013) | 0.121 (0.021) | 0.149 (0.035) |
| Single (1 =yes) | 0.037 (0.010) | 0.000 (0.020) | 0.073 (0.018) | -0.019 (0.028) | 0.042 (0.041) |
| Part-time (1 =yes) | -0.615 (0.019) | -0.426 (0.067) | -0.805 (0.027) | -0.551 (0.045) | - |
| Tenure | 0.011 (0.001) | 0.005 (0.002) | 0.023 (0.002) | 0.004 (0.004) | -0.015 (0.005) |
| Tenure-squared *100 | -0.016 (0.004) | -0.002 (0.006) | -0.057 (0.007) | 0.016 (0.012) | 0.071 (0.014) |
| Experience with NT | 0.021 (0.003) | 0.003 (0.005) | 0.018 (0.005) | 0.032 (0.008) | 0.013 (0.009) |
| (Experience with NT)-squared *100 | -0.105 (0.018) | -0.042 (0.035) | -0.094 (0.033) | -0.145 (0.064) | 0.003 (0.049) |
| Experience | 0.024 (0.002) | 0.018 (0.003) | 0.015 (0.003) | 0.038 (0.004) | 0.076 (0.010) |
| Experience-squared *100 | -0.043 (0.003) | -0.034 (0.005) | -0.028 (0.005) | 0.070 (0.009) | -0.133 (0.018) |
| Firm characteristics | | | | | |
| Number of employees *100 | 0.049 (0.030) | 0.190 (0.057) | -0.014 (0.063) | -0.050 (0.096) | -0.326 (0.104) |
| Profit/assets | 0.157 (0.028) | 0.138 (0.040) | 0.086 (0.051) | 0.379 (0.092) | -0.137 (0.111) |
| Share of managers, technicians and professionals | 0.335 (0.023) | 0.312 (0.042) | 0.197 (0.061) | 0.006 (0.063) | 0.220 (0.090) |
| Share of skilled workers | 0.086 (0.021) | 0.399 (0.035) | 0.058 (0.038) | -0.069 (0.069) | 0.040 (0.107) |
| Total assets $*10^6$ | -0.251 (0.142) | -2.636 (1.209) | 0.254 (0.479) | -0.108 (0.212) | 0.397 (0.446) |
| Export ratio | 0.059 (0.019) | 0.098 (0.032) | 0.080 (0.030) | 0.277 (0.041) | 0.009 (0.063) |
| 6 working-time schedule groups | Yes | Yes | Yes | Yes: 3 groups | Yes: 3 groups |
| 9 occupational groups | Yes | - | - | - | - |
| 14 sectoral groups | Yes | Yes | Yes | Yes | Yes |
| Number of observations | 3845 | 1022 | 773 | 506 | 377 |
| McFadden's Pseudo-$R^2$ | 0.258 | 0.115 | 0.224 | 0.189 | 0.176 |

*Note*: Standard errors are presented in parentheses. The figures are based on a maximum likelihood approach using ordered logit with exogenous thresholds.
*Source:* INSEE: French Labor Force Survey 1987 (Enquête Emploi 1987), BIC-EAE and ESE.

*Table C14:* The NT-wage effect: Detailed results

| NT group | Total sample | Merged sample |
|---|---|---|
| Assembly line | -0.024 (0.018) | -0.038 (0.021) |
| Reception of information | 0.001 (0.018) | -0.030 (0.019) |
| Use of listings | 0.025 (0.009) | 0.037 (0.011) |
| Emission of data | 0.021 (0.021) | -0.013 (0.026) |
| Data entry | -0.017 (0.009) | -0.036 (0.011) |
| Video (supervising) | 0.010 (0.013) | 0.011 (0.021) |
| Automatic transportation | 0.027 (0.020) | -0.004 (0.018) |
| Text processing | 0.018 (0.014) | 0.043 (0.019) |
| Minitel | 0.030 (0.010) | 0.050 (0.013) |
| Micro | 0.035 (0.008) | 0.044 (0.011) |
| Terminal | 0.012 (0.009) | -0.014 (0.011) |
| Machine-tools | -0.014 (0.021) | 0.013 (0.022) |
| Robots | -0.005 (0.023) | -0.038 (0.025) |
| Laser technique | -0.018 (0.033) | -0.002 (0.049) |
| Others | -0.031 (0.011) | -0.026 (0.016) |

*Notes:* Estimated parameters of NT groups; left column: see (6) in Table C12, right column: see Table C13, "total sample", but with detailed information about NT groups instead of aggregate variables (remaining parameter estimates are not reported). Note that the same worker can work with more than one NT (so that aggregate NT categories differ from aggregated disaggregate results).

*Table C15:* Explaining mismatch

Dependent variable: "*Mismatch*" (1 = yes)

| Independent variable | Total sample | Total sample[1] | Middle-level professionals | Skilled blue collar workers | Unskilled blue collar workers | Clerks |
|---|---|---|---|---|---|---|
| Intercept | -0.866 (0.065) | -1.102 (0.084) | -0.377 (0.213) | -0.288 (0.172) | -0.799 (0.173) | -0.625 (0.142) |
| Use of computer-based NT with high autonomy (1 = yes) | 0.179 (0.031) | 0.182 (0.032) | -0.032 (0.103) | 0.283 (0.083) | 0.419 (0.142) | 0.151 (0.079) |
| Use of computer-based NT with average autonomy (1 = yes) | -0.024 (0.040) | -0.020 (0.042) | -0.046 (0.155) | -0.189 (0.091) | 0.141 (0.129) | 0.093 (0.105) |
| Use of production-based NT with low autonomy (1 = yes) | 0.061 (0.053) | 0.068 (0.056) | 0.070 (0.053) | 0.089 (0.090) | 0.095 (0.095) | 0.713 (0.401) |

*Table C15:* (continued)

| Independent variable | Total sample | Total sample[1] | Middle-level professionals | Skilled blue collar workers | Unskilled blue collar workers | Clerks |
|---|---|---|---|---|---|---|
| Hours worked per week | - | 0.007 (0.001) | - | - | - | - |
| Educational degree (1 = yes): | | | | | | |
| None | 0.026 (0.041) | 0.022 (0.043) | 0.325 (0.189) | -0.085 (0.104) | -0.134 (0.104) | -0.062 (0.145) |
| Elementary school | 0.112 (0.041) | 0.130 (0.043) | 0.283 (0.165) | -0.025 (0.106) | -0.085 (0.117) | 0.142 (0.115) |
| Vocational technical school | 0.142 (0.035) | 0.170 (0.039) | 0.181 (0.125) | -0.168 (0.100) | 0.321 (0.106) | -0.097 (0.079) |
| Junior high school | 0.260 (0.046) | 0.182 (0.040) | 0.107 (0.151) | 0.103 (0.147) | 0.124 (0.160) | 0.146 (0.102) |
| Technical college | -0.375 (0.054) | -0.353 (0.059) | -0.401 (0.160) | - | - | - |
| University | -0.482 (0.062) | -0.538 (0.067) | -0.604 (0.200) | - | - | - |
| Working-time dummies (1 = yes): | | | | | | |
| Fixed, all day | - | - | - | -0.274 (0.061) | -0.140 (0.083) | - |
| 2 shifts (2 x 8 hours) | 0.115 (0.048) | 0.124 (0.051) | - | -0.202 (0.100) | -0.195 (0.121) | - |
| 3 shifts (3 x 8 hours) | 0.255 (0.063) | 0.272 (0.067) | - | 0.061 (0.118) | -0.247 (0.164) | - |
| Varying, firm determined | 0.176 (0.032) | 0.184 (0.034) | 0.166 (0.183) | - | - | 0.324 (0.129) |
| A la carte | 0.158 (0.048) | 0.147 (0.050) | 0.139 (0.145) | - | - | -0.011 (0.097) |
| Varying, individual choice | 0.174 (0.039) | 0.139 (0.041) | 0.111 (0.102) | - | - | 0.054 (0.132) |
| Lives in "Ile de France" (1 = yes) | 0.104 (0.026) | | 0.053 (0.093) | 0.047 (0.060) | 0.160 (0.087) | 0.125 (0.071) |
| Sex (1 = male) | 0.218 (0.027) | 0.199 (0.029) | 0.234 (0.093) | -0.073 (0.087) | 0.222 (0.070) | 0.086 (0.084) |
| Single (1 = yes) | -0.095 (0.036) | -0.099 (0.038) | 0.056 (0.128) | 0.068 (0.088) | -0.324 (0.124) | -0.013 (0.101) |
| Part-time (1 = yes) | -0.112 (0.044) | 0.007 (0.055) | 0.180 (0.125) | -0.018 (0.199) | -0.145 (0.119) | -0.017 (0.114) |
| Experience | -0.007 (0.004) | -0.007 (0.004) | -0.016 (0.014) | 0.007 (0.008) | -0.010 (0.011) | 0.007 (0.012) |
| $(Experience)^2$ *100 | 0.008 (0.011) | 0.009 (0.012) | 0.044 (0.041) | -0.043 (0.028) | 0.030 (0.036) | -0.019 (0.040) |

*Table C15:* (continued)

| Independent variable | Total sample | Total sample[1] | Middle-level professionals | Skilled blue collar workers | Unskilled blue collar workers | Clerks |
|---|---|---|---|---|---|---|
| Experience with NT | 0.021<br>(0.009) | 0.018<br>(0.010) | 0.011<br>(0.040) | 0.028<br>(0.020) | 0.016<br>(0.034) | -0.039<br>(0.029) |
| (Experience with NT)$^2$ *100 | -0.090<br>(0.058) | -0.070<br>(0.061) | 0.286<br>(0.321) | -0.136<br>(0.113) | -0.173<br>(0.219) | 0.391<br>(0.223) |
| Occupation: | | | | | | |
| Managers, engineers, professionals | 0.305<br>(0.061) | 0.284<br>(0.065) | - | - | - | - |
| Managers, engineers, professionals / CS | -0.333<br>(0.083) | -0.280<br>(0.089) | - | - | - | - |
| Middle level professionals | 0.421<br>(0.054) | 0.438<br>(0.057) | - | - | - | - |
| Middle level professionals / CS | -0.185<br>(0.058) | -0.153<br>(0.062) | - | - | - | - |
| Technicians | 0.123<br>(0.058) | 0.137<br>(0.060) | - | - | - | - |
| Technical foremen | 0.153<br>(0.061) | 0.145<br>(0.063) | - | - | - | - |
| Clerks | 0.167<br>(0.049) | 0.144<br>(0.051) | - | - | - | - |
| Clerks / CS | 0.169<br>(0.049) | 0.127<br>(0.052) | - | - | - | - |
| Sales workers | 0.418<br>(0.071) | 0.384<br>(0.074) | - | - | - | - |
| Direct personal service | -0.273<br>(0.069) | -0.276<br>(0.071) | - | - | - | - |
| Unskilled blue collar workers | -0.064<br>(0.039) | -0.079<br>(0.040) | - | - | - | - |
| Size dummies (number of workers; 1=yes): | | | | | | |
| 0-49 | -0.066<br>(0.031) | -0.069<br>(0.033) | 0.116<br>(0.124) | -0.197<br>(0.067) | -0.096<br>(0.086) | 0.017<br>(0.089) |
| 50-499 | -0.039<br>(0.036) | -0.060<br>(0.037) | -0.095<br>(0.135) | -0.064<br>(0.072) | -0.165<br>(0.088) | 0.042<br>(0.098) |
| Number of sectoral groups | 38 | 38 | 11 | 12 | 12 | 12 |
| Number of observations | 17184 | 15563 | 957 | 3543 | 2505 | 1808 |
| Number of cases with "event=1" | 4915 | 4490 | 423 | 1049 | 597 | 588 |
| McFadden's Pseudo $R^2$ | 0.065 | 0.064 | 0.070 | 0.040 | 0.062 | 0.027 |

*Notes:* Probit estimates, standard errors in parentheses. 1) The number of observations is smaller than in the first column because observations with missing values for hours worked have to be disregarded. CS = civil servants.
*Source:* INSEE: French Labor Force Survey 1987 (Enquête Emploi 1987).

# 5. Conclusions

This book evaluates evidence of recent mismatch trends reported in the literature, analyses mismatch in terms of matching functions in the Beveridge-curve framework, and provides a microeconomic basis capable of explaining persistent wage differentials between new-technology jobs and conventional positions.

Three main conclusions can be drawn from the preceding chapters:

- I. The risk of spurious results limits the interpretation of tradititional mismatch indices based on aggregate data;
- II. A disaggregate approach to the analysis of economy-wide matching functions is superior to the conventional, aggregate approach; and
- III. Matching of unobserved high and low abilities with installed technologies leads to higher wages of new-technology workers and to a wage differential that increases with the duration of new-technology experience.

The first conclusion is based on the analysis of popular mismatch indexes. Most conventional measures of mismatch indicate falling mismatch in Europe. This macro finding does not fit the conclusions drawn from micro data: According to surveys covering the last twenty years, regional and occupational mobility has decreased.

This work shows that such surprising results can arise when unemployment figures reveal upward trends. Technical time series analysis proves that with both deterministic and stochastic trends, most mismatch indexes are likely to decline without any changes in the *relative* structure of sectors, skills or other groupings criteria.

Empirical tests show that this theoretical result has practical relevance, since (nonstationary) trends and drifts are detectable in the data. The puzzle of contradictory results from different indicators can thus be solved by the observation that the existing measures of mismatch are designed for stationary (more precisely: static) models, whereas measured mismatch indexes are based on data from a dynamic and changing world. Thus, mismatch indexes should be supplemented by alternative measures, taking into account more realistic descriptions of the dynamics of mismatch phenomena.

The Beveridge-curve theory is considered an alternative concept. It proposes to determine aggregate matching functions that stress the dynamic functioning of the labour market, since it maps outflows from unemployment and vacancies (i.e. hires) in dependency of respective stocks. Changes and deviations from an economy-wide matching efficiency are reflected in a time-variant scaling parameter of the matching function (like technical progress in aggregate production functions).

An important disadvantage of aggregate matching functions is the ignorance of disaggregate information. Since teenagers and other high-turnover workers with very brief employment records dominate the matching process, the aggregate models cannot take counterbalancing movements at a disaggregate level into account, which arise due to a changing occupational structure for instance.

Thus, to overcome the aggregation bias, a new panel data set describing the German matching process of 40 occupational groups during the period 1971 to 1992 has been constructed. It yields the following results for economy-wide matching functions:

- 1.) The matching process is dominated by the dynamics of vacancies (which have a higher elasticity than unemployment figures);
- 2.) The matching process is variant to prevailing economic situations (times of high unemployment lead to higher elasticities of hiring with respect to unemployment);
- 3.) Matching efficiency is declining over time (when the scaling parameter is measured as a linear time trend);
- 4) A non-linear analysis of changes in matching efficiency reveal that very deep recessions (as in 1982) coincide with easy match, confirming the "thick" market hypothesis;
- 5.) The general level of mismatch at the end of the eighties and the beginning of the nineties is higher than before 1975 (despite smaller unemployment rates before 1975 and the fact that high unemployment facilitates matching);
- 6) The disaggregate approach to matching functions does not prevent interpretational problems arising due to high-turnover jobs; and
- 7) The analysis of covariates suggests that a higher proportion of workers without a schooling degree (but see the qualification given by conclusion 6.) and improved economic situations lead to lower mismatch, whereas a growing labour force, a higher female participation rate, and a higher share of service jobs deteriorate matching efficiency. Many other potential indicators of mismatch are found to be insignificant (for instance: real wages, the ratio of wages between skilled and unskilled workers, and the share of workers being older than 50 years).

The last point reveals that a growing labour force as well as a growing female labour force are positively associated with mismatch which might be explained by insufficient skills of new entrants in the labour force, so that matching them with with adequate positions is difficult. In contrast, a larger share of people without schooling leads to decreasing mismatch since these people seem to be hired in high-turnover and seasonal jobs. This possibility limits the conclusions that can be drawn from the estimated matching functions. These functions might still be dominated by fluctuations arising from short-term contracts, and do not necessarily reveal information about the matching efficiency of long-term contracts. In

Europe, however, where workers change their jobs much less frequently than in the U.S., matches corresponding to *long-term* contracts are more important for the reduction of unemployment. Thus, matching functions seem to be better suited for the understanding of the U.S. labour market.

Nevertheless, conclusions for economic policy are straightforward. On the one hand, better education and improvement of skills favours the matching process, and, on the other hand, a reduction of wage and of other demands of labour force entrants may lead to increased hiring activities of firms. However, as can be seen from the role of the female participation rate, efforts of hiring firms are also a "conditio sine qua non" for reducing mismatch. Time restrictions of job-seeking women require a larger share of part-time jobs. Up to now, lacking part-time job offers lead to an insufficient number of matches.

Moreover, the analysis of aggregate matching functions is open to generalizations. In order to be more instructive with respect to the role of particular occupational groups in the matching process, the approach is extended to the analysis of reallocation dynamics. A more general matching function based on search theory takes account of the fact that people change their professions. Among other results, the investigation of matching processes in which the pool of unemployed is enlarged by unemployed workers of other occupations reveals that jobless workers from the shrinking primary sector are matched with vacant positions in production and service sectors, that many unemployed service workers find jobs in the production sector and vice versa, and that technical workers seem to take jobs that were previously occupied by less educated production workers. The last result provides some evidence in favour of the "job competition" hypothesis.

The analysis of potential switches between occupational groups reveals a lack of mobility between many occupational groups. This leads to a long-lasting reallocation process with a permanent outward shift of the Beveridge curve, since vacant positions cannot be filled within a reasonable period of time. Improved training facilities would shorten the period of reallocation so that hiring would only be temporarily restricted by wrongly skilled job seekers. Of course, such training opportunities have to be offered to adult and even older workers, and they have to be accepted by both unemployed workers and hiring firms. For a successful balance, it is particularly important that older workers can change their profession and still have the chance to find a new position after a successful training period.

The matching of young school-leavers is another source of persistent reallocation problems. The choice of a profession and the commitment to spend the next three years attending an apprenticeship cause future adjustment problems if changing tastes or technical progress demand a different occupational structure. This conclusion is reinforced by the numerical importance of young school-leavers (according to official data for 1992, 13% of all job seekers are school-leavers), and by the result that firms and apprentices base their decisions on recent labour market experiences, which are given by past occupational unemployment and by occupational vacancies. Thus, the advice is to inform school-leavers about the delayed consequences of their decisions. If many other apprentices choose the same profession because of a good historical performance, future unemployment/vacancy relationships can dramatically change and cause a higher individual probability of becoming unemployed. Labour offices who advise young school-leavers should provide them with "rational expectations", i.e. inform them that other apprenticeship beginners may dispose of the same information set which could worsen their own future income streams.

Chapter 4 of this book adds neglected microeconomic aspects to the analysis of matching phenomena. It aims at explaining the empirical result that new-technology workers receive higher wages than comparable workers at conventional places of work. If prices reflect the relative demand structure, the higher pay for "new technology" abilities reveals that these are still underdeveloped. Thus, one may conclude that the skill structure has still to be changed in favour of more high-tech oriented professions. The results presented in this book do not justify this hypothesis of skill-biased technical change. According to the matching framework presented here, employers learn to evaluate abilities that remain unobservable to the econometrician, and simply tend to hire workers with higher abilities when they fill NT-positions.

This result is based on theoretical predictions from a matching framework dealing with unmeasured abilities. Under the assumption that such abilities are time-variant because of learning, mobility, and because the same ability is higher or lower rewarded by hiring and learning firms, then three predictions can be derived: i) workers who move from a conventional job to a new-technology position experience a wage increase, ii) the wage differential between new-technology workers and conventional jobs grows with the duration of new-technology experience, and iii) workers in high-wage groups are better matched with an eventual new-technology job than are workers in low-wage groups.

The econometric results do not confirm hypothesis i), while ii) and iii) are supported by the data. Since the validity of the matching framework depends heavily on the quality of data and on assumed specifications of estimated wage equations, particular attention is paid to the choice of rich data which allow for the implementation of most common hypotheses of individual wage determination. Using an appendix to the regular French Labour Force Survey on the use of new technologies and the organization of the work place, the specification is capable of introducing variables in the sense of efficiency wage theory, gift-exchange hypotheses, profit-sharing and other wage determinants more directly than standard wage equations do.

An interesting result can be added from the analysis of perceived mismatch in NT positions: Evidently, women accept the use of new technologies more easily than men. They perceive a lower mismatch when working with computer-related techniques. This result should encourage firms to extend the training of women in new-technology professions.

The noted shortcomings of the mismatch frameworks suggest directions of future research. The analysis of the matching process in Europe has to focus on long-run matches which characterize the majority of jobs. Moreover, matching functions inform about the efficiency of installed matching mechanisms, that transform current stocks of unemployed and vacant positions into new hires. This strategy is not very instructive with respect to the reversed causality direction, i.e. how matching activities affect the reduction of unemployment. Of course, matching functions have to be seen in context of a more general Beveridge curve theory, where unemployment is reduced by efficient matching via a dynamic flow equation. A more direct test, however, would need a framework in which unemployment depends on matching activities, and where the matching efficiency itself becomes a function of various economic indicators. This would simplify the search for causes of mismatch and structural unemployment.

## 6. References


Abowd, J. and A. Zellner, Estimating gross labor force flows, *Journal of Business and Economic Statistics* 1985, 3: 254-283.

Abowd, J. and F. Kramarz, An exploration of firm-level heterogeneity: Covariance models for unbalanced panels, working paper, Cornell University and INSEE, 1993.

Abowd, J., F. Kramarz and D. Margolis, High-wage workers and high-wage firms: Compensation and firm performance in France, working paper, Cornell University and INSEE, 1993.

Abraham, K.G. and L. Katz, Cyclical unemployment: Sectoral shifts or aggregate disturbances?, *Journal of Political Economy* 1986, 94: 507-522.

Abraham, K.G., Help-wanted advertising, job vacancies and unemployment, *Brookings Papers on Economic Activity* 1987, 1: 207-248.

Abraham, K.G., Mismatch and labour mobility: Some final remarks, in: F. Padoa-Schioppa, ed., *Mismatch and Labour Mobility*, Cambridge: Cambridge University Press, 1991, 453-481.

Abraham, K. G. and S.N. Houseman, Earnings inequality in Germany, Discussion paper 94-24, W.E. Upjohn Institute for Employment Research, 1994.

Aigner, D.J., C. Hsiao, A. Kapteyn and T. Wansbeek, Latent variable models in econometrics, in Z. Griliches and M. Intriligator (eds.), *Handbook of Econometrics, Vol II*, 1984, 1322-1393.

Akerlof, G.A., Labor contracts as partial gift exchange, *Quarterly Journal of Economics* 1982, 97: 543-569.

Akerlof, G.A., Gift exchange and efficiency-wage theories: Four views, *American Economic Review* 1984, 74: 79-83.

Akerlof, G., A. Rose and J. Yellen, Job switching and job satisfaction in the U.S. labor market, *Brookings Papers on Economic Activity*, 1988, 495-582.

Anderson, T.W. and C. Hsia, Estimation of dynamic models with error components, *Journal of the American Statistical Association* 1981, 76: 598-606.

Balestra, P. and M. Nerlove, Pooling cross section and time series data in the estimation of a dynamic model: The demand for natural gas, *Econometrica* 1966, 34: 585-612.

Banerjee, A. and D.F. Hendry, Testing integration and cointegration: An overview, *Oxford Bulletin of Economics and Statistics* 1992, 54.

Banerjee, A. J. Dolado, J.W. Galbraith and D.F. Hendry, *Co-Integration, Error-Correction, and the Econometric Analysis of Non-Stationary Data,* Oxford: Oxford University Press, 1993.

Barron J.M., D.A. Black and M.A. Loewenstein, Employer size: The implications for search, training, capital investment, starting wages, and wage growth, *Journal of Labor Economics* 1987, 5: 76-89.

Barro, R.J., The persistence of unemployment, *American Economic Review* 1988, 78: 32-36.

Bean, C.H., European Unemployment: A Survey, *Journal of Economic Literature* 1994, 32: 573-619

Bentolila, S. and J.J. Dolado, Mismatch and internal migration in Spain, 1962-86, in: F.Padoa-Schioppa, ed., *Mismatch and Labour Mobility*, Cambridge: Cambridge University Press, 1991, 182-234.

Berman, E., J. Bound and Z. Griliches, Changes in the demand for skilled labor within U.S. manufacturing industries: Evidence from the annual survey of manufacturing, NBER Working Paper No. 4255, 1993.

Berry, M., Taylor et les robots: Les raison d'une incompatibilité, *Gérer et Comprendre*, special issue, 1988.

Beveridge, W., *Full Employment in a Free Society*, London: Allen and Unwin, 1944.

Bhargava, A., On the theory of testing for unit roots in observed time series, *Review of Economic Studies* 1986, 52: 369-384.

Blanchard, O. and P. Diamond, The Beveridge curve, *Brookings Papers on Economic Activity*, 1989, 1-60.

Blanchard, O. and P. Diamond, The cyclical behavior of the gross flows of U.S. workers, *Brookings Papers on Economic Activity*, 1990a, 85-155.

Blanchard, O. and P. Diamond, The aggregate matching function, in P. Diamond (ed.). *Productivity/ Growth/ Unemployment,* Cambridge, Ma: MIT Press, 1990b, 159-201.

Blanchard, O. and P. Diamond, Ranking, unemployment duration, and wages, NBER Working Paper No. 3387, 1990c.

Blanchard, O. and P. Diamond, The flow approach to labor markets, *American Economic Review* 82, *Papers and Proceedings*, 1992, 354-359.

Börsch-Supan, A., Panel data analysis of the Beveridge curve. Is there a macroeconomic relationship between the rate of unemployment and the vacancy rate?, *Economica* 1991, 58: 289-297.

Bound J.and G. Johnson, Changes in the structure of wages in the 1980's: an evaluation of alternative explanations, *American Economic Review* 1992, 82: 371-392.

Bover, O., J. Muellbauer and A. Murphy, Housing, wages and U.K. labour markets, in H. König (ed.), *Economics of Wage Determination*, Berlin: Springer, 1990.

Brainard, S.L. and D.M. Cutler, Sectoral shifts and cyclical unemployment reconsidered, *Quarterly Journal of Economics* 1993, CVIII: 219-243.

Brown, C. and J. Medoff, The Employer Size-Wage Effect, *RAND Journal of Political Economy* 1989, 97: 1027-1059.

Brown, C., Wage levels and method of pay, *Journal of Economics* 1992, 23: 366-375.

Brunello, G., Mismatch in Japan, in: F. Padoa-Schioppa, ed., *Mismatch and Labour Mobility*, Cambridge: Cambridge University Press, 1991, 140-179.

Bundesanstalt für Arbeit (various issues), Amtliche Nachrichten der Bundesanstalt für Arbeit, various years.

Burda, M., Modelling exits from unemployment in Eastern Germany: A matching function approach, forthcoming in: König, H. and V. Steiner (eds.), *Arbeitsdynamik und Unternehmensentwicklung in Ostdeutschland - Erfahrungen und Perspektiven des Transformationsprozesses*, NOMOS-Verlag (forthcoming).

Burda, M. and C. Wyplosz, Gross labour market flows in Europe: Some stylized facts, INSEAD Discussion Paper 90/51/EP, 1990.

Burda, M. and C. Wyplosz, Gross worker and job flows in Europe, *European Economic Review* 1994, 38: 1287-1320 (with discussion).

Buttler, F. and U. Cramer, Entwicklung und Ursachen von mis-match-Arbeitslosigkeit in Westdeutschland, *Mitteilungen aus der Arbeitsmarkt- und Berufsforschung* 1991, 24: 483-500.

Cahuc P. and B. Dormont, Profit-sharing: Does it increase productivity and employment? A theoretical model and empirical evidence of French micro data, in: *Cahier de Recherche Economie, Mathématiques et Applications*, Université de Paris I - Pantheon Sorbonne, 1992, 92-145.

Cézard, M., F. Dussert and M. Gollac, Taylor va au marché, *Travail et Emploi* 1992, 54: 4-19.

Christl, J., Structural unemployment in Austria, in W. Franz (ed.), *Structural Unemployment*, Heidelberg: Physica Verlag, 1992, 107-132.

Currie J. and S. McConnell, Firm-specific determinants of the real wage, *The Review of Economics and Statistics* 1992, 74: 297-304.

Dabouineau, J.-L., C. Gacon, F. Kramarz and S, Lollivier, The hiring difficulties of French firms: An empirical analysis on a panel of firms using simulation techniques, mimeo, INSEE, Département de la Recherche, 1993.

Davis, S. and J. Haltiwanger, Gross job creation and destruction: Microeconomic evidence and and macroeconomic implications, in O.J. Blanchard and S. Fischer (eds.), *NBER Macroecomics Annual 1990*, Cambridge, Ma: MIT Press, 1990, 123-168.

Davis S.J. and J. Haltiwanger, Wage Dispersion between and within U.S. Manufacturing Plants, 1963-1986, *Brookings Papers on Economic Activity: Microeconomics*, 1991, 115-200.

Davis, S.J., Cross-country patterns of change in relative wages, NBER paper No. 4085, 1992.

Delame E. and F. Kramarz, Entreprises et Formation Continue, INSEE working paper, 1993.

Diamond, P., Aggregate demand management in search equilibrium, *Journal of Political Economy* 1982, 90: 881-894.

Dickens, W. and L. Katz, Inter-industry wage differences and industry characteristics, in: K.Lang and J. Leonard (eds.), *Unemployment and the Structure of Labor Markets*, Oxford: Basil Blackwell, 1987.

Dickey, D.A. and W.A. Fuller, Distribution of the estimators of autoregressive time series with a unit root, *Journal of the American Statistical Association* 1979, 74: 427-431.

Dow, J. and Dicks-Mireaux, L., The excess demand for labour: A study of conditions in Great Britain 1946-1956, *Oxford Economic Papers* 1958, 10: 1-33.

Drèze, J.H. and C. Bean, (eds.), *Europe's Unemployment Problem*, Cambridge, Ma: MIT Press, 1990.

Durbin, J., Estimation of parameters in time-series regression models, *Journal of the Royal Statistical Society, Series B* 1960, 22: 799-808.

Durlauf, S. N. and P.C.B. Phillips, Trends versus random walks in time series analysis, *Econometrica* 1988, 56: 1333-1354.

Dussert, E., L'Informatisation des Entreprises, in: *Entreprises 1992*, INSEE, 1992.

EEC, *Employment in Europe*, Luxembourg: Office for Official Publications of the European Communities, 1991.

Engle, R.F. and C.W.J. Granger, Co-integration and error correction: Representation, estimation, and testing, *Econometrica* 1987, 55: 251-276.

Entorf, H., Overtime work, lack of labour, and structural mismatch: Some extensions of the "European Unemployment Programme" framework, *Recherche Economique de Louvain* 1992, 58: 373-398.

Entorf, H., Random walks with drifts, the simultaneous-equation bias, and small samples: Simulating the bird's eye view, Discussion Paper 498-94, Universität Mannheim, previous version: Discussion paper No. 9222, Département de la Recherche, INSEE, Paris, 1994.

Entorf, H., Random walks with drifts: Nonsense regressions and spurious fixed-effect estimation, Universität Mannheim, 1997a, forthcoming in *Journal of Econometrics*

Entorf, H., Mismatch and labour force heterogeneity in Germany, Universität Mannheim, mimeo, 1997b

Entorf, H., W. Franz, H. König and W.Smolny, The development of German employment and unemployment: Estimation and simulation of a small macro model, in: J.H. Drèze and C. Bean (eds.), *Europe's Unemployment Problem*, Cambridge: MIT-Press, 1990.

Entorf, H., H. König and W. Pohlmeier, Labor utilization and non-wage labor costs in a disequilibrium macro framework, *The Scandinavian Journal of Economics* 1992, 94: 71-82.

Entorf, H. and F. Kramarz, The impact of new technologies on wages: Lessons from matching panels on employees and on their firms, INSEE, Paris, CREST Discussion paper 9407, 1994.

Entorf, H. and H. Sneessens, Aggregation in quantity rationing models, mimeographed, Université Catholique de Louvain and University of Mannheim, 1994.

Ermann, K., Arbeitsmarktstatistische Zahlen in Zeitreihenform. Jahreszahlen für die Bundesrepublik Deutschland, Institut für Arbeitsmarkt- und Berufsforschung der Bundesanstalt für Arbeit, *Beiträge zur Arbeitsmarkt- und Berufsforschung* 3.1, 1984.

Ermann, K., Arbeitsmarktstatistische Zahlen in Zeitreihenform. Jahreszahlen für die Bundesrepublik Deutschland, Institut für Arbeitsmarkt- und Berufsforschung der Bundesanstalt für Arbeit, *Beiträge zur Arbeitsmarkt- und Berufsforschung* 3.1, 1988.

Flanagan, R.J., Labor market behavior and European Economic growth, in R.Z. Lawrence and C.L. Schultze (eds.): *Barriers to European Growth. A Transatlantic View,* Washington: Brookings, 1987, 175-211.

Frank, R.H., *Choosing the Right Pond: Human Behavior and the Quest for Status*, Oxford: Oxford University Press, 1985

Franz, W., Hysteresis, persistence, and the NAIRU. An empirical analysis for the Federal Republic of Germany, in: R. Layard and L. Calmfors (eds.), *The Fight against Unemployment,* Cambridge: Cambridge University Press, 1987.

Franz, W., Match and mismatch on the German labour market, in: F. Padoa-Schioppa, ed., *Mismatch and Labour Mobility*, Cambridge: Cambridge University Press, 1991a, 105-135.

Franz, W., *Arbeitsmarktökonomik*, Heidelberg and New York: Springer, 1991b.

Franz, W. and H. König, The nature and causes of unemployment in the Federal Republic of Germany since the 1970's: An empirical investigation, *Economica* 1986, 53 (Supplement): S219-S249.

Freeman, R., Labour market tightness and the mismatch between demand and supply of less-educated young men in the United States in the 1980s, in F. Padoa-Schioppa, *Mismatch and Labour Mobility,* Cambridge: Cambridge University Press, 1991, 360-381.

Freeman, R.B. and L.F. Katz (eds.), *Differences and Changes in Wage Structures*, Chicago: Chicago Press, 1995.

Gibbons, R. and L. Katz, Does unmeasured ability explain inter-idustry wage differentials?, *The Review of Economic Studies* 1992, 59: 515-535.

Gollac, M., L'Ordinateur dans l'Entreprise reste un Outil de Luxe, *Economie et Statistique* 224, INSEE, 1989.

Gollac, M., La Modernisation à Deux Vitesses, in: *Données Sociales*, INSEE, 1990.

Gollac, M., La Diffusion de l'Informatique au Travail, in: *Données Sociales*, INSEE, 1993.

Granger, C.W.J. and N. Hyung, Spurious stochastics in panel models, San Diego, mimeo, 1997

Granger, C.W.J. and P. Newbold, Spurious regression in econometrics, *Journal of Econometrics* 1974, 2: 111-120.

Groshen, E.L., Five reasons why wages vary among employers, *Industrial Relations* 1991, 30: 350-381.

Grubb, D., Topics in the OECD Phillips curve, *The Economic Journal* 1986, 96: 55-79.

Hall, A., Testing for a unit root in the presence of moving average errors, *Biometrika* 1989, 79: 49-56.

Hall, P. and C.C. Heyde, *Martingale Limit Theory and its Applications*, London: Academic Press, 1980.

Hall, R.E., An aspect of the economic role of unemployment, in G. Harcourt (ed.), *Microeconomic Foundations of Macroeconomics*, 1977.

Hall, R.E., A theory of the natural unemployment rate and the duration of unemployment, *Journal of Monetary Economics* 1979, 5: 153-169.

Hall, R.E., The Beveridge curve: Comments, *Brookings Papers on Economic Activity*, 1989, 61-64.

Hansen, B., Excess demand, unemployment, vacancies, and wages, *Quarterly Journal of Economics* 1970, 84: 1-23.

Heckman, J.J., Sample selection bias as a specification error, *Econometrica* 1979, 47: 153-161.

Hsiao, C., *The Analysis of Panel Data*, Cambridge: Cambridge University Press, 1986.

Hylleberg, S. and G.E. Mizon, A note on the distribution of the least squares estimator of a random walk with drift, *Economics Letters* 1989, 29: 225-230.

Institut der Arbeitsmarkt- und Berufsforschung der Bundesanstalt für Arbeit, *Zahlen-Fibel,* Beiträge zur Arbeitsmarkt- und Berufsforschung, 1988.

Jackman, R., R. Layard and C. Pissarides, On vacancies, *Oxford Bulletin of Economics and Statistics* 1989, 51: 377-394.

Jackman, R., R. Layard and S. Savouri, Mismatch: A framework for thought, in: F. Padoa-Schioppa (ed.), *Mismatch and Labour Mobility*, Cambridge: Cambridge University Press, 1991, 44-101.

Jackman, R. and S. Roper, Structural unemployment, *Oxford Bulletin of Economics and Statistics* 1987, 49: 9-37.

Jovanovic, B. and R. Moffit, An estimate of a sectoral model of labour mobility, NBER working paper No. 3227, 1990.

Kahneman, D., J. Knetsch and R. Thaler, Fairness as a constraint on profit seeking: Entitlements in the market, *American Economic Review* 1986, 76: 728-741.

Katz, L.F., Efficiency wage theories: A partial evaluation, *NBER Macroeconomics Annual* 1986, 1: 235-276.

Katz L.F. and K.M. Murphy, Changes in relative wages, 1963-1987: Supply and demand factors, *Quarterly Journal of Economics* 1992, CVII: 35-78.

Katz, L.F., G.W. Loveman and D.G. Blanchflower, A comparison of wages in four OECD countries, in: R.B. Freeman and L.F. Katz (eds.), *Differences and Changes in Wage Structures*, Chicago: Chicago Press, 1995.

Katz, L.F. and L. Summers, Industry rents: Evidence and implications, *Brookings Papers on Economic Activity: Microeconomics*, 1989, 209-275.

Keane, M.P. and D.E. Runkle, On the estimation of panel-data models with serial correlation when instruments are not strictly exogeneous, *Journal of Business and Economic Statistics* 1992, 10: 1-29 (with discussion).

König, H. and H. Entorf, Strukturelle Arbeitslosigkeit und unausgelastete Kapazitäten, *Allgemeines Statistisches Archiv* 1990, 74: 117-136.

Kraft K., The incentive effects of dismissals, efficency wages, piece-rates and profit-sharing, *The Review of Economics and Statistics* 1991, 73: 451-459.

Kramarz, F. and S. Lollivier, Les difficultés de recrutement s'accentuent à la fin de 1989, *Economie et Statistique* 1990, 234: 3-12.

Krueger, A.B., How computers have changed the wage structure: Evidence from microdata, 1984-1989, *Quarterly Journal of Economics* 1993, CVIII: 33-60.

Lambert, J.-P., *Disequilibrium Macroeconomic Models - Theory and Estimation of Rationing Models using Business Survey Data,* Cambridge: Cambridge University Press, 1988.

Layard, R., Human satisfactions and public policy, *Economic Journal* 1980, 90: 737-750.

Layard, J. and C. Bean, Why does unemployment persist?, *The Scandinavian Journal of Economics* 1989, 91: 371-396.

Layard, R., S. Nickell and R. Jackman, *Unemployment*, Oxford: Oxford University Press, 1991.

Leupoldt, R. and K. Ermann, Arbeitsmarktstatistische Zahlen in Zeitreihenform. Jahreszahlen für die Bundesrepublik Deutschland, Institut für Arbeitsmarkt- und Berufsforschung der Bundesanstalt für Arbeit, *Beiträge zur Arbeitsmarkt- und Berufsforschung 3.1*, 1973.

Levin, A. and C.-F. Lin, Unit root tests in panel data: Asymptotic and finite-sample properties, Discussion paper 92-23, University of California, San Diego, 1992.

Lilien, D.M., Sectoral shocks and cyclical unemployment, *Journal of Political Economy* 1982, 90: 777-793.

MacKinnon, J., Critical values for cointegration tests, in: R.F. Engle and C.W.J. Granger (eds.), *Long-Run Economic Relationships,* Oxford: Oxford University Press, 1991, 267-276.

Mortensen, D. and C. Pissarides, Job creation and job destruction in the theory of unemployment, mimeographed, Northwestern University and LSE, London, 1993.

Murphy, K.M. and R.H. Topel, Unemployment, risk and earnings, in: K.Lang and J. Leonard (eds.), *Unemployment and the Structure of Labor Markets*, Oxford: Basil Blackwell, 1987.

Murphy, K.M. and F. Welch,, The structure of wages, *The Quarterly Journal of Economics* 1992, CVII: 285-326.

Nam, C.W., G. Nerb and H.G. Russ, Measurement of regional competitiveness in Europe by survey: Application of survey techniques in a new field, in: K.H. Oppenländer and G. Poser (eds.), *Business Cycle Analysis by Means of Economic Surveys, Part II*, Aldershot: Avebury, 1992, 443-465.

Nelson, C.R. and C. Plosser, Trends and random walks in macroeconomic time series, *Journal of Monetary Economics* 1982, 10: 139-162.

Nickell, S. and S. Wadhwani, Insider forces and wage determination, *Economic Journal* 1990, 100: 496-509.

Padoa-Schioppa, F., ed., *Mismatch and Labour Mobility*, Cambridge: Cambridge University Press, 1991.

Park, J.Y. and P.C.B. Phillips, Statistical inference in regressions with integrated processes: Part 1, *Econometric Theory* 1988, 4: 468-497.

Park, J.Y. and P.C.B. Phillips, Statistical inference in regressions with integrated processes: Part 2, *Econometric Theory* 1989, 5: 95-131.

Phillips, P.C.B, Understanding spurious regression in econometrics, *Journal of Econometrics* 1986, 33: 311-340.

Pissarides, C., Job matchings with state employment agencies and random search, *Economic Journal* 1979, 89: 818-833.

Pissarides, C., Unemployment and vacancies in Britain, *Economic Policy* 1986, 3: 489-560.

Pissarides, C., Loss of skills during unemployment and the persistence of employment shocks, *Quarterly Journal of Economics* 1992, CVII: 1371-1391.

Reyer, L., E. Spitznagel, G. Kretschmer, Das gesamtwirtschaftliche Stellenangebot: Umfang, Struktur und Besetzungsprobleme, *Mitteilungen aus der Arbeitsmarkt- und Berufsforschung,* 1990, 347-372.

Rosen, S., The theory of equalizing differences, in: O. Ashenfelter and R. Layard (eds.), *Handbook of Labor Economics,* New York: North Holland, 1986.

Schettkat, R., Mobilität im Arbeitsmarkt - eine Funktion der Makroökonomie, in: W. Franz (Ed.), *Mikro- und makroökonomische Aspekte der Arbeitslosigkeit, Beiträge zur Arbeitsmarkt- und Berufsforschung* 165, 1992.

Schmidt, C.M. and K.F. Zimmermann, Work characteristics, firm size and wages, *Review of Economics and Statistics* 1991, 73: 705-710.

Schmidt, P. and P.C.B. Phillips, LM tests for a unit root in the presence of deterministic trends, *Oxford Bulletin of Economics and Statistics* 1992, 54: 257-287

Sims, C.A., J.H. Stock and M.W. Watson, Inference in linear time series models with some unit roots, *Econometrica* 1990, 58: 113-144.

Smolny, W., *Dynamic Factor Demand in a Rationing Context. Theory and Estimation of a Macroeconomic Disequilibrium Model for the Federal Republic of Germany*, Heidelberg: Springer, 1993.

Sneessens, H. and J.H. Drèze, A discussion of Belgian unemployment combining traditional concepts and disequilibrium econometrics, *Economica* 1986, 53: S89-S119

Soskice, D., Skill mismatch, training systems and equilibrium unemployment: A comparative institutional analysis, in F. Padoa-Schioppa, *Mismatch and Labour Mobility,* Cambridge: Cambridge University Press, 1991, 386-400.

Spence, M., Competition in salaries, credentials, and signal prerequisites for jobs, *Quarterly Journal of Economics* 1976, XC: 51-74.

Stock, J.H, Asymptotic properties of least squares estimators of cointegrating vectors, *Econometrica* 1987: 55: 1035-1056.

Strand, J., The relationship between wages and firm size: An information theoretic analysis, *International Economic Review* 1987, 28: 51-68

SVR, Den Aufschwung sichern - Arbeitsplätze schaffen, Gutachten des Sachverständigenrats 1994/95, Metzler-Poeschel Verlag, 1994.

Teulings, C. and M. Koopmanschap, An econometric model of crowding out of lower educational levels, *European Economic Review* 1989, 33: 1653-1664.

Troske, K.R., Further evidence on the employer size-wage premia using worker-establishment matched data, Center for Economic Studies, U.S. Census Bureau, 1993.

Turvey, R., Structural change and structural unemployment, *International Labour Review* 1977, 115.

Van Dam, J.W., G.W.M. Ramaekers and A.K.W. Van Der Velden, Skill shortages in Limburg, Research Centre for Education and Labour Markets (ROA), Limburg University, Maastricht, 1991.

Van Ours, J.C. and G. Ridder, Job matching and job competition: Are lower educated workers at the back of job queues? *European Economic Review* 1995, 39: 1717-1731

Van Rijkeghem, C., Unemployment, vacancies, and the female labor force in Belgium, 1953-1988, mimeographed, UC Berkely, 1993.

Von Rosenbladt, Fachkräftemangel und Arbeitslosigkeit. Wann und wie wird Arbeitskräftenachfrage beschäftigungswirksam?, *Mitteilungen aus der Arbeitsmarkt- und Berufsforschung 3/1990,* 1990, 373-385.

West, K.D., Asymptotic normality, when regressors have a unit root, *Econometrica* 1988, 56: 1397-1417

Wirtschaftswoche, Geschäfte durch Arbeitskräftemangel beeinträchtigt, *Wirtschaftswoche* 45 (5 Nov. 1993), 108.

Yellen, J., The Beveridge curve: Comments, *Brookings Papers on Economic Activity*, 1989, 65-71.

Yule, G.U., Why do we sometimes get nonsense-correlations between time series?, *Journal of the Royal Statistical Society* 1926, 1-69.

Zentralarchiv für empirische Sozialforschung, Qualifikation und Berufsverlauf, Maschinenlesbares Codebuch - ZA Nr. 1243, 1979.

Zentralarchiv für empirische Sozialforschung, Qualifikation und Berufsverlauf 1985/1986, Maschinenlesbares Codebuch - ZA Nr. 1790, 1986.

Zentralarchiv für empirische Sozialforschung, ALLBUS 1980-90 (Allgemeine Bevölkerungsumfrage der Sozialwissenschaften), Codebuch - ZA Nr. 1795, 1994.